Praise for *The Priest and the Medium*

*"**The Priest and the Medium** is a wonderfully rich and inspiring tale of two truly exceptional ... nce of two vastly divergent v ... g that you'll find it difficu ...*

— **Sandra An** ...
best-selling a ...

"I had a hard time putting this book down.
***The Priest and the Medium** is a real page-turner."*

— **Joseph A. Pepe**, NYPD detective, retired

---

*"We are all fascinated by priests and mediums.
This book will keep you turning the pages as you follow
the spiritual journeys of two intriguing people. Each grew up
in loving families but took paths that were at times lonely . . .
until they found each other. A wonderful book!"*

—**Ellen Ratner**, bureau chief,
Talk Radio News Service and *Talkers Magazine*

---

*"This book is bound to intrigue you with its
insights into the religions of Spiritualism and Catholicism.
Be ready for tears as a famous medium, the Rev. B. Anne Gehman,
shares stories of communication between spirit and their loved ones
on earth. Belief in God takes the Jesuit priest and the Spiritualist
medium on a rocky path to shared love—of each other and God."*

— **Rev. Lelia E. Cutler**, **NST**, president,
National Spiritualist Association of Churches

---

*"Dr. Wayne Knoll is a legendary teacher at Georgetown University.
One of my problems while chairman of the English department
was consoling students who couldn't find a place in his popular,
over-enrolled classes. Anne Gehman is an extraordinarily sensitive,
perceptive, empathetic person. Their story—sad in places,
inspiring in more—has great human interest throughout."*

— **Paul Betz**, professor of English, Georgetown University

"Suzanne Giesemann has written a wonderful book. The storytelling is expertly crafted. Easy and enjoyable to read, it's an old-fashioned love story, but in following these two spiritual journeys, we learn a great deal about how to deal with some of the most important issues each of us faces as we move inexorably toward our final days. Science-minded people tend to avoid facing such questions, and spiritually minded people tend to pretend science isn't relevant to such questions. Every reader could profit by reading this thought-provoking book."

— **Theodore Rockwell**, nuclear engineer, member of the National Academy of Engineering and representative for 12 years of the Parapsychological Association to the American Association for the Advancement of Science; author of *The Virtual Librarian: A Tale of Alternative Realities*

"Congratulations to Suzanne Giesemann for vividly capturing and telling this intriguing story. Midway through life, this remarkable priest and medium found an unlikely soul mate in the other. They joined forces to continue a fabulous, spirit-filled voyage together, savoring their love affair with God and the infinite and unexpected possibilities of life on multiple planes."

— **Joseph Sparling, Ph.D.**, senior advisor on curriculum and research, MindNurture, Inc.

"An important book."

— **Sophy Burnham**, author of *A Book of Angels*

"Romantics with interest in faith and/or true crime should find this a stirring read."

— ***Publishers Weekly***

⊕⊕⊕ ⊕⊕⊕

The Priest and the Medium

Also by Suzanne Giesemann

CONQUER YOUR CRAVINGS

IT'S YOUR BOAT TOO: A Woman's Guide To Greater Enjoyment On The Water

LIVING A DREAM

Hay House Titles of Related Interest

YOU CAN HEAL YOUR LIFE, the movie, starring Louise L. Hay & Friends
(available as a 1-DVD program and an expanded 2-DVD set)
Watch the trailer at: **www.LouiseHayMovie.com**

THE SHIFT, the movie, starring Dr. Wayne W. Dyer
(available as a 1-DVD program and an expanded 2-DVD set)
Watch the trailer at: **www.DyerMovie.com**

BORN KNOWING: A Medium's Journey—Accepting and Embracing My Spiritual Gifts,
by John Holland

DIARY OF A PSYCHIC: Shattering the Myths, by Sonia Choquette

INSPIRATION: Your Ultimate Calling, by Dr. Wayne W. Dyer

LEFT TO TELL: Discovering God Amidst the Rwandan Holocaust,
by Immaculée Ilibagiza, with Steve Erwin

REMEMBERING THE FUTURE: The Path to Recovering Intuition,
by Colette Baron-Reid

SECRETS OF SUCCESS: The Science and Spirit of Real Prosperity,
by Sandra Anne Taylor and Sharon A. Klingler

YOUR SOUL'S COMPASS: What Is Spiritual Guidance?
by Joan Borysenko, Ph.D., and Gordon Dveirin, Ed.D.

All of the above are available at your local bookstore, or may be ordered
by visiting: Hay House USA: **www.hayhouse.com**®
Hay House Australia: **www.hayhouse.com.au**
Hay House UK: **www.hayhouse.co.uk**
Hay House South Africa: **www.hayhouse.co.za**
Hay House India: **www.hayhouse.co.in**

The Priest and the Medium

The Amazing True Story of
Psychic Medium B. Anne Gehman
and Her Husband,
Former Jesuit Priest Wayne Knoll, Ph.D.

Suzanne Giesemann

HAY HOUSE, INC.
Carlsbad, California • New York City
London • Sydney • Johannesburg
Vancouver • Hong Kong • New Delhi

Copyright © 2009 by Suzanne Giesemann

Published and distributed in the United States by: Hay House, Inc.: www.hayhouse. com • *Published and distributed in Australia by:* Hay House Australia Pty. Ltd.: www.hayhouse.com.au • *Published and distributed in the United Kingdom by:* Hay House UK, Ltd.: www.hayhouse.co.uk • *Published and distributed in the Republic of South Africa by:* Hay House SA (Pty), Ltd.: www.hayhouse.co.za • *Distributed in Canada by:* Raincoast: www.raincoast.com • *Published in India by:* Hay House Publishers India: www.hayhouse.co.in

Editorial supervision: Jill Kramer • *Design:* Nick C. Welch

All rights reserved. No part of this book may be reproduced by any mechanical, photographic, or electronic process, or in the form of a phonographic recording; nor may it be stored in a retrieval system, transmitted, or otherwise be copied for public or private use—other than for "fair use" as brief quotations embodied in articles and reviews—without prior written permission of the publisher.

The author of this book does not dispense medical advice or prescribe the use of any technique as a form of treatment for physical, emotional, or medical problems without the advice of a physician, either directly or indirectly. The intent of the author is only to offer information of a general nature to help you in your quest for emotional and spiritual well-being. In the event you use any of the information in this book for yourself, which is your constitutional right, the author and the publisher assume no responsibility for your actions.

Library of Congress Cataloging-in-Publication Data

Giesemann, Suzanne.
  The priest and the medium : the amazing true story of psychic medium B. Anne Gehman and her husband, former Jesuit Priest Wayne Knoll / Suzanne R. Giesemann.
    p. cm.
  ISBN 978-1-4019-2309-9 (tradepaper : alk. paper) 1. Gehman, Anne, 1936- 2. Women psychics--United States--Biography. 3. Women mediums--United States--Biography. 4. Knoll, Wayne, 1933- 5. Catholic ex-priests--United States--Biography. 6. College teachers--United States--Biography. I. Title.
  BF1027.G44G54 2009
  133.3092'273--dc22
  [B]   2008040017

ISBN: 978-1-4019-2309-9

12 11 10 09 5 4 3 2
1st edition, June 2009
2nd edition, August 2009

Printed in the United States of America

For Susan, whose vibrant spirit could never be extinguished. Thanks for the yellow butterflies.

Author's note: Some names and identifying details have been changed to protect the confidentiality of the individuals involved. When actual names have been used, permission has been granted.

Foreword

What can I say about Anne Gehman? To know her is to understand what it means to truly admire another human being. I learned of Anne through my friend Laurie Campbell, who's also a medium. Laurie spoke fondly of Anne for being a unique person and an outstanding medium, although it would be a few years before I'd have the pleasure of meeting Anne face to face. When I met her, we were in Lily Dale, New York. She invited me to her house for lunch and a little socializing.

Anne's home in Lily Dale looks like a perfect, pink dollhouse; and the six-year-old in me was giddy to be invited inside. We chatted about people we both knew and the paths we walk that sometimes morph into something unexpectedly splendid. We spoke of our girls whom we adore and the husbands who were divinely guided our way.

To try to describe Anne is difficult because she defies words, which are my only tools to share her with you. Anne is not only a timeless beauty on the outside, but she carries her beauty within as well. My assistant Andrea Brooks described her as "dessert for the soul." I'd say she's right. I, on the other hand, am a "kick down the door" kind of medium. Anne uses her gifts with grace, yet her eyes carry secret weapons that put you on notice. I mean that as a compliment, for she's every bit a lady, but even ladies have limits, as they should.

While with Anne in Lily Dale, I had the pleasure of meeting her husband, Wayne Knoll. Wayne is an enigma—a former Jesuit priest now married to a Spiritualist minister and psychic medium. In spite of their different spiritual backgrounds, it's obvious that he and Anne were made for one another. Wayne has dashing good looks, a warm soul, a brilliant mind, an accepting heart, and eyes for only his one spectacular lady.

Our host was most welcoming and immediately took my husband, Joe, and our girls out on Cassadaga Lake for a great kayak experience. The girls loved it. My daughter Fallon brought back a lily that Anne put into a clear "bubble" bowl of water and proudly displayed in her kitchen. Fallon beamed with pride as Anne swooned over the gift. Wayne made that wonderful memory possible for us, as did Anne, and I thank them.

This marvelous book by Suzanne Giesemann is the tale of Anne and Wayne's remarkable lives, but it's also their love story, which must be acknowledged as extraordinary in its own right. Separately, they've inspired countless lives for the better. Together, they're unstoppable. Their positive outlook, coupled with their resilience and humor, comes through on every page, making you feel as though you're there with them through their trials and tribulations.

My favorite parts of the book involve their love story, of course, but also the criminal cases that Anne has helped with over the years and her impressive predictions. I was stunned to discover that Anne and I have an interesting overlap in our own lives, in that we've both brought through the spirit of Apollo astronaut Gus Grissom. How random is that? I wrote about Gus in my third book and was blown away by the coincidence.

I love the clever way in which each succeeding chapter takes you from Anne to Wayne, emphasizing the uncanny parallels in their lives until their two paths merge. The design is organized, yet highly personal, allowing you a glimpse into Anne and Wayne's fascinating lives that will keep you hungering for more.

I recommend this book for anyone grappling with their own beliefs. It offers a candid look at religion and spirituality and draws a picture showing the intersection of the two. From Anne and Wayne, you'll learn firsthand that what you want in life sometimes involves making difficult choices. These two individuals stayed true to their convictions, and I admire them for that. At the end of the story, your faith in people will receive a jump start, and you'll find restored assurance that we're bound by love in life and death.

I'm lucky to call Anne and Wayne friends, and Joe and I plan to do so for a very long time.

— **Allison Dubois**

Preface

John F. Kennedy is going to die.

The thought flashed through Anne Gehman's mind yet again that warm November morning, and her hand slipped. The patient by her left hip jerked his head in surprise as the saliva ejector sucked noisily at his cheek.

"Miss Gehman!" Dr. Collins turned to admonish his young assistant.

Anne shook her head and apologized as she repositioned the tube behind the patient's lower teeth. Try as she might, she simply couldn't concentrate. Her mind was hundreds of miles to the west in Dallas, Texas, where President Kennedy and his beautiful wife, Jackie, were scheduled to have lunch.

Anne moved automatically, handing Dr. Collins the mirror, probes, and gauze before he asked for them. In her mind, she was back in Wilbur Hull's cozy house in Cassadaga three years earlier, watching the big debate between Vice President Nixon and Senator Kennedy on Wilbur's black-and-white TV. That day she'd turned to Wilbur and stated with unwavering certainty: "Senator Kennedy is going to win the election, but he's going to be assassinated."

Her pronouncement may have surprised Wilbur, but he had no reason to doubt her. He was the one who'd given names to the gifts Anne had taken for granted all of her life. To Wilbur, words like *prophecy, clairvoyance,* and *mediumship* were as common as *cat* and *dog.*

When Kennedy won the election, Anne felt no triumph in having been right. Every time she saw the handsome young President on television, her conviction grew that he'd be killed by an assassin's bullet. When news came of the Kennedys' impending trip to Texas, Anne felt the same shroud of dread descending over her that she'd experienced years before.

President Kennedy is going to die . . . in Dallas.

Desperate to do something, she found the number for the White House and called it no fewer than three times. The people on the other end didn't know her the way Wilbur did. They paid no attention to her dire warnings and refused to put her through to anyone who could alert the President.

Now Anne handed a cup to the patient at her side and instructed him to rinse and spit. The man leaned over the little round sink. Dr. Collins sat back. Suddenly, a commotion down the hall caused the three to raise their heads in unison. The door from the waiting room swung open and a woman burst into the hallway.

"President Kennedy has been shot!"

The patient sputtered into the sink. Anne put a hand to her chest and raised her eyes to meet those of Dr. Collins. She'd told him that President Kennedy shouldn't make the trip to Texas. Like the switchboard operator at the White House, he'd laughed off her warnings. The eyes that looked back at her now reflected not just shock, but a touch of wonder.

Anne knew that her boss, a staunch conservative, didn't care as much for Kennedy as she did, but it was hard not to be emotional after such distressing news. With a waiting room full of patients, they continued to work, but Anne could tell that even Dr. Collins was rattled. When she dropped a sterilized probe onto the floor, he didn't say a word.

As soon as they finished with their next patient, Dr. Collins left the room for an update on the news. Anne remained behind, her hands shaking as she prepped a new tray.

Dr. Collins returned to the exam room and stared at her from the doorway. She knew what he was going to say before he opened his mouth.

"He's dead," the dentist said.

Anne choked back a sob and barely managed to speak past the lump in her throat. "I need to excuse myself," she whispered.

She pushed past her boss and hurried down the hall to the restroom. She closed the door behind her and fumbled with the lock. In the privacy of the small room, she felt free to let out the sorrow that had been building for days. As tears rolled down her cheeks, she stared at her reflection in the mirror over the sink. Her long brown hair and delicate features made her look even younger than her 27 years. With her soft, feminine voice, she must have sounded like a child on the phone. It was no wonder the operator at the White House had ignored her.

She pictured President Kennedy with his thick shock of hair and cried even harder. She truly loved him, but had been unable to do anything to save him from his fate. Anne had carried the responsibility within her, and now her heart threatened to burst.

Wilbur Hull had taught her to appreciate her gifts, but what good were they, she challenged herself, if she couldn't use them to help people? Anne knew that she was blessed. As a healer, she was able to relieve others' pain and restore them to health. As a medium, she could sense, and communicate with, spirits who had passed to the other side, bringing great mental comfort to their loved ones left behind. As a psychic, her ability to foresee future events held the potential to change the course of history, but it was useless if no one would listen to her.

She thought back to the first time Spirit had warned her that President Kennedy's days were limited. His death, she knew, had been in motion for a long time, at least since she had watched the televised debate with Wilbur. Through the dark cloud of her grief, she could hear Wilbur's lessons. A *prediction*, he taught her, could be changed and a psychic could intercede. *Prophecy*, on the other hand, is that which is already set and can't be changed. Even if she'd been able to get through to President Kennedy, Anne now began to understand, who was to say that he might not have met the same end at a different time in a different place? These were questions that even a psychic would never be able to answer.

Anne straightened her uniform and reached for the door. She knew that she wouldn't be a dental assistant forever. It was simply the means to an end. As soon as she'd saved enough money, she would be free to dedicate her days full-time to her true calling as a medium. She'd been unable to help her beloved President Kennedy, but she was going to do everything in her power to help those she could.

Chapter 1

Most young children have vivid imaginations. Beatrice Anne Gehman was no exception, but she had a vivid memory as well—so vivid that she remembered her birth.

When Beaty Anne described the maternity room's cheery yellow walls and told her mother that she wanted a picture of an angel like the framed one she'd seen there, she was met with stunned silence. Not because her claims were so outrageous, but because they were right.

Her mother was well familiar with that picture of an angel and those yellow walls. She worked at the maternity home in Petoskey, Michigan, where she'd given birth. But the babies she helped deliver there could barely focus their eyes, let alone see the kind of details her daughter described.

Despite her clear memories, Beaty Anne didn't recall seeing the family doctor on that July morning back in 1936. That's because the good Dr. Engle arrived late, after she was already delivered.

"I remember you were crying, Mama," Beaty Anne said, "but you were smiling, too."

And her mother had reason to smile. Young Beatrice was her namesake, as decided by her older children. The girl's middle name was Dr. Engle's idea. She would be called Beaty, or sometimes Beatrice, or Beatrice Anne by her father; and in her later years, just plain Anne. But her name was never really plain—Dr. Engle had insisted that it end with an "e."

She was the last child born to Beatrice and John Gehman. Their first six each arrived less than 18 months apart, one after the other.

Then after a seven-year hiatus, little Rosina came along, followed by Anne two years later. Anne laughs as she recalls her father rounding up the children. When he called just the girls, he'd string her sisters' names together, often making Anne think her name was "Mary Patricia Aloise Rosina Beatrice Anne."

Looking back, Anne wonders how they all squeezed into their small, wood-frame house with the faded red paint. Her parents slept in a room on the first floor with the children spread between the three rooms upstairs. Being so much younger than the rest, Anne and Rosina had a bedroom to themselves.

One night while her sister slept soundly beside her, Anne awoke to find her grandfather standing by her bed. He only lived about six miles down the road, but he'd never visited her like this before. She smiled as he bent down and kissed her forehead, then he tucked her in and quietly disappeared.

As soon as he left, Anne pulled back the covers and scurried down the dark stairs. She slipped into her parents' bedroom and shook them awake, exclaiming, "Grandpa came to see me!"

"Don't worry, Beatrice Anne," her father said. "You were just having a dream."

"No," Anne insisted, shaking her brown curls. "Grandpa's gone to Heaven."

"Everything's okay," her mother said, and led her back to bed.

Just before daybreak, someone knocked at the front door. It was the neighbors from down the road. John wondered what they could want so early in the morning, but five-year-old Anne already knew. They'd come to tell the family about her grandpa. He'd had a heart attack and had died in the night. The neighbors had found him lying on the steps in front of his house.

Hearing the news, Anne's parents immediately thought of her dream, and they asked her to tell them again what she'd seen. She insisted that his appearance wasn't a dream at all. He'd stood beside her just as real as if he were alive. She hadn't been scared, simply pleased that he'd come to tuck her in.

Seeing spirits was nothing new for Beaty Anne. She couldn't remember a time when they weren't around. Some she knew and some she didn't. Rather than being scared by what others might call ghosts, Anne welcomed these peaceful souls. They were human just like she was. She saw them and sensed them; she simply couldn't touch them. As a child who knew no better, she always found their presence loving and comforting.

⊕⊕⊕

The white-haired woman in the brown-shingle house two streets over never failed to smile at Anne when the little girl walked by. With her pointed nose, pointed chin, and dark, dark eyes, the elderly neighbor might have frightened other children, but Anne looked forward to seeing her. Sometimes she sat in a wheelchair, but mostly she just rocked back and forth in the rocker in one corner of the porch. The two never said much to each other, but Anne knew that the woman's name was Emma.

One day as Anne passed the small house, she saw flames around it. Emma nodded at her from the porch and continued to rock as if nothing were wrong, so the seven-year-old nodded back. Several more times she saw flames surrounding the house, but always Emma smiled.

"The neighbors' house is going to burn down," Anne announced at the dinner table one evening. Her father looked up, shared a glance with his wife, then told his daughter not to have such negative thoughts.

Several days later, as Anne and her mother walked hand-in-hand to the store, they passed Emma's house. Anne turned to her mother and said, "That's the house that's going to burn down."

"You mustn't think that way, Beaty Anne," the older Beatrice said.

"But Emma told me," Anne insisted.

The fire was big news in little Petoskey. The house was a complete loss, but the family wasn't homeless for long. It was the Gehmans' nature to help those who were less fortunate. In spite of their tight quarters, John and Beatrice invited the neighbors they'd never met to stay with them, offering their own bed until the couple could find another place to live.

The big oak table was crowded with the extra guests. John sat at one end and Beatrice at the other. The Gehman children squeezed closer on the long benches to make room. With bowls of home-grown vegetables steaming before them, they joined hands and thanked God for the food they were so blessed to share.

"It's interesting," Mrs. Gehman said as she dished the food onto the plates. "Little Beaty Anne told us your house was going to burn down, but we thought she was just imagining things again."

"I wasn't imagining it, Mama," Anne said indignantly, "Emma told me."

"Emma?" their neighbor asked. "How do you know about Emma?"

The shock in the woman's voice made all eyes turn to Anne.

"She always s-smiled at me from the p-porch," the little girl replied, stammering as she often did in front of strangers.

"She did?" The woman leaned forward. "What did she look like?"

Anne described the white hair, the pointy nose and chin, and those dark, dark eyes.

The neighbor's hand flew to her mouth. "That's *her*—that's my mother, Emma! She was confined to a wheelchair, but she loved to sit on that porch."

"You actually saw her?" the woman's husband asked.

Anne nodded shyly. She saw Emma all the time.

"But she passed away years ago!" the woman said, her eyes wide.

Anne shrugged and took a bite of broccoli.

If the Gehmans thought their youngest daughter was unusual, they didn't share those thoughts with her. If anything, they helped Anne see that her visions and visitations were special gifts from God. She often sat with her father in the living room after dinner to pray, and listen to verses from the Bible.

"Now concerning spiritual gifts, brethren, I would not have you ignorant," John read from the New Testament one evening. "There are diversities of gifts, but the same Spirit."

Anne listened with closed eyes to the deep, full voice. She adored her father. He was a handsome man with black hair, dark eyes, and an olive complexion. Everybody always had such good things to say about him, like the people at the general store. They were still talking about the time her papa walked all the way back from the house when he realized they'd given him two cents more than he was owed.

She remembered when he saw two men stealing potatoes from his field. He ran inside and got her brothers, then they all went out and helped the thieves fill their bags. The table was crowded again that night with the two extra guests, but her Mama never let anyone go hungry. One of those men even joined their church after her Papa finished talking to them.

John Gehman, known to his family by his German baptismal name, Johannas, was a leader in Petoskey's spiritual community. Nobody would have expected that years earlier. He'd been caught in the barn doing something that good Mennonite boys just didn't do: using a typewriter. The correspondence course he was working on got him thrown out of the church.

John's family members, like others in their northern Michigan town, were close to the Amish in dress and beliefs. More than anything, they valued people over material possessions. They rejected technology, not because it was evil, but for fear it might affect the close nature of their community.

After he was shunned, John went to work on a neighboring farm. When his boss saw that the young man spent all of his free time reading, he took notice. Despite the fact that John had only three years of formal schooling, the farmer-professor pulled some strings. He enrolled his young farmhand in nearby Fenton College.

Because he loved nature, John chose to study horticulture. He completed his degree but never accepted the diploma. Instead, he returned to his Mennonite roots, where hard work was more important than a piece of paper.

Over the years, John worked a variety of jobs. He raised bees, chopped down trees, and tried his hand at carpentry. Until the Great Depression came along, he ran an experimental seed farm for Burpee. There, he grew the first yellow geranium folks had ever seen. He could have had it patented, but Mennonites didn't do such things. Instead, he went on to tend the grounds at the big hotels along Lake Michigan. In the winter months, he ran the local skating rink. Like his other jobs, it didn't pay much, but the Gehman children skated for free.

Beaty Anne loved going to the skating rink. She was the only one who could do splits on the ice. Usually shy because of her stutter, the skates transformed her. She'd stand in the center of the rink and jitterbug on one leg while her brothers and sisters laughed.

The highlight was the winter carnival at the end of the season. Every year the children got to wear special outfits and show off their skills. Anne loved the pink satin skirt she wore, with the wide band at the hem and the matching vest. It made no difference that her clothes had been handed down five times. When she put on the colorful costume, she knew that she was glamorous.

Her stint as a star was short lived, though. Once the ice rink closed, her heavy black oxfords replaced the skates. Her drab, dark dress once again became the norm. For the daughter of a former Mennonite, *plainness* was a virtue.

Anne opened her eyes and looked at her father as he read from the Bible. He continued with the verse from 1 Corinthians: "For to one is given by the Spirit the word of wisdom . . . to another faith by the same Spirit; to another the gifts of healing by the same Spirit; to another the working of miracles; to another prophecy; to another discerning of spirits; to another diverse kinds of tongues."

John returned his daughter's gaze and let the words sink in.

His choice of verses could not have been more appropriate. In the years ahead, Beatrice Anne would display the gift of prophecy. She would heal people with her hands. To those she helped, her gifts would seem like miracles. She would continue to discern spirits, and she would speak in tongues.

But miracles or not, as long as she lived under the Gehman roof, the glamorous pink skirts would have to wait.

Chapter 2

Wayne Adam Knoll grew up in the shadow of the Catholic church. The twin brick bell towers that flanked St. Fidelis's façade loomed 140 feet over the town. On hot summer days, when the sun rose high over the Kansas wheat fields, the towers cast a swath of shade across the Knoll house a block away.

St. Fidelis sat on the west side of town, but to the Knoll family, the church was central.

There was never a question about going to Mass. Yes, it was an ordeal getting all those boys washed and dressed in their Sunday best, but Mother Knoll had a system. In true German fashion, she kept things orderly by setting out the children's clothes well ahead. Wayne, the oldest, born in 1933, could always find his things at the top of the stairway. Omer's clothes sat neatly on the next step down, followed on successive stairs by Lester's, Carroll's, and Devon's.

In later years, the family grew to 11 with the arrival of Iris, Terry, Janie, and Larry. The youngest boy was quick to claim that when he came along, his parents reached perfection and stopped. Larry's siblings were quick to correct him: they'd simply run out of steps.

There was plenty of room for the Knoll clan at Mass. St. Fidelis was the largest church west of the Mississippi when it was completed more than two decades earlier in 1911. Nicknamed "the Cathedral of the Plains," its seating capacity exceeded the population of Victoria, a tiny town that stretched less than a mile from end to end. The massive Romanesque building stood as an ever-present testament to the faith of the farmers who built it.

Like so many immigrants, Wayne's ancestors came to America in search of a new life: one free of unfair taxation, free from conscription, and with the freedom to practice their faith. They'd tried to find such liberties on the steppes of Russia along the Volga River. When they discovered more of the same oppression they'd left behind in Bavaria, the German settlers began to think of moving yet again.

A Jesuit mystic in the Russian town of Saratov spoke to several young men from the settlements. He told them that things were going to get much worse for the Germans and encouraged them to go to America. Hearing the dire prediction, the village elders sent a group of scouts by steamship to the New World.

Upon their arrival in Baltimore, the young men climbed aboard a train and headed west. Traveling only with duffel bags and shovels, the scouts got off at each stop. Standing beside the tracks, they thrust their shovels into the soil, sifted the dirt through their fingers, then raised it to their mouths for the ultimate test.

When they arrived in Kansas, the scouts' excitement grew. The land was flat like the steppes in Russia. The vast plains were undeveloped and could be bought from the government at a very good price. Best of all, the soil tasted just right for growing wheat. The young men sent a telegram back to Russia: They'd found their new home. Come!

Twenty-three brave families arrived in 1876, tired but hopeful. They established their town just north of a settlement of gentlemen farmers who'd come from England three years earlier. The British had named their town Victoria in honor of their queen. The Germans named theirs Herzog, after their village on the Volga River.

The British planned to live a life of leisure, playing cricket on country estates like the ones they'd left behind. When they experienced the harsh winters and lack of amenities, most gave up the pioneer life and returned home.

Toughened by their years on the steppes, the German-Russians stayed. They adopted the town's name from the British settlers, but little else. With no trees from which to harvest wood, they built one-room huts of sod to survive the first winters. Frigid winds swooped down from the north, and they burned buffalo chips to stay warm. Mother Knoll told Wayne about the time the Chippewa Indians came to her parents' farm, half frozen. Some Cheyenne had killed six railroad workers several years back, but that didn't stop the family from feeding the starving visitors.

Their Catholic faith had led the immigrants to Victoria. Once their need for basic shelter was met, their desire to worship as a community came next. Within a year of their arrival, they built a church measuring 30 by 60 feet, using sandstone from nearby hills.

By the turn of the century, the German farmers had outgrown the small building. They decided to build a structure that would show anyone who saw it the depth of their love for God. With few funds, but no lack of faith, the parish assessed each family its share of sandstone and labor.

Wayne only had to look at the walls of the cathedral to be reminded of his family's contribution to the monumental effort. There, embedded behind the cornerstone, lay his grandfather Allois's tools. As chief stonecutter, Allois tapped his hammer at spikes inserted deep into the rock. Ten-inch slabs weighing up to 100 pounds sprang free, to be loaded by hand onto the villagers' mule-drawn wagons. Construction continued for three years, with each family hauling up to 80 loads of stone.

It took clever means to maintain such a large church in a town with fewer than 1,000 residents. The parish held fund-raisers and auctioned off benches to raise money for upkeep. Young Wayne was sure it was his father's frugality that bought them the seats right up front. Only in later years did he understand his parents' desire to be more intimately involved in Mass.

Each week, the Knolls filled their pew. Wayne sat mesmerized in the soft glow of the stained-glass windows brought all the way from Germany. Yes, he loved playing ball with his friends, but being in church was special. His mother told him that this was God's home, and he always waited with anticipation for Jesus to arrive.

The nuns taught him that when the priest held up the host and said, "This is my body," the bread actually became the body of Christ. They told him that when the priest raised the chalice with the wine and said, "This is my blood," it became that, too. Wayne liked that part of Mass best, because that's when they rang the special bell. Far different from the *clang-clang* that called his family to worship, the silvery sound was the music of angels. That ethereal tone confirmed to Wayne that God was real! The six-year-old heard the magical bell and knew without a doubt that Jesus Christ was in his house.

⊕⊕⊕

"Did Sister Mary send you here again?"

Wayne nodded and rushed to the shelf by the window. He scanned the spines of the books and pulled down a hardback with a familiar title. He'd started this one the last time his teacher sent him to the library. He took the book to a low wooden table with child-sized chairs and opened the cover. Soon his friends back in the classroom were left behind, and he was floating across the sky in a hot-air balloon.

The nuns in Victoria's grammar school didn't know what to do with such a bright young student. When he finished his lessons ahead of the others, they said what they always did: "Go to the library, Wayne."

Their request was far from punishment. He'd discovered the magic of books at four years old. Sitting with three-year-old Omer beside him, Wayne read to his brother. The words carried the boys far from the wheat fields of Kansas, where nothing ever changed, to exciting worlds they could explore in their minds. When he came to a word he didn't understand, Wayne spelled it aloud. Mother Knoll would lift her head from her kitchen chores and call out the meaning.

The ringing school bell brought his balloon back to earth. Wayne returned the book to its shelf and ran outside. Varian Wellbrock was already waiting for him. It was time for softball, a game he and his friends played until they couldn't see the ball through the darkness.

Spying his friend standing in the school yard, Wayne thought back to another day, years earlier, when he and Varian had faced each other in the same spot. The Knolls had just moved from the town of St. Peter, a short distance beyond Hays to the west. They'd decided to return to Mother Knoll's hometown where Wayne's father managed the grain elevators.

Wayne was anxious to make friends with the local boys, but they held him at arm's length. Their taunts and mocking left him feeling puzzled and lonely. One day as he was going down the stairs when school let out, he had to push past the boys on the landing.

"Where are you going, new kid?" one asked. Wayne turned to answer just as a foot shot forward.

He landed on his face. The boys' laughter filled the stairwell as he rolled over and looked up. Varian Wellbrock stood at the center of the small crowd, his arms crossed in smug satisfaction.

Wayne got to his feet and brushed off his clothes. He turned his back and continued outside. He could hear the boys behind him, laughing and jeering. Halfway across the yard, with his house in full sight, he stopped. Slowly he turned, his face as red as the schoolhouse bricks, and raised his fists.

A cheer went up as Varian dove at Wayne. The others formed a ring around the two fighters, but they kept their distance. The boys traded blows equally, but weeks of frustration gave Wayne the advantage. In the back of his mind, he worried that the nuns would see them, but nothing was going to stop him. Enough was enough.

Then, out of the corner of his eye, he saw something far more frightening than the sisters' habits: his father's car pulling up to the curb. Wayne knew he was going to get it when he arrived home.

It wasn't his father that stopped the fight, however, but the sight of blood. The cheap ring Wayne had found in a Cracker Jack box had proven valuable, cutting into his opponent's skin. As the combatants separated, the circle of boys closed in around them. Wayne and Varian stared at each other wordlessly as Varian wiped the blood with the back of his hand. He nodded his head, then turned and walked away.

From the next day forward, they were bosom buddies.

"You ready?" Varian asked, tossing a softball into the air.

"You bet," Wayne answered. "Back in a minute!"

He ran the short block to his house and vaulted across the floor of the blue-roofed porch. He flew upstairs to his room, changed out of his school clothes, and grabbed his bat. He met his father coming in the front door just as he was heading out.

Wayne tossed a greeting into the air, then stopped as an unanswered question popped into his mind.

"Dad," he said, turning back, "do you remember the time I had that fight with Varian in the school yard?"

His father nodded. "Yes, I sure do."

Wayne cocked his head. "Why didn't you ever say anything? I saw you watching from the car."

Adam Knoll glanced toward the school. "I was just checking to see if you were all right, son. It looked as if you were handling things just fine from where I sat."

Wayne held his father's gaze, his face flushed with pride.

"You boys going to play ball?"

"Yes, sir," Wayne said, moving toward the door.

"Too bad. I have to run over to Hays. Thought I might stop by the library."

Wayne's hand froze on the knob.

"Hear they got in another Zane Grey book," his father said slyly.

Wayne pulled his hand back and set his bat by the door. The boys could play without him.

Wayne sat in the front row of the classroom, head bent as he scribbled the last line. He set his pencil down, raised his head, and looked around. All of the other sixth graders were still writing. He couldn't help that he finished so fast; learning just came easily to him. His mother said it was a gift from God.

He stared out the window at the church towers. Easter was coming up. Holy Week was always a special time, but it was even better since he'd become an altar boy. Now, each year on Good Friday when the cathedral bells hung silent, he and the other boys paraded through town. The racket they made with their clappers let everyone know it was time to head to church.

The noisy procession continued through the weekend, with the clappers announcing each sacred service. Their fun culminated on Monday, when the boys added their own voices to the commotion, shouting, *"Geld oder eier!* Money or eggs!" The gifts they received from the townspeople paid for the altar boys' picnic.

He looked up from his daydream as a shadow fell across his desk.

Sister Frances gazed down at him over her glasses. "Why aren't you working?" she asked.

"I'm finished," he said.

Normally, he loved this moment—anticipating the excitement of being sent down the hall and reading a new book. This time, he felt a cold draft of dread as the nun nodded toward the door and said, "Go to the library, Wayne."

He stepped into the empty corridor. He made the familiar right turn and shuffled slowly ahead. He glanced in the seventh graders' room and swallowed past a lump in his throat. He passed the eighth graders, and his lip began to tremble. The door to the library loomed before him, but instead of going in, Wayne turned his face to the wall and cried.

He had two more years to go in grammar school, and he had read every book in the library.

Chapter 3

The Gehmans didn't have the money for a car. If they had, her father would have taken it to fetch Doc Engle the time Anne became so ill. When the doctor felt her burning forehead, he gathered her in his arms and carried her outside. He laid her on the back seat of his Buick and headed for the hospital. It was the first time the eight-year-old had ridden in a car, but she was too sick to care.

The diagnosis was pneumonia, and it was serious. For two weeks, Anne lay in bed with little sign of improvement. One morning, she heard her parents talking with Dr. Engle in the hallway. If they'd known she could hear them, they probably would have closed the door. She listened as the doctor told them that she might not make it through the night.

Later that day, Anne looked up and saw a bright beam of light streaming through the window. It was the most dazzling light she'd ever seen, and it filled the corner of the room by her bed. *Is that the sun?* she wondered, but no sunlight had ever been so brilliant. She stared, transfixed, as it condensed into a large ball, then formed a body.

The vision reminded Anne of the angel she'd seen when she was born, but this was no painting. The luminous winged figure with the beautiful face drifted to her bedside, and neither of them said a word. They simply connected with their eyes, and Anne felt a surge of love. The angel swept one wing the length of the sick girl's body, then floated away through the ceiling.

Later in life, Anne would question the reality of winged angels. She'd wonder why the one who came to her bedside that day in the hospital had wings. It bothered her because she knew that these beings didn't need wings to move about. In time, however, she realized that angels, like the spirits of loved ones, appear in the form that a person is most likely to recognize. If an uncle who always wore a straw hat passed to the other side, the mention of that hat by a medium would be evidence to his family that the uncle lived on. Likewise, if a beautiful light appeared at the side of a dying child, she would know by the wings that she'd been touched by an angel.

A nurse came into the room shortly after the spirit visitor had left. She checked her patient's temperature, then called Doc Engle right away. He, like her parents, was weak with relief to discover that Anne's fever had broken. When she told them about the angel, they didn't laugh, nor did they blame her story on a feverish delusion. They said it was the answer to prayer.

Two days later, Beaty Anne was back at home with her brothers and sisters.

Other than her sister Rosina, Anne had few friends close to her own age to play with. When no one was around, the old woodshed attached to the back of the home became her playhouse. There she piled scraps of wood one atop the other to make a table and chairs. She propped her favorite teddy bear on a makeshift seat. The bear was one her mother had made. It had no face, for the Bible warned against graven images.

Instead of sharing tea, Anne took her place across from the bear and simply chatted. She told him about the spirits who came to visit and passed along their messages of love. She didn't know that she was practicing her future vocation; she was simply doing what came naturally.

Anne never told her parents about the readings in the woodshed. Maybe her father noticed the tiny table and chairs, or maybe a neighbor saw her talking with an imaginary friend. But one day while she and her mother were folding clothes together, Mama mentioned that Mrs. Swenor wanted to speak with Anne. Although the woman lived nearby, Anne had never spent much time with her, but if Mama wanted the two of them to talk, Anne would never say no.

Beatrice set two chairs in a corner of the dining room. Mrs. Swenor came in, and Anne sat across from her. The little girl didn't know what they were supposed to talk about, so she told Mrs. Swenor about the old lady standing at her side who had green eyes just like hers. She mentioned a name that popped into her mind and passed along a greeting.

"And she suffered from a problem here," Anne said, rubbing her small hand on her chest.

Anne didn't know if she'd said the right thing, but Mrs. Swenor seemed satisfied. She thanked Anne's mama, then got up and left. Soon more neighbors came to call, one after the other. They knocked at the door and said, "I want to talk with little Beaty Anne."

And Beaty Anne talked. She didn't understand why nobody else could see the people she saw, nor why some of her neighbors cried when she described the friendly spirits. But after they dried their tears, the visitors always left smiling.

Her mother didn't initiate the visits, nor did she ask for money. With their faith as a guide, she and John simply stood back and supported their daughter as she developed her natural abilities.

Much of Anne's training took place in the shade of the big tree in the front yard. While she rested on a blanket, spirits introduced her to a world beyond her five senses. She thought of these adventures as dreams, for she didn't know what else to call them. Often, an Indian boy rode toward her on his pony. He'd reach out his hand to pull her up beside him, and they'd gallop away to what Anne later realized were different realms of reality.

Other times, while fully awake, she enjoyed the company of a young Indian woman. The spirit wore her dark hair in two long braids and told Anne to call her Honto. The two would leave the shade of the tree and wander through the nearby woods. Anyone watching would see Beaty Anne walking with one arm held out to the side. She was simply holding hands with Honto.

⊕⊕⊕

Many Indians called northern Michigan home. The Chippewa tribe had long ago given up their birch-bark wigwams in favor of houses, and one family lived next door to the Gehmans.

The first time Anne went inside the neighbor's house, she was frightened by the crippled woman huddled on the bed. Ella May had raised several children, then suffered a tragic illness that left her trapped inside a useless body. Although permanently bent, with her arms frozen across her chest, her friendly smile soon made Anne feel welcome.

The family often asked Anne to sit with Ella May when they went out. They only wanted someone to keep their mother company, but Anne was happy to feed Ella May her oatmeal or help her with a bedpan. The woman's body had failed her, but her mind was still sharp. She filled the hours by telling Anne stories that had been passed from one generation to the next.

Anne listened, enthralled, to tales from the sacred history about the spirit Nanabozho. The legends reminded Anne of the Bible stories her papa read. She listened to how Nanabozho caused the great flood, then escaped the high waters in a canoe filled with animals. Later, a giant fish came along and swallowed many people. Nanabozho taunted the fish until he, too, was swallowed. Once inside the fish's belly, he used his arrow to mortally wound it. The great hero came out of the fish, went home, and smoked his pipe, happy that he had saved his tribe.

Until she spent time with Ella May, Anne had only known the spiritual beliefs of her own family. From her Indian friend, she learned about a world governed by the Great Spirit. The Chippewa faith was much more personal than the Mennonites'. Their knowledge came from dreams and visions not unlike those in Anne's naps under the tree.

Anne grew to love Ella May. She sometimes gave her readings, just as she did for the neighbors in her dining room. An elderly member of the family, known to everyone as Grandma White, would often listen as Anne passed along the spirit messages.

"There is a light that surrounds you," Grandma White said one day from across the room. "It is the light of your spirit, not of your body, and it has the colors of the rainbow. You will help many people in your lifetime."

Anne hadn't yet learned about auras, but she was pleased by the observation. She felt a strong connection with this woman who saw visions and heard voices.

Grandma White went to the yard and returned with a long green frond. She crossed to Anne's side and looked down at her.

"You are like us," she said.

Before Anne could react, the old lady took hold of Anne's wrist and whisked the frond across it. Tiny barbs on the reed cut into Anne's skin, drawing blood. The Indian woman quickly pressed her hand over the small wound and held it there.

"Now you are one of us," she announced.

Like her Indian friends and her father, Anne loved the outdoors. She often took long walks through the forest and fields along the nearby Bear River. Her parents never questioned the young girl's extended absences nor her whereabouts. Just as they did with her gifts, they let her discover the world on her own.

One evening while wandering, Anne passed the Pentecostal church a mile from her house. She stopped, enthralled, and listened to the music. The hymns she sang with her parents on Sundays seemed lifeless compared to the joyous noise that flowed from the windows.

Anne opened the door cautiously and slipped into a pew in the back. Shouts of "Hallelujah!" and "Praise the Lord!" filled the air. She soaked up the vibrant energy as those around her raised their arms in jubilation. Such open displays of emotion would never be allowed in the Mennonites' somber service, where men and women sat separately and the pastors preached most often in German.

Looking at the altar, Anne recognized the preacher with the dark skin and long black ponytail. He was the Indian everyone talked about who had married a white woman. The mixed marriage was quite the scandal in Petoskey, but it didn't seem to bother the parishioners at the Foursquare Gospel Church. Like Anne, they hung on every word as he spoke about the joy of being saved. She didn't know what that meant, exactly, but she longed to be part of it.

The preacher exuded the power of a healer, and Anne was drawn to his energy like a bee to pollen. The following week, she snuck out again to the little log church, and she worked up the nerve to move closer to the front. Soon she was attending services regularly. She wasn't sure what her father would say about her drinking the Pentecostals' wine, but that was part of being saved.

When she reached her 12th birthday, Anne chose to be confirmed in the Mennonite faith. As a symbol of her confirmation, she pinned a net cap to her hair. Beneath the cap, her young mind swirled. The Mennonites worshiped God one way, the Pentecostals, another. The Chippewa honored the Great Spirit. Who was right?

She settled her bonnet over the netting, and suddenly Anne's thoughts settled as well. Perhaps it was Honto whispering in her ear, but at the tender age of 12, she knew the answer to her question: the Bible stories might differ; the names in the legends might sound strange, but it was all the same God.

Chapter 4

Even after countless hours on the bus, Anne couldn't sleep. Most of the passengers nodded off before they left northern Michigan, but she had too much to think about on this, her first long trip. She hoped her new dress wouldn't get too wrinkled. She wanted to look nice when her father saw her. It had been so long that he might not recognize her, especially in her bright, colorful clothes.

Anne never believed that Grandma White's words would come true. "Soon you'll move to a land to the south," Grandma had said. "There will be white sand and trees with branches like a fan."

When she heard the prediction, Anne had nodded just to be polite. Most everything Grandma said about Anne's life came true, but she couldn't imagine ever leaving Petoskey. It was all she knew. Her school was there. And her church.

Then, not too much later, in 1948, when Anne was 13, her parents started talking about making some changes. They pulled back from their spiritual roots. Anne continued to attend services, but her parents stopped going along.

Her father worried more and more about money. He almost always had a job, but nothing seemed to last for long. He said the season was too short up north—that he could make more money with year-round work. When he announced that he was leaving for Florida, Anne ran straight next door to tell Grandma White that she was right.

John left soon after and found work as a surveyor. Anne missed him terribly. She missed hearing him sing his German love songs to her mama and having him gather the family around him each evening. She studied her Bible nightly, but it just wasn't the same as when her father read the verses aloud. The spot at the head of the big oak table sat empty for 12 long months.

It took him that long to get a small cabin near the tiny town of Paisley, some furniture, and just enough money for two tickets on the Greyhound. The school year was starting soon, so Anne and Rosina went first. Had Anne known she wouldn't see her mother for a year, she wouldn't have been so excited about leaving.

The ride through Indiana wasn't too much different from Michigan. In Kentucky, things started to change, but when they got to Tennessee, Anne and Rosina sat spellbound. They'd never seen anything as beautiful as the craggy mountains covered in forests that made the woods back home seem dull.

The window at their seat wasn't big enough to take in all of the beautiful sights. Behind them, the glass ran from one side of the bus to the other, framing the view like a moving picture show. There was one empty seat in the back and Anne scampered down the aisle. She climbed onto the seat and kneeled, facing backward. The road shot out from under the bus; the life she'd left behind a diminishing dot on the horizon.

When the bus stopped, she stayed in her seat, still staring at the scenery. Suddenly, she became aware of a presence. She turned around and blinked up in surprise at the bus driver. He'd smiled nicely every time they stopped for food, but now his face twisted into a scary scowl.

"What do you think you're doing?" he demanded.

Anne gaped at him, too afraid to speak. Rosina sat a good ten rows away.

The driver shook his finger at Anne. "You can't sit back here," he said.

Anne's chest tightened. She looked down the aisle and noticed for the first time that the passengers were arranged by the color of their skin. When had that happened?

She locked eyes with the lady by her elbow—long enough to see a strength and dignity just like her mama's. Then the woman slowly lowered her head, leaving behind a memory that would linger in Anne's mind forever.

⊕⊕⊕

In spite of the sunshine, the palm trees, and her brighter clothes, Anne's days seemed colorless. Yes, she was happy to be reunited with her father, but she'd never before lived without her mama. She spent her first year in Florida with a constant ache in her heart.

Everything was so different from the life she'd known. The cabin had just one room. A curtain in the corner gave the girls their only privacy. They took their baths outside under the hand pump near an outhouse that wasn't nearly as nice as the three-holer back in Michigan.

Worst of all, there was no community. Their little home sat along a remote country road with only a few small cottages nearby and not a single Mennonite church. Anne's bonnet lay unworn in a drawer beside her Bible.

Anne and Rosina rose each morning far earlier than they were used to. The ride to Umatilla on the yellow county bus took the better part of an hour. Anne longed to go to school in DeLand, only ten miles away, but that was a different county.

School was the bright spot in Anne's days. Just like back home, she did well in her studies, even though the words in her books looked so jumbled. She could read them easier when she turned the pages sideways, but the teacher always came along and turned them back.

One Friday afternoon, Anne's English teacher gave the class a special assignment. They were to choose someone they thought was interesting and write a paper about that person over the weekend.

On Saturday, when Anne's father announced he had to buy supplies, she jumped at the chance to go with him. She climbed into their rusty Model A and held her breath. Sometimes the old Ford ran and sometimes it didn't. This time the engine started on the second try, and they rumbled down the road.

When they got to the small general store, John went inside. Anne trailed behind him, then stopped. On a bench beside the red Coca-Cola machine sat the most interesting man. She stood off to the side where he couldn't see her and studied him with growing excitement. She'd found the perfect subject for her English assignment.

He wore blue coveralls like a working man, but his face was wise and knowing. She watched as he carved a piece of wood, focused on his task with total concentration. The gnarled black fingers that gripped the knife looked like the knobby branches of an old tree. She couldn't wait to get home and write about him.

The 30-mile bus ride didn't seem so long on Monday morning. Surely none of her classmates had found a subject as interesting as hers. She waited anxiously all day to turn in her paper. When she got to English class, the teacher announced that each student would read his or her essay aloud.

Normally, Anne would worry about her stutter. But assured by the words on the page, she stepped to the front of the room with confidence and began. The students listened quietly at first, then they began to laugh. When Anne glanced up, she saw them whispering across the aisles. The teacher clucked her tongue, the class settled down, and Anne continued reading.

The boys and girls clapped politely when she finished, but their smirking faces told a different story. Anne took her seat and discovered a small square of paper on top of her English book. She looked to her left and right and saw her classmates watching her. The boys and girls covered their snickers as she turned the note over. Anne felt as though her heart had stopped when she read the ugly words scrawled in lead.

When school let out, her classmates' laughter resumed. Out of earshot of their teacher, they unleashed the full force of their adolescent cruelty, shouting "Nigger lover!" at Anne's heels like a pack of hungry dogs.

All the way home, Anne held back her tears. Her parents had taught her to love others and to treat everyone the way she wanted to be treated. She had no idea that people could be so unkind. Rosina asked her what was wrong, but she didn't dare to speak.

Like a reflection of her mood, the sky darkened as the bus neared their cabin. Just before they reached their stop, the clouds burst open, releasing a torrent of rain. Rosina ducked onto the porch, but Anne didn't follow. She held her arms over her head and ran for the big shed out back where her father's boss stored his wood.

She dashed under the roof and climbed on top of the lumber. Finally alone, she released her tears. She cried for the man in her essay, and she cried for herself. She thought of the woman on the Greyhound bus, and she cried some more. She cried for her mother, whom she missed more than ever.

Rain was leaking through the roof, but Anne ignored it. Her tears dripped from her cheeks, but she didn't bother to wipe them away. She let them fall onto the wood, leaving tiny dark splotches like the darkness in her heart. She watched as two tears fell into a puddle and blended with the rainwater. She stared at the spot, transfixed, as a thought began to take form.

As the puddle expanded, so did her mind. The water began to spill onto the ground, and Anne's thoughts spilled over with it. She felt as though she'd merged with the water, and she traveled along as it flowed through the earth to a stream, then on to a river and out to the ocean. There, it evaporated to form the clouds and fall once again to the earth as rain.

Anne became aware that water, like everything else that existed, was never lost—it was merely transformed.

She'd traveled to different realms with her spirit guides, but this was an awareness she'd never before experienced. She suddenly understood that she and everyone and everything were all intimately connected. The biggest mountain and the smallest stone, the trees and the flowers, all of the animals and all of the people . . . their essence was the same! Beyond the things she could touch and see, beyond the atoms and the molecules . . . *everything was one.*

It was what her guides had tried to show her in her dreams, what her father had tried to teach her from the Bible. She hadn't understood the message before, but now it seemed so clear: Her family whom she loved, the students who teased her, the black man on the bench . . . no one was better, no one was worse . . . like drops of water in the same ocean, they were each unique, but all of the same Source.

She sat back and ran her hands over her face, then she slowly climbed down from the lumber. She turned toward the cabin and looked around as if seeing the world with new eyes. She wanted to rush inside and tell her father that she finally understood, but she knew that she could never put into words what she'd experienced.

Instead, she took her time and slid her shoes through the wet grass. Until that day, her life had seemed normal. Now, for the first time in her 13 years, Anne realized that she not only saw things differently from others . . . she would never see things the same way again.

Chapter 5

Adam Knoll used to introduce his seven sons as his basketball team. With nine mouths to feed, Wayne's father bought some land near the center of town. He put a few cows there to graze, then added a ball field and a couple of hoops for the boys.

Being the oldest, Wayne never lacked for chores. The cows had to be milked every day, but his duties as an altar boy came first. During the week, he helped with 6 A.M. Mass. He'd rise with the sun, dress quickly, and run down the block to the church. He went first to the small room to the left of the main altar, where he donned his surplice and cassock. The priests vested in a sacristy on the right.

To get from one side of the altar to the other, Wayne had to go through a corridor that ran around a separate chapel for the monks. Traversing the pitch-dark passage added an aspect of danger to his morning. Wayne would feel his way along the wall, inching forward step by step. Then, just when he thought he'd made it past the peril, his buddy Robert Brungardt would dive from the darkness, assaulting him with shrieks and laughter.

Wayne knew when to have fun, but he also knew when to be serious. He could recite his Latin forward and backward and took his duties at the altar to heart. He never failed to be awed by the sheer grandeur of the cathedral and the honor of assisting the priests. The silvery bell that had mesmerized him years earlier was now his to ring, as were the larger ones that called the faithful to worship.

Wayne and his brother Omer often raced their friends to the bell tower. The lucky ones who got there first grabbed the wrist-thick ropes and heaved. Once they got the big bells going, they hung on tight for the best ride in town. The ropes lifted them like an elevator, legs dangling from their robes, high above the floor.

Every so often, the boys pulled too hard and a bell got stuck. They'd hear the brassy gong change to a sickly clank and know they were in for it. It wasn't so much the wrath of God they feared, as the hand of Brother Wendolyn. Tall, thin, and bearded, the cantankerous Capuchin would never hit or yell, but he'd grab an ear and yank so hard it hurt.

The gruff old monk was a tough taskmaster, but he had to be. He was German, just like the 100 rowdy youngsters in his care, and he understood them far too well. His boys were on their best behavior at the altar, but out of sight of the priests, the little angels' halos came off.

High on the sacristy shelf sat the Mass wine. Out of reach for good reason, the temptation proved too much for Wayne and his gang. With his friends egging him on, Wayne boosted his buddies onto his shoulders, laughing as they replaced the wine with water. If the priests noticed that the wine was diluted, they never said so.

Their drinking days came to an abrupt end the time Bob Brungardt gave Vernie Stang a lift. Just as Vernie reached for the cruet, the boys heard the slap-slap of Brother Wendolyn's sandals on the hard stone floor. Loyalty went out the door, along with Bob, leaving Vernie caught red-handed, dangling from the ledge.

With no more wine to quench their thirst, the boys turned to the church garden to satisfy their hunger. No doubt Mother Knoll had to force her sons to eat their carrots at home, but the ones behind the fence belonged to Brother Wendolyn. For Wayne, Omer, Varian, Bob, and Vernie, that was enough to transform the vegetables into forbidden fruit.

The pointed wooden slats proved too daunting for the bigger boys, but smaller Vernie scaled the fence with ease. Soon carrots, radishes, and giant turnips came flying from the enclosure as Vernie tossed the stolen salad to his comrades. The boys helped him back over the fence and ran to hide their stash. Their dirty deed complete, they brushed off their hands and reset their saintly smiles.

The next morning, Wayne waited with his cohorts on the sacristy benches. Brother Wendolyn was due any minute to give them their altar assignments. Omer's belly rumbled, and the others snickered. The fibrous feast the night before had taken a toll on their bowels, but it was worth it. They'd gotten away with their stunt, and no one was the wiser.

The familiar slap of the sandals announced Brother Wendolyn's approach. The boys wiped the grins from their faces and checked their posture. The brown-robed monk entered the room and stopped in the doorway. His face was glum as he slowly passed his gaze from one boy to the next. Wayne stiffened with apprehension as the old monk glowered.

"*Mein Gott,*" he said, "this world is really something."

Wayne lowered his eyes, lightheaded from a full dose of Catholic guilt.

Brother Wendolyn clucked his tongue. "Now even women are stealing my vegetables."

Wayne looked up, confused, and exchanged glances with Omer, Bob, and Varian. Then Vernie solved the mystery by turning his foot ever so slightly to the side. The boys had to cover their mouths to keep from laughing. Their friend's cowboy boots still had dirt on the soles. It wasn't the grace of God that saved them, but Vernie Stang's high heels.

The Sisters of St. Agnes ran the public schools in Victoria. In a town where every student was Catholic, it made no sense to hire secular staff. The fact that the state paid the sisters' salary didn't strike anyone as unusual: They didn't fit the stereotype of Catholic-school nuns to begin with. Instead of rapping knuckles with a ruler, the sisters encouraged their students with love and kindness.

Wayne's seventh-grade teacher, Sister Mary Teresa, would discipline when necessary, but with Wayne she never had to. His close brush with Brother Wendolyn had been a wake-up call. He realized that he couldn't keep taking such chances or he was going to get caught. He'd always been a good student, but from the seventh grade onward, Wayne thrived.

Mary Teresa recognized Wayne's insatiable desire to read. She fed that hunger with books he'd never seen in the school library. He usually took the treasures she brought him to a favorite spot beneath a row of trees. There he felt God's presence as he read and prayed, a habit his eighth-grade teacher, Sister Thomas Aquinas, further encouraged.

Most bookish boys were the butt of jokes, but like the nuns who taught him, Wayne defied the stereotypes. During his first year in high school, he became a starting end on the varsity football team. He tackled his teammates in practice, then followed the roughness with quiet contemplation alone. The more he prayed, the more Wayne felt that he was made for something more than what Victoria had to offer.

His parents insisted that their children go to college. His mother and father had grown up in the Depression and understood the value of a good job. Wayne knew that he'd get a degree eventually, but at 14, he hadn't given much thought to what he'd study. He was content to play ball, milk the cows, and help his father at the grain elevators.

Then Sister Mary Teresa gave him a book that changed the course of his life.

The Seven Storey Mountain became a classic, but it was newly published in 1948 when Wayne first opened the cover. Immediately, he knew he had found something different. The author, Thomas Merton, wrote with such eloquence that his prose seemed more like poetry. The book began with the story of Merton's early life, from his years with his parents in Europe, to his college days at Cambridge and Columbia. As a young student, Merton was an atheist and dabbled in Communism. He drank, smoked, and caroused with his friends.

Wayne read, enthralled, about places he could only imagine and people far different from any he'd met. Merton's world was captivating, but too removed from Wayne's life on the plains of Kansas for him to identify with. The one thing he shared with the author was his love of literature. Merton freely quoted texts and authors Wayne had never heard of, yet now longed to read.

Page by page, as Wayne immersed himself further in the book, Merton's life and Wayne's began to merge. He read with fascination of Merton's growing interest in spiritual reading . . . how he devoured books, making notes and remembering words that might be useful. When Merton described his decision to work on a Ph.D., Wayne's pulse quickened. He'd never imagined that a person could do more than just enjoy reading books—that one could actually focus on the *study* of literature with the goal of someday teaching it.

A third of the way into the book, the author's life took a momentous turn. Merton discovered God and became a Catholic. Now, more than just his love of books, Wayne shared his respect for the doctrine and traditions of their faith—a faith, Merton wrote, that he had come to by grace.

"I was to become conscious of the fact that the only way to live was to live in a world that was charged with the presence and reality of God,"[1] Wayne read.

Merton's writing described the very reason Wayne immersed himself in hours of daily prayer.

"I began to want to take the necessary means to achieve this union, this peace. I began to desire to dedicate my life to God, to His service."[2]

Wayne stared at the book, riveted. The page was a mirror of his private reflections.

"Meanwhile, there had been another thought, half forming itself in the back of my mind—an obscure desire to become a priest."[3]

Here, Wayne stopped. In spite of his faith, in spite of his years as an altar boy, in spite of the Capuchin seminary mere blocks from his home, he'd never before thought of becoming a priest. Yes, he felt drawn to God and a life in closeness to God, but he hadn't considered the priesthood. Now, just as it had formed in Merton's mind, the idea stirred for the first time in Wayne's.

Was this why he felt so drawn to prayer? Was this why he loved spiritual reading? The priesthood was a vocation, which the nuns defined as *a calling*. All this time, Wayne wondered, had God been calling him?

"It took me about a minute to collect my thoughts about the grace that had been suddenly planted in my soul . . . yes, I want to be a priest, with all my heart I want it. If it is Your will, make me a priest—make me a priest."[4]

Absorbed in the book for days, Wayne thought of little else. He finished his chores, completed his lessons, and returned to the pages. In between chapters, he talked with the nuns. Sister Mary Teresa encouraged him to trust the promptings of the Lord. Sister Thomas Aquinas advised him to surrender the decision into God's hands.

Wayne read that Merton's searching led him to a one-week retreat at a monastery in Kentucky. The Abbey of Gethsemani was home to one of Catholicism's most austere orders, the Trappists, more formally known as the Order of Cistercian of the Strict Observance. Men like Merton who entered for temporary seclusion prayed separately from the monks who lived there, yet the experience exposed him to monastic life. To Merton's great surprise, it took his breath away.

Wayne had heard about these monks who lived in silence. From what he knew, they resided in monasteries around the world, out in the country, where they raised their own food and ate little more than bread, cheese, and vegetables. The life held no appeal until he read Merton's eloquent descriptions.

"Because they had nothing, they were the richest men in the world, possessing everything . . . And the Poor Brothers of God, in their cells, they tasted within them the secret glory, the hidden manna, the infinite nourishment and strength of the Presence of God . . . And grace was in them, suddenly, always in more and more abundance."[5]

With the power of his words, Thomas Merton planted the seed of desire in Wayne's heart. He felt powerfully attracted to this life of prayer and contemplation, as well as to the work in the fields.

To be so fully dedicated to God struck him, and he hoped he'd also be able to continue studying like Merton, whom he now recognized as a true kindred spirit.

At 14 years of age, the vows of priesthood presented no problem for Wayne. As far as poverty, he had no money of his own, other than the dimes his father gave him to go to the theater. As for chastity, he was young and naïve. He'd danced with Helen Baker a time or two at parish picnics, but the love affair he longed for was one with God. As for obedience to the Lord, that would be the easiest vow of all.

After his retreat at Gethsemani, Thomas Merton withdrew from the university where he taught, gave away his belongings, and entered the monastery. He would remain there until his death, praying, working, studying, and writing. As Wayne finished reading *The Seven Storey Mountain,* he wanted nothing more than to follow Merton's path.

Wayne knew that he'd have the full support of his mother and father. His family's faith had always been the center of their lives, and he looked forward to seeing the pride in his parents' eyes when he informed them of his decision: he was going to apply to Gethsemani, the very monastery where Thomas Merton still lived and wrote.

He waited until he was alone with his mother and father. He cleared his throat and paused, fully savoring the anticipation of their reaction, then solemnly announced, "I've made up my mind. I'm going to become a Trappist."

There was a moment of stunned silence before his mother burst into tears. Wayne was shocked. He thought she'd be ecstatic. Caught up in Merton's rapture, it never occurred to Wayne to see his decision from a mother's point of view.

"Wayne," she said, her face aghast, "you'll be buried alive!"

She hadn't read Merton's words, but Barbara Knoll knew about the Trappists. Once her son entered the monastery, she'd never speak with him again.

His mother's despair cut to the core, but Wayne had made up his mind. He'd been called to dedicate his life to God, and he was going to be a priest. With full faith that all would turn out well, he penned a request to the Abbot of Gethsemani.

Chapter 6

Anne's second year in Florida proved better than her first. Her oldest brothers and sisters had moved out to live on their own by then, but her mother and two remaining sisters rejoined the family. In anticipation of their arrival, John built another house a short distance from the cabin. The separate bedroom and indoor plumbing would come later, but in the meantime, the 16-by-20-foot home with a small porch in the front was a step forward.

Although much had improved, Anne still got up early for the long ride to school. She knew that she didn't have to go if she decided not to. By choice, most of her brothers and sisters hadn't attended school beyond the ninth grade. Yes, her father had earned his college degree, but for reasons she struggled to understand, he never encouraged his children to do the same. It confused and upset Anne that her parents didn't place more value on her schooling, but she didn't feel she could discuss it with them.

In spite of her family's attitude, Anne enjoyed the ninth grade. Her studies were interesting enough, and being a majorette and a cheerleader made it even better. Her baton didn't cost much, but the boots were a problem. Anne's mother had left her job to move to Florida, and money was tighter than ever. Anne was given a choice: new shoes or the majorette boots. Her old shoes had holes in the soles, but for Anne, there was no question.

She wore her boots when she twirled, and every hour in between. Her classmates started calling her "Boots," and it stuck. Anne didn't care much for the nickname, but it was better than the way they said her real first name down south. "Be-AT-riss" was dreadful.

Rosina, Aloise, and Mary all got married that year. Her father joked that if you had daughters to marry off, you just had to move to Florida. To Anne, it was no laughing matter. She and Rosina had always been especially close. After Rosina left, Anne cried for months.

The next summer, her father lost his job. Whereas before there had been little encouragement for Anne to continue her studies, now her parents discouraged her outright—which made no sense, since an education would only help her get ahead in life. Anne's resentment built, along with her guilt for having such negative thoughts. She loved her parents, but she wanted desperately to finish high school and go on to college.

The long bus ride from Umatilla gave Anne plenty of time to think about the future. She could stay with her family and do nothing, or she could strike out on her own and get the schooling she longed for. Feeling guided as she did so, Anne took a different bus into DeLand.

No one at the high school questioned the pretty young girl who wanted to enroll in the tenth grade. A friendly teacher named Mrs. Foster told Anne about the work-study program.

"If you work real hard, you can have a Buick like mine some day," Mrs. Foster said.

Anne had no interest in a car; she simply needed a way to support herself. The teacher told her about an opening for a nurse's aide and lined up an interview.

Scott's Nursing Home was about a mile outside of town. The bus didn't run that way, so Anne walked. Mrs. Scott greeted Anne politely and invited her into the office. She seemed to think that Anne might find the duties distasteful, but it was nothing worse than she used to do for her neighbor, Ella May. Anne confirmed that she could start right away, but she didn't have the money for a uniform. Mrs. Scott agreed to let her wear her street clothes until she could afford a plain white dress.

On her way back to town, Anne marveled at how things had come together. School didn't start for another two months, yet she was already enrolled. She had a job, and if she could only find a place to stay, her plan would be complete.

Near the center of town, she passed a millinery shop. She glanced at the fancy hats in the window, then stopped. A hand-lettered sign taped to the glass held the answer to her problem: "Room for rent—inquire within."

She pushed open the door and asked for the owner. Mrs. Perry had no difficulty maneuvering her wheelchair between the display racks, but she couldn't climb the stairs to show the room. Anne took the key and went on her own. The small chamber held a bed, a chair, and a chest of drawers. A bathroom connected the bedroom to another room on the far side.

Anne returned to the shop and told Mrs. Perry it was perfect. She didn't mention that she hated the gray bedspread and the awful, drab paint. With no money in her pocket, she couldn't afford to be choosy. The room was clean and comfortable, and Mrs. Perry agreed to wait for the first week's rent.

The only thing Anne told her parents that evening was that she'd found a place to stay in DeLand so that she could go to school. Just as they'd stood back and let her develop her spiritual gifts on her own, they stood back as their youngest daughter packed her belongings. She placed her clothes in a brown paper bag and laid her baton beside it. Then, determined that no one in DeLand would ever call her "Boots," Anne picked up her tattered shoes and carried them to the porch. Using her mother's scissors, she cut two pieces of cardboard to patch the soles.

The 14-year-old had full faith that things would work out. She knew that she'd be guided. She no longer felt the anger she'd struggled with before—simply a steely determination to do as she'd decided. DeLand was just ten miles away. She could always go home if she wanted to, but Anne knew that she wouldn't be coming back.

She stood in front of the fruit stand and stared longingly at the bright, red apples. The sight of food made Anne's empty stomach ache. After paying for her room, she earned just enough at the nursing home to buy a few groceries. A few pieces of bread and baloney were never enough to take away the hunger completely.

The fruit stand belonged to Mr. Santilli, and Anne could see that he was busy with a customer. Her heart racing, she looked left, then right. With nobody else in sight, she grabbed an apple and shoved it under her arm. Painfully aware that she'd committed a crime, she rushed around the nearest corner and devoured the evidence.

The apple took the edge off her hunger, but now guilt gnawed at her conscience. In all her life, she'd rarely even told a white lie, yet in a moment of desperation, she'd broken one of the Ten Commandments. Surely Adam himself hadn't felt as bad when he ate the forbidden fruit.

As she walked through town, she thought about her short career waiting tables. Walt Walker's was the best restaurant in DeLand. The pay would have supplemented her income quite well. She might even have eaten some free meals if she'd worked a bit longer, but after what had happened the other day, she could never show her face there again.

Even thinking about the incident made Anne shudder. It was her first time working in a restaurant, and she'd wanted to make a good impression on Mr. Walker. She didn't know much about serving customers, but she knew how to be kind to people. It was only natural to ask the man in the seersucker suit if he'd enjoyed his meal. He'd smiled up at her nicely, but when he put his hand on her belly and pinched her bottom with the other, Anne reacted without thinking. She took the pot of hot coffee she was carrying and poured it right on his shiny, bald head.

Everyone in the restaurant had turned to see the commotion, including Mr. Walker. The nasty man was still jumping about and cursing as Anne grabbed her purse and fled. She cried herself to sleep that night, embarrassed, ashamed, and out of a job.

Now she'd resorted to stealing food. She felt the tears burning her eyes once again, but she refused to cry in public. Anne walked on through town, then stiffened as she spied Mr. Walker directly in her path. With her heart in her mouth, she averted her eyes and quickly crossed to the opposite sidewalk. When she dared to look up, she saw with dismay that he had crossed the street as well. She started to turn the other way, but Mr. Walker called out her name.

Unable to escape, Anne stopped. She lowered her head and waited, terrified, for the verbal lashing.

"Young lady," Mr. Walker said as he caught up to her, "I've never had one of my waitresses treat a customer like you did the other day."

Anne's lip started to tremble. When she worked up the courage to meet his eyes, she saw a twinkle there that took her aback.

"All the girls want to thank you," he continued. "You did exactly what they've wanted to do to that man for a long time."

Mr. Walker reached into his wallet and pulled out some bills. "Here are the two days' wages you earned, and your job's still waiting for you if you want it."

Flustered, Anne took the money and slid it into her purse. "Thank you," she said. "I'll think about it."

Mr. Walker shook his head and laughed, then continued on his way. His offer echoed in Anne's ears, but she didn't really have to think about it at all. No matter how hungry she was, she wasn't cut out to be a waitress.

With the unexpected pay in her purse, Anne turned around and walked back to the fruit stand. Taking a deep breath, she approached Mr. Santilli and held out the money with a shaking hand. Her stutter worse than ever, she told him that she'd stolen an apple and wanted to pay for it.

He walked around the counter, frowning. Anne was sure he was going to call the police. Instead, he put his arms around her.

"My family came to America when I was a boy, not much younger than you," he said. "We had no food then either, but people, they always helped us."

From that day on, whenever Anne walked by the fruit stand, Mr. Santilli would nod his head toward a special bag meant just for her.

After the school year started, Anne found a second job that suited her much better than restaurant work. Each afternoon she worked at the nursing home until 8:30, then she babysat from 9 P.M. till midnight. Her boss, Mrs. Ross, had two small children, ages three and four. They were usually asleep when Anne arrived, allowing her to study. It was an easy way to earn money, and Mrs. Ross paid surprisingly well.

Anne had never seen such a fancy woman. Very much a lady, Mrs. Ross left the house each night in colorful dresses that Anne would never have the nerve to wear. Her high heels made her long legs look shapely, and she applied her makeup like a movie star.

Anne noticed that Mrs. Ross often looked somewhat different when she came home than when she left. Her makeup would be a bit smeared and her hair disheveled. Anne began to wonder what her employer did each evening, but she thought better of asking. The more mussed up Mrs. Ross was when she returned, the better she paid.

The only problem with Anne's second job was walking home so late at night. As a little girl, Anne had enjoyed walking the streets of her neighborhood. Things were different in DeLand. It wasn't so bad when she walked to school in the morning or to the nursing home when classes let out. But when she'd leave Mrs. Scott's and walk to Mrs. Ross's, the town took on a different feel. The men who whistled and called out made Anne's skin crawl. It was even worse after midnight.

She did her best to keep a low profile. She never reacted to the cat calls or encouraged the men's rudeness in any way. In spite of her efforts not to be noticed, somebody did. The school principal called Anne to his office and got straight to the point.

"You have to get off the streets at night," he told her.

At first she thought he was being kind—that somehow he'd found out she was working two jobs. Then she grew scared, thinking he'd discovered that she was living alone. But when she realized his words had a different meaning, she flushed with embarrassment. The disapproval in his eyes told Anne he thought she was like Mrs. Ross.

Within days she found a car—a black Studebaker—for $210. She barely had enough money for food, but she could afford the $10 monthly payment if it kept her off the streets. At 14, she wasn't old enough to have a license, but once again, no one asked her age. Afraid to be caught driving illegally, she only used the car to get to work.

She could have driven down the highway to her parents' house, but as much as she missed them, she couldn't bring herself to do so. Her mama and papa had never said, "Don't come back," but Anne convinced herself that she wouldn't be welcome. She was going to school now and had made choices for another way of life.

The girl who cried for a year when first separated from her mother now cried every night. The dreary gray room where she slept was cold and empty compared to the loving and spiritual home where she'd grown up. Away from the room, men leered and whistled and tried to touch her. At Mrs. Scott's, the nurses talked badly about the patients and used foul language. Anne couldn't understand this new world in which she lived. Didn't people care about each other?

She didn't belong at home, yet she didn't belong where she was. Overwhelmed with despair, she prayed to God, but she didn't see how He could help her.

Lying in her lonely room, she thought back to when she used to lie under the big tree in Petoskey. There, her spirit friends would take her to other worlds, but try as she might, Anne could see no place for herself in this one.

Anne sat on the edge of her bed. She'd given her decision a lot of thought. It had taken weeks to save enough money for the pills. Every time she set the coins aside, she wondered if she was doing the right thing, and every time the answer was yes. The depression that plagued her would not go away. Now she had just the right prescription to banish her sadness forever. It was simply a matter of doing it.

In spite of all of the tears she'd shed, Anne's eyes now were dry. Two by two, she placed the pills on her tongue and washed them down with water. When she'd swallowed the last one, she set the glass on the night stand and lay back. She had no expectation other than to finally be free of her pain.

She didn't remember entering the darkness, but she became aware of floating toward the ceiling. She hovered over the bed and found herself looking down at her body. She noticed that there were spirits dressed in white standing at both sides of the bed. They seemed to be doctors of some sort, and they were pressing on her stomach.

Her eyes were drawn to a rosy, golden glow beyond the bed. Enchanting music filled her ears, more beautiful than the finest symphony. Loving faces smiled at her, beckoning. Anne had been out of her body before, accompanied by her spirit guides, but these sights and sounds were of a dimension far beyond her past experiences.

None of the beings around her spoke, but Anne knew she was being given a choice: she could continue toward the magnificent light or return to her body. She stared down at the bed where the spirit doctors were still working. She could see that their pressing had caused her body to release what was inside.

She looked longingly toward the radiant light. It pulled at her as if there were a string attached to her soul. *I have to return,* she thought, in spite of the powerful urge to go on. *I have to go back and tell everyone about this!*

Her thoughts had the desired effect. Within moments, the intense beauty was gone and she was back in her body. She could physically feel the spirit hands pressing on her until she drifted back into darkness once more.

Anne awoke to find herself lying in her own feces and vomit. She stumbled to the bathroom and washed her body. Disgusted by the smell and afraid someone would see the sheets, she scrubbed them in the tub. Still drugged and dizzy, she returned to the bed and collapsed on the bare mattress.

She slept for what could have been days or mere hours. When she finally opened her eyes, a woman stood at the foot of her bed. She was small and very feminine. Gray hair framed a pretty face that was wide at the brow and tapered at the chin.

The woman drifted to the side of the bed. She laid her fingers on Anne's arm, then gently touched her hand. "If you will follow me," she said softly with a foreign accent, "I will lead you to a new way of life."

Her eyes were gentle, and Anne immediately felt comforted and safe. A sense of peace enveloped her like a warm blanket. She questioned nothing; she simply got out of bed, bathed again, and got dressed.

Without knowing why, she then went to her car and got behind the wheel. The woman stayed with her, and Anne began to drive. Whether from the chemicals or the spirit's presence, she felt as if she were in a trance, but still she pressed on.

She drove southeast, no more than ten miles, and came to an open gate. A large sign read: "Cassadaga Spiritualist Camp." Anne had never heard the name. She drove through the entrance and down the tree-lined streets. There were only a few commercial buildings and what looked like a meeting hall. Mostly, there were just houses. Many had small signs in front with "Medium" or "Healer" painted in neat letters.

As she drove past a square white cottage with green trim and a white fence in front, her car suddenly stalled. When she turned the key, the engine started right up, and she continued on. At the end of the camp she felt compelled to circle back.

The Studebaker had never given Anne any trouble, yet as she passed the white cottage where she'd stalled before, the engine died again. Flustered, she restarted the engine. Round and round she circled through the small community, not knowing what compelled her to do so. When the car stalled twice more in the same spot, Anne could no longer deny the message.

She parked beside the white fence and slowly stepped out. The spirit woman was no longer with her, but Anne followed her instinct. Never one to talk to strangers, she still approached the screened-in porch at the end of the walkway. She had no idea why she was there or what she was meant to do, but she raised her hand and rapped. The screen door opened a mere moment after her knock.

A white-haired man with pleasantly full lips looked down at Anne and smiled. He pushed the door open wider and beckoned her inside.

"I don't know who you are or where you've come from," he said, "but they told me you were coming."

Chapter 7

Barbara Knoll needn't have worried when her son announced that he intended to become a Trappist. To Wayne's great disappointment, the Abbot of Gethsemani denied his request. Cistercians didn't accept 14-year-old novices.

Wayne found consolation in the very book that had led him to the Trappists. He knew from reading *The Seven Storey Mountain* that Thomas Merton hadn't been granted his first choice either. Merton originally wanted to join the Carthusians. The Trappists kept silent, but they worked, ate, and prayed as a group. The Carthusians, being the strictest of the monastic orders, did everything alone in their solitary cells. Unfortunately for Merton, all of the Carthusian monasteries were in Europe, which was then in the throes of the second world war.

Just like the writer who had sparked his interest in the priesthood, Wayne turned to his own second choice. Through the nuns at his school, he learned about the Passionists. They considered themselves both contemplative and active, attempting to blend the meditative life with missionary work. Teaching was not one of their main missions, but they taught their own students. Their Seminary of the Holy Cross in St. Louis trained future Passionist priests for their four years of high school and the first two years of college.

With Wayne's strong academic record and service as an altar boy, gaining admittance to the seminary as a sophomore was the easy part. Leaving home at such a young age proved far more difficult. Not only was he the first of nine children to depart the nest, he was the first boy in Victoria to leave for what was the equivalent of a prep school. He got through the painful good-byes by forcing himself to focus on his future. The vows of priesthood were still years away, but the minor seminary was the first step in fulfilling his vision.

On the morning of his departure, Wayne gathered his courage and headed for the station. As the train pulled into town, the squeal of the wheels took him back to when he'd crouched under the nearby trestle, hot cinders from the steam engine showering over him as the train roared past. Those cars had been filled with soldiers and sailors on their way to war. Now it was he, too young to wear the uniform of a soldier, who boarded the train bound for Missouri. He would serve his country by praying for the souls of all humankind—his uniform the black robe of a Passionist seminarian.

Like the Trappists, the Passionists eventually realized that high school boys are too young to make decisions about a life of poverty, chastity, and obedience. But for Wayne, with his love of prayer and academics, the first few years with the Passionists proved to be the perfect choice.

In Victoria, Wayne had always been ahead of his class. At the minor seminary, he found the studies challenging, but intensely stimulating. There, the priests laid the foundation for a lifetime of study, teaching him not just how to write and read spiritually, but how to analyze and use his mind. Because he arrived in his sophomore year, he missed the freshman Latin course. The Latin he had learned as an altar boy didn't make up the difference, so one of the priests tutored him privately. By his junior year, Wayne had packed two years of study into one. Rather than balk at the extra work, he soaked it up, just as he did the other aspects of monastic life.

Initially, he felt out of place beside boys from big cities like Chicago and St. Louis, but he held his own in the classroom as well as on the ball fields. Later, his background worked to his benefit. Because he came from the country, the priests appointed Wayne superintendent of the grounds in his senior year. While his classmates did the dirty work, Wayne drove the tractor. Because it wasn't his nature to gloat, he simply sat behind the wheel and smiled.

That same year, his brother Carroll entered the seminary as a freshman. From Wayne's description of the school, Carroll thought he'd love it. In his eyes, however, the place was practically medieval.

Had Wayne gone into more detail about the daily drudgery, Carroll might never have applied. They slept in open dormitories with their cots lined up one beside the other. The priests slept on beds of straw, and there wasn't a chubby one among them, what with all their fasting.

The boys rose at 5:30 and showered without speaking. They donned their black robes, then went straight to the chapel. After Mass, they ate their breakfast as they did all of the other meals: with heads bowed in total silence. They were allowed to talk in the classroom, but only with the teacher. Periods of physical exercise and work on the grounds provided the only break from their silent and sedentary class work and prayer. Carroll's first thought was: *What have I done to myself?* He didn't know how Wayne could stand it.

Carroll decided after one short year that the path to priesthood was not for him. He later joined the Army, where he found boot camp a breeze compared to the Seminary of the Holy Cross. Wayne took much longer to question his choice of schools, but in his first year of collegiate studies, he began to rethink his future direction. It wasn't the rigors of the order that caused him to waver, but a visit to the Cathedral of St. Louis.

Built in the Romanesque style like Wayne's beloved St. Fidelis Church, the green-tile domes made the cathedral a distinctive landmark near St. Louis University. Wayne was excited about the opportunity to sing Gregorian chants in the magnificent basilica along with his fellow seminarians. The young Passionists often sang the sacred songs on important religious occasions. Members of other organizations had been invited to share in the event, and there was quite a crowd.

Standing amid the mosaic glass inside the cathedral, Wayne met members of the largest order in the Roman Catholic Church, the Jesuits. He'd heard of them in passing, but information was hard to come by in the early '50s. Wayne knew little about the Society of Jesus, other than what he'd been told. That day in the Cathedral, he learned that the Jesuits were involved in ministries like the Passionists, but they were best known for their work in education. His pulse quickened when he heard that they engaged in and encouraged intellectual research and cultural pursuits.

Wayne returned to the seminary and saw it in a new light. He loved and respected the Passionists, but they lacked the opportunity to interact with others intellectually like the Jesuits did as a matter of course. Deep inside, he knew the Passionist lifestyle would not allow him to pursue the path he was truly meant to follow: that of an academic. He still felt the calling for the priesthood, but the strong desire to complete graduate studies and to teach caused him to question if he should remain at Holy Cross. The Passionists were giving him an excellent education, but for the priests, the seminary was the end of it. Study, research, and teaching was not their mission.

In spite of his indecision, or perhaps because of it, he returned to the Passionist seminary for one more year. The summer break at home had done little to help him make up his mind, for he hadn't felt free to discuss his dilemma with his parents or former teachers. He lay awake on his cot at night, his doubts too strong to ignore. He'd only been back at the seminary a few days when he knew he had to leave.

The next morning he consulted his superiors. They encouraged him to go to the chapel and make his decision in the presence of God. There, in prayer and meditation, Wayne's picture of the future finally came into focus. He'd leave the seminary and return to Victoria. Eventually, he'd join the Jesuits, but after four years with the Passionists, he needed a break. A little time off would allow him to clear his head and make room for his bigger, brighter vision: that of becoming a Jesuit priest and professor.

The priests gave him money for the Greyhound bus. On the ride to Victoria, he made the decision to enroll immediately at Fort Hays State University, just ten miles from home. What he needed was a break from the Passionists—not from his personal passion. For Wayne, learning was as vital as breathing.

The bus pulled into Victoria just after dawn. It was too early for anyone in his family to be up, so Wayne went to the only other place where he always felt at home: St. Fidelis church. He arrived just a few minutes before the start of the 6 A.M. Mass. He entered the cathedral at the west, between the two tall towers. He started down the center of the nave toward the altar, but stopped in surprise. His mother and father were seated in the front.

He paused at the end of their pew, genuflected, then slid onto the bench beside his mother. She couldn't have been more surprised if the Pope himself had joined her.

"Wayne!" she whispered. "Wayne! What's the matter?"

On her far side, Wayne's father sat forward and eyed him silently.

Barbara Knoll's body twitched as she tried to hold her emotions in check within the confines of the church. "Are you all right?" she asked under her breath.

"I'm fine," he whispered, but offered no explanation. There would be time for that later; Mass was about to begin. The altar boys and the priest paraded past their pew while Wayne's father sat back and chuckled.

When the service was over, Wayne walked with his parents back to the house. He waited for his dad to say something, but just like years earlier when he was caught fighting in the schoolyard, his father didn't say a word. Now, as then, he simply needed to know that his son was okay. Satisfied with what he saw, the matter was closed.

The three entered the kitchen, and Wayne sat at the table. It felt good to be home, but it would be even better when the house filled with the happy noise and energy of his brothers and sisters.

"Give him some breakfast," Adam said to Barbara.

Wayne's mother busied herself at the sink. His father stood with his hands in his pockets. Wayne wondered how his parents would react to the news that he intended to go to the local college instead of the seminary.

What Adam did next proved to Wayne that fathers sometimes know their sons even better than the boys know themselves. Adam pulled his hands from his pockets. In them was a hundred-dollar bill and the keys to his car.

"When you're ready," he said, offering Wayne the gift, "you can enroll at Fort Hays State."

Chapter 8

Anne had felt compelled to approach the house where her car had stalled repeatedly. Still, she worried that if someone came to the door, she wouldn't be able to speak. What if she opened her mouth and nothing came out? Her stutter always got worse when she had to talk to strangers.

When the white-haired man spoke first, Anne was relieved, but she didn't understand: *Who* told him she was coming? And how could they have known such a thing, when she hadn't known it herself?

"Why don't you come in," the man said, "and we'll just sit and talk."

Still unsure, Anne studied him. He was old enough to be her father. He wore a long-sleeved blue shirt and khaki slacks, as if he were dressed for company. His body was thin, but his face was full. His eyes were warm and inviting.

Anne stepped past him and took the seat he offered her on the porch.

"I'm Wilbur," he said as he sat on a wicker chair across from her. "Wilbur Hull."

Anne nodded.

"And you are?"

She blushed. "Beatrice Anne Gehman."

"Beatrice Anne." He said her name correctly and Anne flashed her first shy smile.

"Well, Beatrice Anne, I sense that you're a natural medium, and they brought you to me so I could help you."

Help me do what? Anne thought. She'd seen the word *medium* on the signs as she drove through the surrounding streets, but she had no idea what it meant.

"I'm going to help you use your spiritual gifts," Wilbur said.

She squinted, trying to figure out how this stranger knew so much about her.

"This is Cassadaga," Wilbur said, indicating with a wave of his arm the area beyond the porch. "It's a community for Spiritualists. It's named after Cassadaga Lake in Lily Dale, New York—our largest Spiritualist community."

Anne recalled the sign at the gate.

"Are you familiar with Spiritualism?" Wilbur asked. Then he added, ". . . with a capital *S*?"

She shook her head.

"It's a religion," Wilbur said. "Just like Christianity and Judaism, Spiritualism seeks to answer the question of what God is and what our role is in relationship to God. But it's also a science and a philosophy because it studies the laws of nature and analyzes and classifies facts demonstrated to us from the spirit side of life."

Anne listened intently, sensing now that she was meant to hear his words.

Wilbur told her that Spiritualists had no creed. They followed a Declaration of Principles that set forth their truths.

"We'll go into all of the principles later," he promised, "but I'll summarize them for you."

He went on to explain that Spiritualists believed in a supreme power. Some called this power God, or Spirit, but officially they referred to it as Infinite Intelligence. This Intelligence was everywhere, he said, and everything that lived was a manifestation of it. Just as scientists had proved that nothing is ever destroyed—merely transformed—Spiritualists affirmed that life continues after the change called death.

Anne couldn't help but recall the wondrous glimpse of the world she'd nearly entered just hours earlier when she came so close to taking her own life.

"And," Wilbur said, pointing his finger for emphasis, "we affirm that communication with those who've passed to the other side is a scientifically proven fact as well."

I know that. Anne thought of the spirits she'd been talking to for as long as she could remember. Nobody needed to prove that fact to her.

"It's the communication with those on the other side that gives us our knowledge. We don't need inspired writings or teachings from years past to tell us what to believe. For us, knowledge takes the place of faith." Wilbur leaned forward and rested his elbows on his knees. "The ability to speak with those in spirit is a gift, but it's normal and natural."

Anne wrinkled her nose at such an obvious statement. *Of course it is.*

"I want you to do something for me." Wilbur removed the gold band on his left hand and held it out to her. "Hold this ring and tell me what you sense."

The moment Anne touched the metal, the woman who had guided her to Cassadaga appeared before her.

"I see a small woman with gray hair," she said, no longer fearful of speaking. "Her face is very pretty."

She stared past Wilbur as if he weren't there and brushed a hand across her brow. "It's wide across here, and she has the most beautiful eyes. Her nose is pointed, and her face tapers here, through the chin."

Anne half closed her eyes for a brief moment, then said, "Her name is Rose."

"Yes," Wilbur said, nodding and smiling.

"She has an accent. It's French."

"She was Belgian-French."

"And she was a teacher. She taught you, I think."

Tears pooled in Wilbur's eyes. "She was a medium. And you're right: she was my teacher many years ago, when I was new to Spiritualism, just as you are now."

Anne's eyes widened as she realized that what she'd sensed earlier was true. "She guided me here."

Wilbur inhaled deeply and glanced at the ceiling. "Rose taught me while she was here on the Earth plane, and now she's come back to teach you. She told me that she was sending me a pupil . . . a girl who is a natural medium."

Anne stared back at the man and blinked. He was talking about her.

He reached out his hand. Anne returned the ring, and he slid it back on his finger. "What you just demonstrated is called psychometry. It's the ability to sense the energy associated with an object simply by touching it."

"Psychometry," Anne repeated, testing the new word.

"It comes from the Greek word *psyche,* which means 'spirit' or 'soul'; and *metron,* which means 'to measure.'"

A long-forgotten memory flashed through Anne's mind. Back in Petoskey, she used to ride her bicycle to her Grandpa Riegle's house. He was blind and lived alone. One day, she wondered what it was like to not be able to see, so she closed her eyes and moved around her grandfather's house using only her hands to guide her. She'd groped her way through the kitchen and stopped when she bumped into the table. She ran her fingers across the smooth surface until they touched the sugar bowl that had belonged to her grandma. The moment her hands wrapped around the cool glass, her eyes popped open and Grandma Riegle appeared, just as clear as Wilbur sat before her now.

"I've done that psychometry before," Anne said.

"It's only one of several phenomena that Spirit uses to express itself. I have a feeling you've experienced many things that you simply haven't put a name to yet, Beatrice, like clairvoyance and clairsentience." Wilbur waved his hand. "But we'll get to all that soon enough."

He was right: the terms were completely new, and she grew increasingly excited about learning more, but there was one word that Anne needed to understand right away. "You said I'm a natural medium and that mediums sense departed spirit entities." She paused, somewhat embarrassed. "What is a medium, exactly?"

Wilbur shook his head. "We do have a lot to cover, don't we?"

He explained that most people aren't able to see, hear, or sense spirits; and that the spirits themselves often have difficulty communicating their messages in a way that physical beings can understand.

"A medium is an intermediary between both sides," he said. "Like an interpreter."

Anne felt a surge of excitement welling up inside of her. *This is what I'm meant to do.*

"All religions believe in life after death," Wilbur said. "Spiritualism just takes it a step further by giving proof of the continuity of life through mediumship."

"The continuity of life . . . ," Anne said under her breath.

"Exactly." Wilbur rose to his feet. "The most frequent message we receive from spirits is that *there is no death.*"

Anne stood and walked with him to the door. He stopped before reaching for the knob and turned to face her.

"Just imagine how the world would change," he said, "if every person understood that simple message."

Anne's depression lingered for a time, but after her near-death experience and meeting Wilbur Hull, she no longer wanted to leave the world. "I'll see you soon," Wilbur had said when she left him at the door. One week later she returned.

Just as she sat silently for most of her first visit, Anne didn't need to say much on her second. Wilbur seemed to have a plan for her. He began by telling her about the books she needed to read for her development.

"To be a good medium, you have to expand your awareness of philosophy," he said as he pulled a book from his shelves and handed it to her.

He continued perusing his collection. "You'll need to study psychology, comparative religion, and a bit of history. I recommend some knowledge of music and art as well."

Oh shucks, Anne thought as the pile on her lap grew. She liked learning well enough, but reading was still hard for her. Maybe if she turned the pages sideways. . . .

Wilbur ran his fingers along the top shelf, then pulled down a small volume. "Ah, yes, *The Rock of Truth.*" He turned to Anne, tapping the turquoise cover. "You should start with this one. It's by Arthur Findlay, a British historian and philosopher who's also a Spiritualist."

He handed the book to Anne and nodded. "This will lay the foundation for you."

She took the stack and drove back to her room. Between her two jobs and her studies, Anne began to work her way through the little turquoise book. At first the words puzzled her, then she felt the slightest stirrings of discomfort. Soon her hands were trembling as she turned the pages.

This man—this Arthur Findlay about whom Wilbur had spoken so highly—had written some truly awful things. He argued that the Bible was not the true word of God, and he dared to question the way churches interpreted the Good Book. Everything he wrote went directly against what Anne had learned from the Mennonite Church and from her father.

"The Church today," Anne read, "is supported only by people who have always accepted what it has taught and never reasoned for themselves."[1]

Anne had never read anything remotely anti-Christian, but the further she got into the book, the more the author seemed to question her core beliefs.

"What right has the Church to add conditions to salvation, which Jesus did not think necessary?"[2]

Anne slammed the cover shut, sure that the devil had gotten ahold of her. She grabbed her purse and the tiny New Testament she carried with her always and stormed out to her Studebaker. Rather than putting the wicked book in her handbag beside her Bible, she set it on the seat and drove directly to Cassadaga. She parked along the white-picket fence and marched up the walkway. Her forceful knocking on the screen door held none of the trepidation of her previous visits.

Wilbur pushed open the door. Seeing Anne's distress, he started to speak, but she beat him to it.

"This book is from the devil!" she said, thrusting it at him.

He invited her onto the porch and pointed at the wicker chair.

"I don't know why you wanted me to read that," she said with sparks in her eyes. "It's evil, and I refuse to finish it!"

Wilbur sat in the chair opposite Anne and set the book on an end table. He leaned back with his hands in his lap and closed his eyes as if Anne weren't there. She glared at him, wondering why he didn't respond to her accusations. As she watched, his face began to change. The muscles and his features twisted and moved in such a way that they transformed his appearance. With his eyes still shut, Wilbur began to speak. The voice that came from his mouth was his own, yet slightly higher pitched. It had a French accent, and Anne immediately knew that she was seeing and listening to Rose.

"Do not be afraid of thoughts that are new to you," Rose said. "The things that you shall learn are based on nature's law, which is God's law."

Thus, Rose began a lecture that lasted well over an hour. Anne sat enthralled as a male voice who identified himself as Benjamin joined the conversation, followed by another female who called herself Louise. They spoke to Anne as if they knew her, addressing and calming each of the fears she'd felt when reading Findlay's book. They spoke respectfully of Jesus, identifying him as a great prophet, a great healer, and the greatest medium to have walked the Earth. They encouraged her to be open-minded and to accept the teachings she'd receive in the coming months and years as Divine wisdom.

Looking back years later, Anne realized why Wilbur wanted her to read Findlay's book before the others. *The Rock of Truth* was meant to get her to rethink her old beliefs so she could make way for the new teachings of Spiritualism.

When Wilbur opened his eyes, he smiled and asked Anne if she had learned anything. She told him about the voices that had spoken through him. Wilbur had no recollection of their words, but he was pleased to hear that Rose and her friends had helped Anne understand his intentions.

Anne nodded and retrieved the book from the table. Armed with the perspective of the spirits who spoke to her through Wilbur, she returned to DeLand, eager to read the remaining pages. It would be a while before she stopped carrying her New Testament, but by the time she finished *The Rock of Truth,* the seeds of Spiritualism had begun to take root.

Rose had promised to lead Anne to a better life, and within a short period of meeting Wilbur, her life indeed began to improve. She met a boy in school named Phil Harper. He lived with his grandparents across from the nursing home where she worked. She didn't have time for dating, but she enjoyed talking with Phil. He introduced Anne to his great-aunt, Mary Mason, who lived alone in a house behind his grandparents'. Mary was able to do most things for herself, but she needed someone to stay with her at night. Anne felt an immediate connection with the elderly woman and agreed to move in.

It was a happy day when Anne left the dreary room above the millinery shop. The four walls held too much sadness from the long nights Anne had spent there alone. The free room at Mary Mason's was the equivalent of a salary, but Anne never considered it real work. The two spent many an evening sitting in the rocking chairs on the small front porch, chatting like old friends. Anne often saw spirits around Mary and described them to her in exacting detail. Mary was open to the spirits' messages and would cry with happiness as Anne provided first and last names that she had no way of knowing.

Anne was comfortable talking about such things with Mary and Phil, but that was because she knew them. She couldn't imagine sitting down with strangers to do the same thing, as Wilbur said she would. She'd never get past her stutter.

One afternoon, Anne stopped at the Ben Franklin Five and Dime to pick up some things for Mary. She was having trouble finding an item on her list and approached the clerk for help. When she tried to tell her what she needed, she got flustered and the words would not come out. Embarrassed, she turned to leave, but a tiny woman with a hunched back blocked her way. The stranger stepped to Anne's side, put an arm around her waist, and looked up at her with piercing blue eyes.

"I'd like to help you," the woman said.

Help me with what? Anne wanted to ask, but she feared her tongue would fail her again.

The woman reached into her purse and pulled out a business card. "I want you to come and see me." She handed the card to Anne, then turned and left the store.

Anne stared at the card. The black embossed letters read: "Lillian Wells, voice and piano." Tiny print along the bottom showed an address in downtown DeLand.

Anne kept the card in her purse for two weeks. Occasionally she pulled it out and reread the words. Finally, her curiosity overcame her shyness, and she walked to the address on Rich Avenue. She lingered in front of a gift shop next door, admiring the beautiful china and silver in the display. Such fancy things were beyond her means at the moment, but Anne knew that if she finished her education, one day she'd be able to afford anything she wanted.

Finally, Anne rang the bell of a door that led up a set of stairs. She shuffled her feet as she waited. She heard the soft tap-tap of footsteps, then the woman from the five and dime opened the door.

Lillian Wells's face brightened with a welcoming smile. As if sensing Anne's awkwardness, she held up a finger. "I don't want you to say anything; just come in."

Anne followed her up the stairs. They crossed a small foyer and stepped into a studio. An upright piano stood against the near wall with a music stand beside it. Across the room sat a table stacked high with sheet music. A chalkboard hung on the wall by a small window that looked onto the street below. A pretty lace curtain softened what was otherwise a businesslike room. Beyond the studio was a much larger and cozier parlor with the first grand piano Anne had ever seen.

"I'm so glad you decided to come," Lillian said. "As you can see, this is where I give my lessons."

Anne still wasn't sure why the woman had invited her. The only music she'd ever sung was in church, and she had no need to play the piano.

Then Lillian solved the mystery: "I'd like to teach you to sing," she said, choosing a sheet of music from the stand. "It will help you with your speech."

Anne's eyes widened. She had no idea that singing could help her with her stutter, but the more she thought about it, the more she realized it might just work. She'd never struggled with a single hymn in church, where the words seemed to float off her tongue. Anne tried to contain her excitement. Speaking normally would be a dream come true. She imagined herself talking to anyone and everyone with no more shame or fear.

Then Anne remembered the purse on her arm. The wallet inside was almost empty. Her heart fell as she realized that the happy dream was not meant to be. Even working three jobs she couldn't afford a single piece of china from the shop downstairs, let alone a private teacher.

With downcast eyes she explained the problem.

Lillian made a clucking sound with her tongue. "I just want you to come, and we'll work it all out."

Anne started the lessons immediately. She showed up at the studio twice a week. Sometimes Lillian was busy with a paying client, but she always told Anne when to return. Years later, after Lillian had long since retired, Anne found a way to repay her teacher's kindness. She would show up at Lillian's door with tickets to local concerts by the Civic Music Association and the Florida Symphony. The two would attend the musical performances together. Lillian always tried to pay her own way, but Anne steadfastly refused. She never did learn to carry a tune, but she would forever be grateful for the two years of voice lessons that cured her embarrassing stutter.

Anne's ability to discern spirits was so pronounced that she never sat in a development circle with other budding mediums. What training she received came from her mentor, Wilbur Hull.

She fell into a routine of visiting Wilbur daily. She learned that what he called a *reading* was nothing more than what she did on Mary Mason's porch and what she'd done for her neighbors and teddy bears back in Petoskey. She had only one question that her personal experience had not yet answered.

"If spirits are always around us . . ." Anne asked, then stopped mid-sentence and stared at her feet.

"Yes?" Wilbur prompted her. "Don't be embarrassed."

She still couldn't meet his eyes. "I know that spirits are everywhere, but do they watch us when we go to the bathroom and . . ." she cleared her throat, ". . . kiss?"

Wilbur laughed at her discomfort. "From what they've told me, they honor our privacy."

Anne exhaled, then added to his laughter with a giggle of her own.

With that important detail out of the way, they moved on to issues that would help her give readings to strangers. They covered the philosophy, psychology, and professional ethics of mediumship. Anne already knew the "how to" of being a medium; Wilbur and the spirits who spoke through him taught her the professional side.

Finally, Wilbur announced that Anne was ready. As clients came to call at his house, he suggested that Anne give them a reading. He observed her only a few times, then satisfied that she needed no more supervision, he left her to work on her own.

Soon Anne was invited to participate in services at the Cassadaga community hall and Colby Temple. At first she found the platform intimidating, but the spirits who appeared to her sent her waves of loving support. She pushed back her nervousness and passed along their messages one by one, feeling honored to unite members in the congregation with their loved ones from the other side. It didn't take long for word to get around about the young medium who was dazzling visitors to Cassadaga.

The summer before Anne's senior year in high school, Wilbur invited her to go with him to Wonewoc, Wisconsin, home to another Spiritualist camp like Cassadaga. Wilbur had a wife, but she lived in a mental hospital and he didn't talk much about her. Wilbur himself suffered from muscular dystrophy. He'd had trouble getting around when Anne first met him, and eventually he spent more and more of his days in a wheelchair. The drive to Wisconsin would be long, and Wilbur couldn't do it on his own. His son, Brian, wasn't old enough to drive. When he suggested the trip to Anne, she readily agreed.

The two-day journey left Anne drained, but all discomfort vanished when they arrived at Wilbur's hometown of Stevens Point. In spite of his chronic illness, Wilbur had enjoyed a long career there as a banker. Anne hadn't realized how well loved her mentor was until she saw the marquees on the main street flashing, "Welcome home, Wilbur Hull!"

He was equally welcomed in Wonewoc, where people didn't know him as a banker, but as a great teacher and healer. He was slated to deliver several lectures about Spiritualism in the assembly hall, and Anne sensed his embarrassment at being seen in a wheelchair. She hoped he would remember his own wise teaching that Spirit worked through people regardless of their own physical conditions.

Anne was surprised to see her name listed beside Wilbur's on the program. She thought he had only brought her along to share the drive. At first she blanched, thinking she was expected to give a lecture. Her pulse slowed when she noted the word *medium* after her name. She would only have to pass along spirit messages like she did back in Cassadaga—something she was far more comfortable with than speaking before a congregation.

When Wilbur's turn on the platform arrived, he asked Anne to sit beside him. She helped him from his chair to the podium, then took her seat under the lights. She sat stiffly with her hands in her lap as Wilbur adjusted the microphone.

"Ladies and gentlemen," he began, "I know you came to hear me speak, but I'd like to introduce the real speaker this afternoon— one of the most gifted mediums I've ever had the pleasure of knowing—Miss Beatrice Anne Gehman."

Anne was sure she'd misheard, but as the people in the congregation applauded, she saw that they were smiling directly at her.

What do I do? she thought with horror. She'd never given a sermon or a speech in her life.

She was sure her legs would never support her, but suddenly she felt propelled from her chair as if firm spirit hands were pushing her forward. She stumbled to the podium and hung onto it with a grip that was sure to break the wood. She stared at all of the people who were waiting expectantly for her to say something, but her mind was blank with fear. Time seemed to stand still as an impatient rustle passed through the audience.

Without warning, Anne felt herself swirling. Later she would learn to recognize this as a sign that she was entering a trance state, but at that very public moment, the world around her simply disappeared.

She was unaware of time passing. She regained awareness in the same spot at the podium and returned to her seat in a daze. From the front row she heard a woman say, "Wasn't that remarkable!"

The woman's companion nodded enthusiastically. "It was so unusual to hear that deep German voice coming from that little girl!"

Wilbur later told Anne that the spirit of a German doctor had spoken through her at great length, giving a highly technical discourse on the scientific aspects of Spiritualism. The information he shared was nothing Anne had ever learned nor could have known by herself.

She went to sleep that night in her cabin reflecting on the momentous day. In a brief period of time, she'd become a minor celebrity. People smiled and nodded at her everywhere she went in the camp. As amazed as she was by the experience, Anne couldn't help but wonder at the irony: She'd taken years of singing lessons to be able to speak with confidence, only to have a spirit do the talking for her.

Chapter 9

Wayne wasted no time getting on with his life after leaving the seminary. The very day he returned to Victoria from St. Louis, he took his father's car and enrolled at Fort Hays State. His brother Omer was a freshman at the school and shared an apartment in Hays with some baseball buddies. Wayne knew he wouldn't be sticking around long enough to need his own place like Omer. Instead, he moved into his old bedroom. It was nice to be home, but unlike those at the seminary, his brothers and sisters knew little about maintaining silence.

At school, he jumped in with both feet, taking on a full load of classes as well as signing up for football and track. He may not have been first string on the field, but in the classroom, as always, Wayne excelled. The four years he spent with the Passionists had instilled in him a focused discipline. He found the work so easy that he routinely read beyond his normal assignments.

His favorite class was philosophy, thanks in no small part to the department chairman, Dr. Anderson. Just as the nuns had encouraged Wayne years before, professor Anderson took Wayne under his wing. The two spent hours discussing the world of thought, and Wayne signed up for all of his classes.

Wayne was used to studying hard and playing sports, but there was one facet of college life that set it apart from the seminary: at Fort Hays State, Wayne was permitted to date. A petite senior from the local high school was the first girl to catch his eye. Yes, he was destined for the priesthood, but he couldn't deny the attraction. With his vows still years in the future, Wayne saw no harm in asking the pretty young blonde out to dinner. He was thrilled, but nervous, when Betty Jane said yes.

Most young men had honed their dating skills by their second year of college; Wayne had spent his teen years in a monastery. He knew that he was inexperienced, but he'd heard enough about wooing the opposite sex to know what to do. The first step in gaining a girl's admiration was to impress her with skillful conversation.

He picked Betty Jane up and launched into the one topic he felt most comfortable talking about: philosophy. For the rest of their date he shared the intriguing ideas that he and Dr. Anderson bounced back and forth in their daily discussions. Fueled by her apparent interest, he chattered on about truth, knowledge, and the meaning of life. At the end of the evening, he was the perfect gentleman, taking her home well before dark.

Buoyed by his success, Wayne asked Betty Jane for a second date. He was surprised when she declined. Instead, she started going out with Tommy Younger, a German farm boy he'd known for years. A short while later Wayne overheard Tommy bragging to his cousin.

"Ja," Tommy crowed, "she doesn't want to go out with anyone but me."

Wayne pulled back, chagrined. He'd done his best to impress Betty Jane, but apparently Tommy Younger's philosophy was more to her liking.

Omer was happy to have his brother back from the seminary. Wayne was still talking about the priesthood, but that didn't stop the two from enjoying themselves. One evening they heard about a German polka dance in town. There would surely be lots of pretty girls, and Omer suggested they find something to help them loosen up. One of their friends had just the thing: a bottle of liquor that they passed around between them.

Wayne had no more experience with alcohol than he did with women and drank a bit more than he should have. Omer drank his share and then some. Somehow the two made it home and stumbled to their beds. The next morning, feeling as bad as he looked, Omer went downstairs first. His father got one whiff of Omer's breath and chewed him out. When Wayne walked into the kitchen a short while later, red eyed and pale, Omer knew his brother was in for it.

Their father studied Wayne for a moment, then his face broke into a smile. "Did you have a good time, son?" he asked, patting Wayne on the back.

Omer stared, incredulous.

"Maybe you'll forget about going back to the seminary now," was his father's only rebuke.

Omer shook his head at the injustice. All his life, Wayne had been a tough act to follow.

Contrary to his father's comment, a minor hangover had no effect on Wayne's desire to join the Jesuits. After a year of study at Fort Hays State, Wayne mailed his application to enter the Society of Jesus. This time Mother Knoll was pleased with the choice. She rejoiced with the rest of the family when a letter of acceptance arrived by mail sometime later.

Wayne was slated to enter the seminary as a novice in the fall. He could hardly wait. As if in answer to his prayer for the time to pass faster, he received an offer from his Aunt Anna. She lived in Washington, D.C., and asked him to come for a visit. The thought of seeing the capital for the first time was enticement enough for Wayne, but the fact that it was his favorite aunt who asked gave the invitation special appeal.

His father's sister was Wayne's role model. Like him, she had grown up in Kansas, in a town even smaller than Victoria. She left the family farm to go to college, where she worked as a janitor's assistant to pay her way. It was rare enough in her day for a woman to earn a degree, but Aunt Anna then joined the Navy and became a WAVE.

She accepted an assignment to Washington, where she completed her active service, then stayed to become a Lieutenant Commander in the Naval Reserves. She earned a master's degree at American University and got a job with the Veterans' Administration. Wayne admired his aunt immensely for her accomplishments, but he respected her even more for having the gumption to leave Kansas and pursue her dreams.

Anna's apartment was on Massachusetts Avenue in the heart of the city. She lived within sight of the stately National Cathedral. Built at the same time as Victoria's Cathedral of the Plains, it stood on the most commanding spot in Washington. As Wayne admired the cathedral's tall towers, he noticed another distinctive spire no more than two miles away to the east.

The spire, Anna told him, was on the campus of Georgetown University. Hearing this, Wayne's ears perked up. Georgetown was not only one of the most prestigious institutions in the nation, it was the country's oldest Jesuit university.

"Do you think I could visit the campus while I'm in town?" he asked, voicing a thought he'd entertained on the long trip east.

Aunt Anna was one step ahead of him. "You'll do better than that," she said with a sparkle in her eye. "I've arranged for you to have a private tour tomorrow afternoon with the rector of the Jesuit community."

Wayne let out a hoot. His introduction to the Jesuits in St. Louis had only been cursory. Even though he'd made the decision to join the order, this would be his first chance to speak with a Jesuit priest in person. The rector was the executive director of all of the Jesuits at Georgetown. Aunt Anna had gone straight to the top.

The next afternoon, Wayne set off for the campus. As directed, he entered through the south gate off 37th Street and approached the statue of Archbishop Carroll straight ahead. The founder of the university stared down from his stone seat as Wayne gazed at his surroundings. Directly behind the statue, stretching nearly 100 yards to his left, stood the building with the spire he'd seen from afar. The 19th-century red-brick façade exuded a collegiate air far loftier than any of the buildings at Fort Hays State.

"Excuse me," said a voice behind him. "Are you Wayne Knoll?"

"I am," Wayne replied, turning to face a tall man in a long black cassock.

"I'm Father Hunter Guthrie," said a kind but authoritative-looking priest. "Welcome to Georgetown."

Wayne couldn't help but feel a stab of nervousness mix with his excitement as he returned the man's handshake.

"I understand you've made the decision to become a Jesuit."

"Yes, Father, I have."

The priest nodded, pleased. "There's nothing more rewarding than to dedicate one's life to God." He looked Wayne up and down, then said, "Tell me a bit about yourself."

Wayne filled Father Guthrie in on his family and his school years. He told him about the time he'd spent with the Passionists at the Holy Cross Seminary and his desire to lead a more active life as both a priest and an academic.

"I'm sure you'll find that the Jesuit superiors will support you in all of your life's decisions," Father Guthrie said, "so long as they deepen your relationship with Christ. Here at Georgetown, the Jesuit community does this through service and education, in the tradition of St. Ignatius."

Wayne scanned the courtyard and inhaled as if to fill his lungs with the almost tangible atmosphere of learning.

"I see you've met our founder, Archbishop Carroll." Father Guthrie indicated the statue in front of them. "Perhaps you know he was America's first Catholic bishop. He acquired the deed to this land to build an institution open to students from all classes and religions. In his day, Archbishop Carroll was one of the leading proponents of religious tolerance."

Wayne nodded and watched the well-groomed young men walking purposefully along the tree-lined sidewalks.

Father Guthrie moved toward the building with the spire, and Wayne fell in step beside him.

"This is Healy Hall, the showpiece of the campus. It's named after Father Patrick Healy, the first Negro president of a major university."

"Impressive," Wayne said.

"Until the construction of this building, Georgetown was known as a small, rural academy." He motioned toward a set of stone steps. "Come, we'll have a look inside."

They entered through a portico at the far right end of the building. Brick archways like those in an outdoor colonnade lined an interior hallway to the left. Wayne longed to peek in the classrooms, but his guide was already heading for a door ahead of them.

"We'll come back to Healy Hall later. For now, we're just passing through to the Quadrangle."

They exited into a cobblestone courtyard. Straight ahead stood a small nouveau gothic church. Father Guthrie explained that Dahlgren Chapel wasn't just the physical center of the campus, but the spiritual heart as well. He identified the building to their right as Old North. They stepped past a railing onto a wide porch where the priest pointed out a brass plaque by the entrance to the hall.

"This is President's Porch, named, as you can see, for the American presidents who have addressed the students and faculty from this very spot."

Wayne blinked as he scanned the plaque. At the top of the list was none other than George Washington, with the year 1797 engraved beside the name. It was all he could do not to gape as he read the long list of leaders straight from his grammar-school textbooks. For a farm kid from Kansas, this was heady stuff.

Across the courtyard, perpendicular to Healy Hall, stood the Jesuit residence. Father Guthrie explained that both priests and lay brothers lived together on the campus. Each had a private bedroom, but they ate their meals in a communal dining room. The priests, he explained, served as faculty in a number of disciplines within the college of arts and sciences. Because of their vow of poverty, their pay went directly into the Jesuit community's common treasury. All of their needs were taken care of, allowing them to focus on God and their work.

Wayne turned in a slow circle. The spirit of the university—the overwhelming aura of scholarship—filled him with a sense of excitement that threatened to burst from his chest. The opportunity for growth here was limitless. Wayne longed to dedicate himself to God and learning, and Georgetown University was the perfect fit.

This is my life, Wayne thought. *This is my future.*

As promised, they returned to Healy Hall, where Father Guthrie led Wayne up a flight of steps. He pointed out the president's office before continuing up another flight and through a set of heavy double doors.

"This is Gaston Hall, named after Georgetown's first student. It's one of the city's historic landmarks."

The two stood at the front of an auditorium far more ornate than any Wayne had ever seen. Rows of upholstered seats filled the ground floor and a wraparound balcony above. The dark wood and rich red carpet gave the large hall an air of elegance, but it was the museum-quality artwork on the four walls that held his rapt attention.

"Everything you see here was painted by one of our own lay-brothers, a former house painter, Brother Francis Schroen," the rector explained. "Around the walls are the coats of arms of 60 Jesuit colleges and universities throughout the world."

Wayne surveyed the beautifully painted shields, reading them one by one until his eyes came to rest on two large murals above the stage. He stared at the Greek figures, but looked straight through them, seeing instead his future clearly painted before him: He would continue his education to the doctorate level, if the Jesuits so allowed. Then, he would return to this very campus as a professor, teaching either English literature or philosophy.

Ecstatically happy, he thanked Father Guthrie for the tour and hurried back to his aunt's apartment. When Anna arrived home from work, Wayne assaulted her with the full force of his enthusiasm.

"I've decided that after I become a Jesuit priest and finish my schooling, I'm going to come back to Washington and teach at Georgetown."

His aunt smiled smugly, almost as if she'd expected this announcement.

"I'll need the best degree possible," he said, "maybe from Harvard." The idea had just occurred to him, and it further fueled his excitement. "What do you think?" he asked.

Anna nodded wisely and said, "The Holy Spirit will provide."

Wayne had to believe she was right. He'd spent only one afternoon on the campus, but that was all it took to bring his vision of the future into perfect focus.

Once Wayne received approval to enter the Society of Jesus, it was up to him to decide where to undertake his studies as a novice. St. Louis was the obvious choice for a resident of Kansas, but after his trip to Washington, Wayne wanted to be as close as possible to the hallowed halls of Georgetown. He applied to the Maryland province and received approval to enter the nearest novitiate to the nation's capital, in Wernersville, Pennsylvania.

He passed the remaining summer months working with his brother Omer. A neighbor with a moving and hauling business had broken his leg and hired the boys to run his truck. The two brothers drove around Hays delivering desks to the college, cargo from the trains, and giant drums of Coca-Cola syrup to the local bottling plant.

The work was strenuous, so Wayne didn't pay much attention to the ache in his side after he lifted a particularly heavy box one afternoon. After a while, the pain intensified, focusing in his lower right belly. He'd had some trouble with his appendix in the past, but it had always cleared up on its own. This day was different. By the time he and Omer got home, Wayne was bent over and nauseated. He'd never felt pain so severe.

His father took one look at Wayne and helped him to the car. They drove to the hospital in Hays, where Wayne was admitted and taken to surgery after a brief exam. He awoke to learn that his appendix had burst. Hoping that the problem would resolve itself, Wayne had waited too long.

The poison from the infection spread throughout his abdomen, causing a raging infection that took him to the brink of death. As his body fought the toxins, Wayne lay in bed unable to eat or drink. Antibiotics flowed into his veins from bottles hung at his bedside. The surgeon deliberately left the incision open, and the stench was almost unbearable. The only thing that brightened the endless hours were visits from his family and a pretty blonde nurse's aide named Mary who came in every day.

Wayne lay in bed as the weeks passed, worrying and wondering about his future. He was supposed to report to the seminary in the fall. Thirty new novices would begin their training together, but Wayne was too weak to even get out of bed.

Little by little, he improved. After the doctor closed the incision, he was able to eat solid foods. As the infection cleared up, his strength slowly returned. Finally, after more than a month in the hospital, he was well enough to go home, but he was far from strong. The former football player had entered the hospital weighing 206 pounds. He left leaning on his father's arm, weighing only 120. Had it not been for penicillin, his doctor told him later, Wayne wouldn't have survived.

As soon as he was well enough, Wayne went to Mass at St. Fidelis church and gave special thanks to God for his health. As he was leaving, he saw a familiar figure in a brown robe and sandals standing at the back of the cathedral.

"Brother Wendolyn!"

The corner of the monk's mouth turned upward for a brief moment before he squinted and frowned down at Wayne.

"You've been sick," he said in German.

Victoria was a small town, and the news had quickly spread by word of mouth. Even so, Wayne's illness would have been obvious to anyone by the way his clothes hung on his emaciated body.

"Yes, but I'm better now. I'm waiting to find out when I can report to the Jesuit seminary."

Brother Wendolyn clucked. "So it's true what I hear?"

"It's true." Wayne grinned. "I'm going to attend the Novitiate of St. Isaac Jogues."

"Ach, the Jesuits," Brother Wendolyn said, shaking his head. "All they do is study and study, then they write a book, and then they die."

With that, the old Capuchin shuffled off, leaving Wayne smiling at his back. The monk's words were meant in jest, but Wayne couldn't imagine a more perfect existence.

After such a long hospitalization, Wayne was ready to get his life back to normal. He hadn't yet heard from the seminary whether he'd be allowed to start late or if he'd have to wait a full year and begin with a new class. While awaiting an answer, he stayed at home, eating his mother's home cooking and trying to regain his strength.

Omer was embarrassed by his brother's sallow skin and sunken cheeks, but he thought it might do Wayne some good to get out of the house. When Omer suggested a double date with a couple of sisters from the apartment next to his, Wayne agreed.

They had a good time, but when Wayne said good night to his date, he knew he wouldn't be seeing her again. She was nice enough, but at this point she would have to be mighty special to make him change his plans. He felt equally safe when his former nurse's aide called and invited him to visit. Wayne accepted, but he was still too weak to drive. With his mother and father as chauffeurs, he visited Mary at her home in Hays.

"You look good in real clothes," Mary said, seeing him for the first time without his hospital gown.

"So do you," Wayne agreed, for until that moment, he'd only seen her in her uniform. He couldn't deny that Mary was pretty, nor that she seemed to have taken a special liking to him. Worried that she might grow too attached, he felt he should remind her about his plans. In the many visits she'd made to his bedside, he'd told her of his calling and his dream of teaching at Georgetown.

"I hope to leave soon for the seminary," he said.

Instead of getting upset when he talked about the priesthood, Mary smiled sweetly and said, "I respect your decision, Wayne, but I'll wait for you."

He stared at her, confused. Perhaps she didn't know about a priest's vows. He chose not to explain them to her at that moment, hoping she'd eventually understand. Once he left Kansas, he'd live a life of chastity, poverty, and obedience among his fellow Jesuits. Mary was a sweet girl, but intimacy with a woman was not in Wayne's future.

Chapter 10

Anne gathered her bags as the train pulled into Jacksonville. It had been a fast trip and a busy weekend. Hugh Gordon Burroughs, a trustee of the National Spiritualist Association of Churches and pastor of the Church of Two Worlds, had invited her to Washington, D.C., to serve his church. She was the youngest medium certified by the NSAC, and at the age of 19, she'd already been giving readings for several years.

Reverend Burroughs, a gifted medium himself, delivered spirit messages to the congregation before giving a glowing introduction to Anne. She now felt at ease speaking from the platform, and enjoyed connecting those in attendance with their departed loved ones.

After the service, a crowd gathered around to meet the young sensation.

"Do you see spirits all the time?" asked a woman in white church gloves.

Anne smiled, as this was one of the most common questions people asked her. "Not all the time," she said. "It's like being a radio, where you tune in to different stations. I can sit in a room and everything is tuned out, but when I stand on the platform, I tune in to a certain frequency and communicate with those on the other side just as you and I are doing now."

She explained that sometimes spirits appeared spontaneously, without any deliberate attunement on her part. When that happened, she knew to listen for a message of special importance.

"I sometimes feel as if I'm walking between two worlds, and I can live in both of them or just one," she concluded. "You probably do it and don't know it."

When the group dispersed, Reverend Burroughs escorted her back to Union Station. He talked excitedly along the way about his new church. The Georgetown section of Washington was pricey, but it was the perfect home for Spiritualists living in the nation's capital.

As he put Anne on the train, he thanked her for making the long trip. "There'll be a day when you live here in the Washington area," he said. "You'll be back on our platform again."

Anne acknowledged his comment politely, but inside she laughed. Georgetown was nice, but who would ever want to live there?

A weekend in the city had been more than enough. Now, as she climbed down from the train, she breathed in the humid Florida air and smiled. Jacksonville was a big city compared to Cassadaga, but even so, the folks here were more friendly than in Washington. People laughed when they heard that she lived in a dormitory called Sleepy Hollow, but it suited Anne just fine.

Her work as an aide at Mrs. Scott's nursing home had shown Anne how much she liked helping people. She'd been fortunate to get a scholarship to St. Luke's School of Nursing. Mrs. Foster at the high school had helped make it happen, but it didn't hurt that Anne had graduated from high school with honors.

Nursing school seemed like the perfect way to further her education. Unfortunately, the program was not all she'd hoped for. Perhaps it was her uniform with the stiff collar and pretty apron, but she seemed to get no more respect than a chambermaid. To Anne, it felt as if she and her fellow students were simply free labor for the hospital. It was bad enough that all they did was change bedpans and give back rubs, but when she was told to wash down the walls in surgery and clean the toilets, Anne drew the line.

"I did those things to get here," she told her supervisors with unaccustomed fury.

The hospital was ready to kick her out, and Anne was ready to leave. Then the other students rose up and joined her revolt. Faced with a walkout, the administrators relented.

A couple of the girls nodded and smiled at Anne as she entered the dorm. Her actions had gained her the respect of her fellow students. Even so, she wasn't sure why she stayed at the school. Every weekend, she traveled 100 miles to Cassadaga to study with Wilbur. When she couldn't take the time to go, he sent her lessons on reel-to-reel tapes.

Ever since she'd pretended to give readings to her teddy bears in the woodshed, Anne had known what she ultimately wanted to do with her life. As a child, she hadn't realized that there was a name for what she did. Now she understood that she was meant to be a medium, but she wasn't sure she could make a living at it. Wilbur and most of the residents of Cassadaga had retired from lifelong careers. Anne was just starting out.

In her heart, she knew that she'd never be a nurse, but she continued with the training. At the very least, she felt that a greater understanding of anatomy, death, and dying would help her with what she knew was her true calling.

She had just settled in and opened a textbook when she heard a soft rapping. She crossed the room and opened the door to find the dormitory housemother peering back at her.

"May I come in?" Mother Burnette asked, glancing furtively down the hall.

Anne smiled conspiratorially and ushered the woman in.

When word first got around that Anne was a Spiritualist and a medium, Mother Burnette took her aside and asked if the rumors were true. She clasped her hands together with excitement when Anne confirmed the news. The housemother was familiar with Spiritualism and had visited churches and mediums in her home state of California. Now, she waited until the other girls were tucked in each night, then sneaked down the hall to Anne's room.

Anne didn't need props to communicate with Spirit, but Mother Burnette loved to experiment. Together, the two would sit with their hands on a table, inviting spirits to tilt and tip it. Other nights, they'd use a Ouija board and wait for messages.

This particular evening, it didn't take long for their fingers to move the plastic planchette over the letters on the board. The process was tedious, but one by one the letters formed words, then sentences.

The message they pieced together came from a man named Richard. Anne intuitively knew it was from her brother-in-law, Dick Bonsteel, married for several years to her sister Aloise.

The last she'd heard, Dick and Aloise were living in St. Lucia, where he earned his living as a pilot flying passengers around the Caribbean. Anne had had little contact with her family since she left home years earlier, but if anything had happened to Dick, she was sure she would have heard from someone.

Seeing the name spelled out before her, Anne recalled that Wilbur had recently asked her if she knew a Richard in the spirit world. He'd been receiving messages for her from someone by that name. He'd also been hearing insistent rapping on his walls.

The sound of rapping was nothing new for a Spiritualist. In the mid-1800s, Kate and Margaret Fox, two young sisters living in Hydesville, New York, heard unexplained sounds in their house. At first Kate was frightened by the knocking and by what sounded like furniture being moved. Kate challenged whatever entity was making the noise to repeat the snaps of her fingers, and it did. Night after night, with their family and neighbors as witnesses, Kate and Margaret experimented with the knocking. They eventually worked out a code to signify "yes," "no," and letters of the alphabet.

The rapping at the Fox house spelled out a clear message from the spirit of a man who claimed he'd been murdered five years earlier and was buried in the basement. Twenty years later, neighbors found the remains of a skeleton under the house. The Fox sisters were subsequently credited with giving birth to modern Spiritualism.

Anne hadn't heard any rapping recently, and she'd told Wilbur she didn't know to whom he was referring. Now she realized from the Ouija board that the Richard whom Wilbur mentioned was indeed her brother-in-law, Dick.

She and Mother Burnette stared intently at the board. The planchette moved faster and faster, as if alive. Richard's message was clear: He'd gone into the ocean in his airplane. His body was consumed, and it was unlikely that anyone would ever find a thing.

For the next few days Anne could think of nothing else. She and Mother Burnette worked the board each night. When the messages from Dick kept coming, Anne knew she had to go home.

The following weekend, she traveled south en route to Cassadaga, but turned west when she got to DeLand. The little house she'd left was bigger than the cabin she'd shared that first year with her father, but it still pained her to think of her mama living in such a place in 1955.

Nervous yet excited, Anne knocked on the front door, then walked in. She wasn't surprised to find Aloise *there* instead of in St. Lucia. Her father wasn't home, but her mother's face brightened at the sight of the daughter she hadn't seen for so long. The three women shared tearful hugs and kisses, but in spite of the happy reunion, Anne felt an undercurrent of sadness. She knew in her heart that the messages from Richard were correct.

Her mother put water on the stove for tea then joined Anne and Aloise at the table.

"Did you know something was wrong?" Mama asked.

"I just had a feeling," Anne said. She knew that telling them she'd heard from Dick through a Ouija board wouldn't be well received.

Aloise described what happened, confirming that Richard's plane had disappeared three months earlier. The Coast Guard searched for more than a week, but they never found a thing.

Anne's father arrived while the women were visiting. He seemed as pleased to see Anne as her mother had been. After greeting her with a kiss, he joined them at the table and brought Anne up-to-date on all of the family news. Anne told them about nursing school, even though she'd sent them a newspaper clipping back when she won the scholarship.

When they finished their tea, Aloise went into the bedroom and got her children up from their nap. It was Anne's first time meeting the two babies, born just ten months apart. She cooed and fawned over the adorable children, but inside her heart ached, knowing that they'd grow up without their father.

After a few hours, Anne looked at her watch. She needed to get back to school. As she stood on the porch and said good-bye, she knew without discussing it that whatever rift there had been between herself and her parents was mended. Yes, the little communication she'd had with them over the years had been strictly one-way, but she held no bitter feelings. Anne had done what she'd set out to do and had finished her education. She returned to Jacksonville knowing that her family was there for her, as if she'd never left.

⊕⊕⊕

Healing came naturally to Anne. She'd become aware of her abilities one day in the third grade when she suddenly got the feeling that something was wrong at home. She told her teacher that her mother was sick and ran out the door. When she got home, she found her mama writhing on the floor. Following her intuition, Anne placed her hands on her mother's stomach and prayed. Slowly, Anne's hands began to turn dark and her mother's face relaxed. It was as if Anne had drawn out whatever toxins were causing the pain.

Wilbur taught Anne that it wasn't the healer, but Spirit, that did the actual healing. Anne wanted to tell that to the doctors at the hospital who seemed to think they were God. She could often tell without looking at a patient's chart what was ailing the person, but her opinion mattered little to the men in the long white coats.

Anne noticed one woman who came into the hospital almost monthly. The doctors could never find anything wrong with her and sent her home each time. Anne didn't need a degree to come up with a diagnosis; her intuition told her what the problem was.

"I think she needs some counseling," she told the attending physician. "She's having trouble with her husband, and she comes in here to get away from him."

The doctor looked down his nose at the young nursing student.

"Miss Gehman," he said, reading her name tag, "you would do well to keep your opinions to yourself."

Anne hung back as he entered the exam room, then she quietly followed behind him. When the doctor asked the patient what was bothering her, the woman started to cry. Through her tears she described the fight she'd had with her husband and said that their disagreements were an ongoing issue.

The doctor kept his eyes from meeting Anne's and recommended counseling.

Later that week, he stopped Anne in the hallway and nodded toward a patient's room. "Well, Miss Gehman, would you like to tell me what's wrong with the man in bed one?"

Anne knew he was teasing, but she stared at the covered chart in his hand, then glanced in the room. "He has a diseased liver."

The doctor opened the chart, read a few lines, then blinked up at her in surprise. From then on, they played the game often, and Anne was usually right.

The doctor must have talked with his colleagues. When Anne began her rotation in the emergency room, several of the interns had already heard about her uncanny diagnostic abilities. They offered to buy her lunch if she could correctly guess what an x-ray would show before it was taken. Anne earned many a free meal by correctly describing the type and location of a patient's fracture simply by seeing it clairvoyantly.

When it came to her schooling, Anne followed in her father's footsteps. John Gehman completed college but never accepted his degree. Anne finished the nursing school's requirements but didn't bother to take her exams. Instead, she used her training to become a licensed x-ray technician.

She moved back to DeLand and got a job at Fish Memorial Hospital, where she could be closer to Cassadaga. What Anne loved most was giving readings, but at $2 per client, being a medium didn't pay the rent. It pained her to charge anything at all, but if she wanted to help as many people as possible, she'd eventually have to give up her job to do what she did best. To reach that goal, she first needed financial security.

She found a room to rent on the top floor of a pretty yellow Victorian home on Rich Avenue. The owner, Dr. Fisher, was a retired professor from nearby Stetson University. His live-in housekeeper did all of the cooking and cleaning, but the woman's specialty, Anne noticed, was taking care of Dr. Fisher's personal needs.

Anne was much happier being closer to Wilbur. He allowed her the use of his house to give readings when she wasn't working at the hospital. She continued to give messages from the platform at the assembly hall on Sundays and always drew a crowd. She began sending her parents literature about Spiritualism, hoping they'd take an interest in it now that they'd reestablished their relationship with her.

Her work as an x-ray technician was interesting enough, but like nursing, Anne's heart wasn't in it. It didn't help that the chief radiologist was temperamental and demanding. Like the doctors back in Jacksonville, he expected more from Anne than her job entailed. He regularly brought his three children to the hospital and expected her to keep an eye on them.

She was polite at first when she informed him, "That's not why I'm here." Later, she grew more insistent and told him in no uncertain terms that she was not his servant.

He paid no attention to her complaints and continued to take advantage of the free babysitting. Anne loved children and his were beautiful, but highly spoiled. Finally, when she could stand it no more, she turned to the classifieds.

An ad for a mature, middle-aged dental assistant caught her eye. Anne was none of these, yet she felt compelled to apply for the position. Perhaps it was Mrs. Collins who placed the ad for a matronly helper for her husband. For whatever reason, Dr. Collins overlooked Anne's lack of qualifications and hired the pretty young x-ray technician.

It didn't take Anne long to learn her duties, and she found the work rewarding and fun. Dr. Collins had a great sense of humor, but the patients made Anne laugh just as much. One day, an elderly man showed up without an appointment. When Anne greeted him at the door, he uncurled his fingers to reveal a gold crown in the palm of his hand.

"Is that yours?" Anne asked.

"Yes, Miss Gehman, I swallowed it."

Anne stared at the nugget. "You swallowed it?"

He nodded and proudly announced, "Yes, ma'am. I panned four days for this piece of gold."

What she thought would be a temporary job lasted for years. From the start, she knew what instruments to hand the dentist before he asked for them, but where she truly earned her marks was for her "chair-side" manner. Dr. Collins was a "Bircher," an avid member of the John Birch society. He would stuff his patients' mouth full of cotton, then regale them with his radical views. Anne would wait until he finished, then pat their arms and smooth their ruffled feathers.

She tried to stay out of politics, but one day in 1963, Anne couldn't help but express her concerns to her boss: "I don't think President Kennedy should go to Dallas," she said.

"Why do you say that?"

"I think he's going to be killed."

Dr. Collins looked at her strangely. "You're serious, aren't you?"

"Yes, I am. I've had a bad feeling about this for days."

She was so serious, in fact, that she called the White House three times. The switchboard operator ignored Anne's warning and refused to put her through.

Her frustration grew as the President's trip approached. Psychics could predict the future, but that didn't mean the future was set in stone. Wilbur had taught her that people were free agents and could change any outcome by exercising their will. Anne's knowledge served no purpose if no one would listen to her.

She mourned with the rest of the country when the news arrived from Dallas. Dr. Collins started calling her "Spooky."

Anne earned enough money working for Dr. Collins that she began to consider a lifestyle change. After years of renting rooms and living in a dormitory, she longed to have a place of her own. She knew of a house in Cassadaga that was available for purchase. The owner was willing to give Anne a good deal, but it was still a major move.

For her entire life, Anne had relied on her intuition to make her decisions. All the jobs she'd held and all the places she'd lived had been based on how she felt about them. Buying a house, however, was a financial matter. Concerned about what she should do, she turned to Wilbur for advice.

"When you tune in to Spirit or follow your intuition," he told her, "that's a different way of thinking from when you base your decisions strictly on known facts."

Anne followed Wilbur's instructions and drew a line down the center of a large piece of paper. She wrote "Positives" at the top of one column and "Negatives" atop the other. Then she closed her eyes and asked Spirit for advice about the house. As thoughts and feelings came to her, she opened her eyes and wrote them in the appropriate column.

When she finished, the list of positives far outweighed the negatives. Property in Cassadaga was cheap compared to DeLand. Anne could rent out one side of the duplex and apply the rental income toward her mortgage. It was close enough to DeLand that she could continue to work for Dr. Collins. The house had the perfect room where she could give readings on the weekends.

She made a deal with the owner, then shared her good news with Dr. Collins. The next day, Fanny Collins came into the office and pulled Anne aside.

"Now, Miss Gehman," Mrs. Collins said through pinched lips. "I understand you're moving to Cassadaga."

"That's right," Anne said.

The older woman drew in her breath and put a hand to her chest. "I hope you don't go over there and get mixed up with all those crazy Spiritualists."

Anne raised her chin. "Well, Mrs. Collins, I am a Spiritualist, and I am a medium. I intend to be fully involved within the community, and I intend to work publicly as a medium."

Mrs. Collins pulled back, then she clasped her hands together and leaned in close. "Oh, really?" she said. "I'm so fascinated . . . tell me all about it!"

Anne named her little white house "Avalon." She turned the room off the porch into her office and lined the shelves with her growing collection of books. A neighbor painted her a sign that she hung out front: "B. Anne Gehman, Certified Medium, NSAC."

Now that she had her own home, she had the room to invite friends over to visit. The little black-and-white TV with its eight-inch screen wasn't much, but nobody seemed to mind. The snowy picture made it even harder to see an old rerun that was playing one evening, but the group simply moved in closer and passed the popcorn.

The young woman to Anne's right took a sip of her Coke. "I just love these Bonzo movies," she said.

Anne looked at the handsome actor holding the funny monkey. Suddenly, a thought popped into her mind. She hesitated to share the vision with her friends, remembering how the operator had scoffed when she'd called the White House. But then, just like now, she knew that she was right.

"That man is going to be President of the United States one day," she announced to the group.

Her friends turned to her in surprise. When they saw that she was serious, they burst out laughing, just as she'd known they would. Not all of her predictions came true, but Anne knew that this one was just a matter of time.

One morning, she awoke to a voice with a different kind of message. Things had been prepared, it said, for her to resign from her job with Dr. Collins. The thought was nothing Anne hadn't considered herself. She enjoyed her work, but she wasn't making enough money. She wanted to have enough savings set aside that she could dedicate all of her time to Spiritualism.

Once again Anne turned to the newspaper. Her gaze fell on an ad from a company in need of a real-estate consultant. *Why am I even looking at this?* she wondered. Anne knew nothing about property, other than what she'd learned while buying her house. But like the other jobs she'd held, this one felt right. She put on a pretty shirtwaist dress and reported to the address given in the paper. The building sat directly across Woodland Boulevard from Dr. Collins's office.

Looking far more professional than the other applicants in their blue jeans and cut-offs, Anne was hired on the spot. She gave notice to Dr. Collins and started working for Gulf American Land Corporation two weeks later. The company's goal was to sell property in the newly developed Cape Coral community on Florida's west coast. Their statewide advertising campaign resulted in a flurry of interest, and it was Anne's job to reel in potential clients.

The first morning, Anne's boss handed her a stack of cards filled out with names and contact information. He instructed her to call the phone numbers and invite whoever answered to visit Cape Coral. For every client who came in for a tour, Anne would earn a hefty commission.

Anne took the cards and sat with the other consultants. Her colleagues got straight to work on the phone, but Anne leafed through the stack and sorted it into two piles. She had a good feeling about the cards in the smaller pile and set those by her phone. She took the larger pile and returned them to her boss.

After a few days of this process, Anne was summoned to the head office. The man who hired her sat behind his big desk. When he saw her come in, he held up a stack of cards.

"You don't seem to want to do the work we're giving you," he said, frowning.

Anne lowered her eyes, not sure if she should try to explain.

"If you want to stay here, we expect you to do what we ask of you."

Anne recalled the phone calls she'd made. The people had reacted with great enthusiasm to the offer to tour the property. It would only be a few days before they started showing up.

She apologized, took the cards, and returned to her desk. She put the stack off to the side and went back to her original sorting method. Each morning she continued to divide the cards into a feel-good pile and those she knew would be a waste of time, but now she kept the latter to herself.

At the end of the first week, when her boss handed Anne her paycheck, he looked at her smugly. "Do you see what happens when you work hard, Miss Gehman? You earned 80 percent more than any of the other consultants."

Anne stared at the number on the paycheck. Two thousand dollars! It was far more than she'd ever earned working for Dr. Collins, and a veritable fortune for a girl who could barely afford to eat just a few years earlier. She put the money away and continued to work as she had been.

After a few more months of making phone calls, Anne realized that calling prospects one by one was inefficient. She knew that if she could speak to local women's clubs and organizations like the Rotary, her commissions would skyrocket.

When she approached her manager with the idea, he agreed to let her try. She heard him laugh behind her back as she walked out the door, but it was Anne who laughed in the ensuing months as she sent clients to Cape Coral by the busload.

While working for Gulf American Land Corporation, she took a course in real estate in preparation for getting a Realtor's license. When she realized the endless hours that agents worked, however, she abandoned the idea. After six months with Gulf American, Anne's nest egg grew so big that she could afford to stop working. She quit the job, but she had no intention of simply sitting around.

She'd gone to nursing school because she wanted the education. She'd become an x-ray technician simply to earn the credentials. She then worked as a dental assistant and a real-estate consultant, knowing that neither was what she wanted to do for the rest of her life. In all that time, she had never been completely satisfied. She'd continued to study with Wilbur in the hopes that one day she'd be able to use her gifts to help others.

Now that day had finally arrived. She went home to Cassadaga and hung out her shingle full-time. Until then, Avalon had been a cozy home, but it hadn't quite lived up to its name. Now that she was finally able to live the life she'd dreamed of, Avalon truly became her *terrestrial paradise.*

Chapter 11

Wayne chose the novitiate of St. Isaac Jogues in Wernersville, Pennsylvania, because it was located in the Maryland Province, one of the Jesuits' nine geographical areas in the United States. The province included Georgetown University, and he wanted to be as close as possible to the school where he dreamed of teaching one day.

The Jesuits chose Wernersville because of its secluded setting. There, the young novices could focus solely on their training, as far removed from the mainstream as possible. Had Wayne known that he signed up to spend three and a half years outside a town not much larger than Victoria, in an area populated mostly by farmers, he might have chosen differently.

Any reservations Wayne had about his decision disappeared at the first sight of his new home. Built in the English Renaissance style, the novitiate resembled a palatial estate more than a seminary. Inside, the building boasted smooth marble, carved oak, and coffered ceilings. Outside, the magnificent grounds and gardens were modeled after the finest royal residences in Europe.

Because of his appendicitis and lengthy recovery, Wayne arrived halfway through the first year. He entered his assigned classroom and knew without asking where he was supposed to sit. The thick dust atop one of the empty desks showed evidence of the swirly swipe of a fingertip posing a question from his fellow classmates: "Wayne, where are you?"

The novice master knew where Wayne had been, but he wasn't sure how to handle the latecomer from Kansas. Father Gavigan was a demanding but kind Irishman. He wrestled with the decision of whether to allow Wayne to stay with the current class or start fresh in the fall.

Wayne held his breath. He'd had one year of college at the minor seminary and three semesters at Fort Hays. Now he faced four more years of schooling, and none of them would result in a degree. A diploma would come during the next phase of training, but that would only be further delayed if Father Gavigan held him back.

Novitiate training was divided into two years as a novice, followed by two years in the juniorate. For the first year Wayne would be a postulate—living with the Jesuits, but not yet a member of the order. Novices used this time to become accustomed to the monastic life of obedience, poverty, and chastity. When Father Gavigan discovered that Wayne had spent four years honing these skills at a Passionist seminary, he decided in the young man's favor.

Wayne had no problem adjusting to life at Wernersville. He easily fell back into a reflective, prayerful existence where the novitiates maintained silence while indoors. If he needed to talk, he was permitted to do so, as long as he spoke in Latin.

Rather than sharing an open dormitory as he had in St. Louis, Wayne slept in a solitary cell. A simple cot, a wooden armoire, a small desk, and a chair filled the 8' by 10' room. A curtain hung across the doorway for privacy.

The only major difference from his days with the Passionists was that the Jesuits didn't chant the Divine Office. The founder of the Jesuits, St. Ignatius himself, was the first to propose doing away with the traditional reciting of prayers at fixed hours of the day. The radical idea caused great conflict at the time, but Ignatius of Loyola found it more important to stress study and contemplation.

Wayne identified with the saint's emphasis on meditation. As much as he loved the frequent sports competitions with his fellow novices, he felt most exhilarated during the quiet hours of prayer. Sitting outside in the magnificence of the gardens or walking the well-tended paths in his long black cassock, he experienced the same closeness to God that he'd felt under the trees in Victoria or during Mass at the Cathedral of the Plains.

In addition to his walks and prayer time, Wayne and his classmates spent two hours outdoors each day tending the grounds.

Once again, the farm boy from Kansas earned the honor of driving the tractor and the school dump truck. He threw himself into the daily labor with exuberance, unaware that his enthusiasm was drawing attention.

Once a week, the novices participated in a special session designed to smooth out whatever rough edges kept them from fitting in. They met in a classroom where they gathered in a circle. A novice would kneel in the center, surrounded by his peers. The others were expected to state the young man's faults. He was then given an opportunity to either correct himself or leave. The comments were often brutal, and several young men left as a result.

When Wayne's turn arrived, he hesitantly moved to the center of the circle. He got down on his knees and held his breath. He scanned the solemn faces, wondering what egregious faults they'd raise. Had he been unkind to another? Was he too impatient? His only consolation as he waited was knowing that all of the novices were eventually subjected to the same fate.

Father Gavigan stood outside the circle, watching. The seconds ticked by, but nobody spoke. The priest crossed his arms and cleared his throat. Finally, Peter d'Alessandro, standing by Wayne's right elbow fidgeted. Wayne hung his head, ready to accept whatever his fellow novice said.

"Brother tends to run to work," Peter announced gravely.

Wayne kept his eyes riveted to the floor.

"Brother runs to work?" Father Gavigan asked.

Wayne sucked on his upper lip to keep from smiling. Yes, it was true. He loved the daily labor so much that he always rushed to get to his tractor. With so much time spent praying and studying, he had an abundance of energy.

When no other novice spoke up, Wayne got to his feet and rejoined the circle. He didn't dare to look at Brother Peter. If fitting in at the novitiate meant slowing down to a walk, Wayne would save his running for the sports field.

Life at the novitiate continued uninterrupted, year-round. There were no semester breaks nor summer vacation. As much as he enjoyed the emphasis on spiritual study in his first year, Wayne looked forward to the juniorate years when the focus would be more academic. He'd heard that the classes were intense, with three years of college condensed into two. Among other subjects, they'd read Homer's *Iliad* and the *Odyssey,* the poetry of Horace, and Virgil's *Aeneid,* all in the original Latin and Greek.

His future as a priest looked exciting, but it was still years away. Wayne first had a major hurdle to jump. The Jesuit superiors wanted to make sure that the young postulates were mentally prepared for the life that lay ahead. Before they were invited to enter the order, Wayne and his brothers endured a 30-day retreat in silence. During this time, they followed a strict routine of prayer, reading, reflection, and exercise. Their sole task was to decide whether to commit to the society or not.

Wayne loved his life among the Jesuits. He was in awe of his superiors. He felt called to be close to God and to help all of humankind through his service. There was just one problem: the vow of chastity.

It wasn't that he knew exactly what he'd be giving up. A year after his failed date with Betty Jane, Wayne was no more experienced with women than he'd been at Fort Hays. Certainly, he worried about the longings that every man experienced, but his needs went beyond the physical. Wayne had grown up in a large, loving family. He had trouble picturing a life devoid of the kind of emotional intimacy he'd witnessed between his parents. Would he be able to endure a life without the love of a woman?

The silence of the retreat was broken during daily meetings with a spiritual director. Confused by his troublesome doubts, Wayne consulted Father Gavigan. In true Jesuit fashion, the novice master made no effort to influence Wayne's thoughts. Instead, the priest told Wayne that his qualms were normal. He encouraged him to use the various methods of meditation he'd been taught and to let God direct his decision.

As part of his training, Wayne had learned about the Spiritual Exercises of St Ignatius: a monthlong program of prayers and practice designed to bring the Catholic faith more fully alive. The sports in which the novices participated exercised their bodies. The saint's exercises gave their spiritual minds a mental workout with the goal of determining God's will for their lives. Ignatius described two ways of making a major decision. Wayne decided to try each one in hopes of solving his dilemma.

He first drew a line down the center of a piece of paper. At the top of the left column, he wrote "Positives"; at the top of the right column, he wrote "Negatives." Then he entered into prayer and reflected on the issue at hand: Was he willing to take the vow of chastity; to be available to all people, not exclusively to one person or to one family?

Unable to answer his question with Ignatius's more pragmatic approach, Wayne turned to the second method taught in the exercises: the discernment of spirits.

Ignatius of Loyola developed the practice of spiritual discernment long before he founded the Jesuits. In his early years, he served as an officer in the Spanish army. In 1521, at the age of 30, Ignatius left to defend his Basque homeland from the French. A cannonball severely injured both of his legs. The French were so impressed with his valor in battle that they sent him home to Loyola to recuperate.

With little to occupy his mind during the long weeks of his recovery, Ignatius asked for something to read to pass the time. The history of the Catholic Church would thereafter be marked by the fact that the only reading matter in the castle was two books: one about the life of Christ and another about the saints. Ignatius read both books from cover to cover. He found the spiritual life of Christ and the saints intriguing and began to contemplate such a path for himself.

Lacking the distractions of his daily routine as a soldier, Ignatius became far more aware of his feelings and emotions. He noticed that when he thought about women, he felt agitated and unsatisfied. When he thought about the lives of Jesus and the saints, he felt calm and content. He realized that focusing on one's feelings rather than one's intellect was a useful way to make a decision. He would spend the rest of his life passing on this discovery to his students.

Wayne sat in the gardens of the novitiate and applied the Spanish saint's wisdom to his own dilemma. He reflected on how he would feel as a teacher and as a Jesuit priest, living without a family of his own. Then he contemplated how he would feel if he were a teacher, but not a priest. He prayed and listened to his emotions, allowing them to rise from deep within his subconscious mind.

The exercise proved definitive. The answer didn't come immediately, but over the course of the retreat, it became clear to Wayne that he should commit. When he pictured himself as a priest, he no longer felt hesitancy—instead, he felt happiness. He returned to Father Gavigan's office and announced that he'd made his decision: he would dedicate his life to God and to the Society of Jesus.

The ceremony took place in the novitiate chapel. Wernersville was too far away for his family to attend, but Wayne felt ecstatically happy surrounded by his brother Jesuits. One by one, the 36 eager young men went through the timeless ritual. They'd repeat the same vows each year for the rest of their lives, but this ceremony—their first vows—would hold a special place in their memories forever.

When his turn came, Wayne walked to the altar and knelt before it. Father Gavigan and his superiors stood in witness. Holding the script in his hands, Wayne read the solemn words aloud in Latin:

"Almighty and eternal God, I, Wayne Adam Knoll, though altogether most unworthy in your divine sight, yet relying on your infinite goodness and mercy and moved with a desire of serving you, in the presence of the most Holy Virgin Mary and your whole heavenly court, vow to Your Divine Majesty perpetual poverty, chastity and obedience in the Society of Jesus; and I promise that I shall enter the same Society in order to lead my entire life in it, understanding all things according to its Constitutions."[1]

Joy welled up from Wayne's chest as the true meaning of the words and the moment sank in. The emotion rose to his throat, threatening to choke his voice. He took a deep breath and continued:

"Therefore I suppliantly beg Your Immense Goodness and Clemency, through the blood of Jesus Christ, to accept this total offering of myself; and that just as you gave me the grace to desire and offer this, so you will also bestow on me abundant grace to fulfill it."[2]

The trembling in his limbs came not from uncertainty, but from pure elation. During the monthlong retreat, he'd come to terms with his doubts. He knew that taking the vows wouldn't eliminate the longing inside him. That was a natural desire that he could neither deny nor willfully make disappear. The issue of celibacy would surely remain a cause for personal struggle for the rest of his life. Knowing and accepting this, he went forward with his plans.

Wayne stepped to a table covered with a white linen cloth. On it lay a document with the same vows he'd just spoken before God. He had to blink away his tears to see the line awaiting his signature. He picked up a pen, scratched it across the paper, and sealed his future.

He was officially a Jesuit.

Chapter 12

The reporter held a pen poised over her notepad. "Will you tell me how old you are, Miss Gehman?"

Rather than answer, Anne sat back in her armchair and asked, "How old do you think I am?"

The question caught the woman off guard. "Well, uh . . . I'd guess about 27."

Anne simply smiled. Had the woman known that she was born in 1936, it would have been an easy matter to tick off the three decades to the current 1966. Anne wouldn't lie about her age, but she was more than happy to let the journalist think whatever she wanted.

The article appeared the following week in the *Orlando Sentinel* and featured "Anne Gehman, 27, the pretty young psychic from Cassadaga."

Anne was no stranger to the press. Her many appearances at local service clubs and organizations where she delivered messages from spirits and discussed Spiritualism had made her a minor celebrity in central Florida. Most articles mentioned her good looks and gentle nature. Anne was thankful they didn't dwell on her marital status, the way her family did.

Anne rarely dated. Young Spiritualist men were few and far between. Marvin Stuckey, the neighbor who painted the sign that hung in her front yard, did little to hide his crush on her, but Anne wasn't attracted to him. Of course she longed for human companionship and affection. Her little mutt dog, Foot Prince, was good company, but it wasn't the same as being in a relationship. Rather than dwell on her lack of a husband, Anne decided that she would stay single forever and dedicate herself fully to her work.

From the day she started giving readings full-time, Anne never lacked for clients. All of her visitors learned about her by word of mouth. One successful reading would result in dozens more when an excited sitter shared the results with friends and family. Her phone rarely sat silent for long.

Father Yannis, a Greek Orthodox priest from Tarpon Springs, visited Anne shortly after the death of his brother. The priest believed in spirit communication and was open to what Anne had to say. When she delivered a message not only from his brother, but from several other loved ones who had passed over, he began to send a regular stream of members of the Greek community to Cassadaga.

One day, Anne received a call from one of Father Yannis's parishioners. Eleni Papadopoulos explained that her cousin Sophia was visiting from Greece and wanted an appointment. Sophia didn't speak English, but Anne agreed to allow Eleni to sit in on the reading and translate.

On the day of the reading, the three women gathered in Anne's cozy office. Anne began with a prayer, as she always did. She waited while Eleni translated her words into Greek. She continued in this manner, speaking a few words, then pausing. The introductory phase of the reading took twice as long as usual.

Anne was beginning to question whether she should have agreed to the unusual meeting, when an older woman from the spirit world appeared in the room. Anne knew intuitively that the spirit was Sophia's mother who had recently passed over.

"Saghapó, Sophia, ti kanis?" Anne said. When she heard herself talk, her eyes widened in surprise. The voice was her own, but she was speaking in Greek.

What's happening? she wondered, as more foreign words flowed from her lips. She'd spoken in other languages in the past, but always while in trance. This time, fully conscious, she didn't merely repeat what her spirit guest said—she spoke the woman's thoughts directly. Anne had no comprehension of the individual words she was saying, but somehow she understood their overall meaning.

The two cousins sat in front of Anne crying tears of happiness and wonder as she passed along the woman's message in their native tongue. With no further need of a translator, the reading progressed far more smoothly. Anne heard herself telling Sophia where to find her mother's will and how to implement it. She then passed along what the woman wanted done with her jewelry and other personal belongings and relayed messages for family and friends.

When the reading concluded, Anne was as dazed as her clients.

"I didn't know you spoke Greek," Eleni said, shaking her head.

"I don't!" Anne replied.

Anne treasured the moment and gave thanks for the unique opportunity. As a medium, she was almost always a go-between. What had started out as an ordinary reading turned into one of the rare times that her clients were able to speak directly with a loved one on the other side.

She and Foot Prince escorted Eleni and Sophia to the door. As her clients walked to their car, another couple brushed past them. Anne had never seen the man and woman before. It wasn't unusual for strangers to stop by without an appointment. The sign in front made it clear that Anne gave readings from the house, and she welcomed walk-ins when she had the time.

The couple's clothes were shabbier than most who came to call. The way they dressed didn't matter to Anne, but the two had an unusually rough look. The man was unshaven, and the woman's eyes kept darting back and forth. Prince, who was usually loving and friendly with all of Anne's clients, sniffed at the door, then bared his teeth and growled.

The man asked if they could have a reading. Anne glanced down at Foot Prince, who was clearly on guard. Even though she was free for the next few hours, she told the couple that she had another client who was due any minute. Prince watched their backs, a soft growl rumbling from his chest until they were out of sight. Later, Anne didn't know whether to feel guilty or relieved when she learned that the strangers had gone to another medium's home where they beat the woman and took her television set.

With Foot Prince at her side, the only problem Anne encountered on a regular basis was her clients' skepticism. She understood that people who'd never consulted a medium might be wary, but she personally had no doubt that there was another reality beyond the one most people experienced. Just because physical humans couldn't see the spirits didn't mean they weren't there. Like the blades of an electric fan that were visible when the fan was turned off, yet invisible when spinning, spirits simply vibrated at a frequency that most human eyes were unable to detect. Anne was able to tune in to these higher frequencies and welcomed the nonbelievers.

Just such a young man arrived at her door one afternoon without an appointment. He was tall, thin, and nicely dressed in khaki pants and a collared shirt. Anne had an opening in her schedule, but she hesitated. When Foot Prince checked out the stranger and responded with a wagging tail, she invited him inside.

As soon as he sat down in her office, the man buried his face in his hands and began to cry. He described how his wife had recently died from a rattlesnake bite. He looked up through teary eyes and told Anne that he was desperate to communicate with the only woman he'd ever loved.

Foot Prince lay calmly at Anne's feet. She knew the man posed no danger, but she frowned. Even though his acting was good enough for the stage, she clearly sensed that his tears were fake.

"Your wife isn't in spirit," she said bluntly. "She's 5'5", weighs about 120 pounds, and is very much alive. She works as a secretary in an office, where she's taking dictation from her boss as we speak."

The man's mouth opened, but no words came out.

"There are several spirits here who actually have passed over," Anne said. "They'd probably like to speak with you, but I don't have time for people who lie to me."

She stood and waited for the man to join her. He rose and clasped his hands as if in prayer. "Please—I'm sorry—I just wanted to see what you'd say."

"So you made up a story about your wife dying?" She started walking toward the foyer. "That's not very nice."

"I swear I'm sorry," he said as his fake tears turned to real ones. "I can tell you're the real thing, and I'd really like to hear from whatever spirits you see."

"They don't like liars either," Anne replied as she showed him out the door.

A short time later, she sensed that something was once again amiss when a new female client with long, straight black hair and equally dark eyes arrived for her appointment. She had called Anne weeks in advance and gave her name as Mary Margaret Murphy.

The moment Anne took her seat, she knew the woman had used a false name. Anne didn't care what people called themselves, but she hated when they tried to trick her.

"Your name isn't Mary Murphy; it's Darina Magdalena Kratochvilova." She spelled the surname letter by letter, then said, "You live in Ft. Myers, and you have a calico cat named Bella. I know you want a reading, but I can't work with someone I don't trust."

The woman stammered and begged for forgiveness, but Anne had made up her mind. "This concludes our reading," she said. "I really don't care to be placed in the category of a fraud. I take my work very seriously."

As she spoke the words, two books on the shelves beside them shuffled forward toward the edge, as if someone were pushing them from behind. Physical phenomena weren't new to Anne, but even so, she stared in surprise as the books stopped moving just before falling off the edge, then retreated to their original position.

Darina sprang to her feet, her eyes large like a frightened deer. She crossed her shaking hands in front of her legs, but she wasn't fast enough to hide a dark stain of urine spreading across her flowered skirt.

"I can see you're not a fraud," Darina said with a trembling voice. "Please, may I come back another time for a reading?"

Anne felt sorry for the woman's embarrassment, but she shook her head. "I don't like the way you handled this."

Darina began to cry. "I'm sorry I lied about my name. It's just that I've visited so many mediums who made up all kinds of nonsense." She glanced at the bookshelves. "You're not at all like those others. Please give me the reading."

It was late in the day, and Anne was tired. She stood her ground and showed Darina to the door. When the woman was out of sight, Anne left the house and walked to Wilbur's.

Her former teacher listened quietly as she poured out her frustration. She could always count on Wilbur to help her when she had a difficult client. This time, he surprised her by laughing.

"You'd better get used to it," he said. "Not everyone who calls themselves a medium is as ethical as we'd like to believe. As long as there's money to be made through trickery and deceit, people have good reason to be cautious."

"But I'm not like that," Anne said. "I'd never lie to a client."

Wilbur knew she was sincere, but he enjoyed teasing his favorite student. From that day forward, he took great pleasure in embarrassing Anne by telling people in her presence: "Anne Gehman's not happy with her readings unless she can make the men cry and the women wet their pants."

Darina Kratochvilova spent the night at the Cassadaga Hotel. The next day she appeared at Anne's door wearing a fresh skirt and a genuine look of remorse. Anne remembered what Wilbur said and invited the woman inside. She gave her a meaningful reading, then tacked on a little advice: "The best way to find a good medium is by word of mouth."

Darina, still dazed by the evidential information Anne had shared with her, merely nodded.

"If a medium advertises a lot, that means the person doesn't have a following," Anne said. "Someone who has a good reputation won't have to advertise."

Anne never sought out clients. They came to her in droves. She learned early on to limit herself to five readings a day; any more than that was simply too tiring. It was the nature of a medium's work to help people deal with grief. Even though she was able to prove to her clients that life was eternal, emotions still ran high.

In the early days, she'd come away from a session as drained as those she read for. Finally, when the stress threatened to overwhelm her, she once again turned to Wilbur for advice. She shared with him the story of a client who was trying to connect with her deceased husband. During the reading, the husband came through clearly, but Anne also sensed a large mass in her client's stomach. She recommended that the woman see a doctor as soon as possible. The client called back two days later to report that tests had revealed a large tumor in her stomach. Anne was pleased that she might have saved the woman's life, but since then, she couldn't get the encounter off her mind.

"Now, young lady," Wilbur said with a stern face, "you've got to learn to let go . . . to release. You can't allow your readings to become part of your consciousness." He warned that if clients ever came back for subsequent readings, Anne shouldn't recall anything about them.

"You don't want to carry the information over," he advised, "so it's important to cleanse your thoughts after each reading."

From that day forward, Anne trained herself to follow Wilbur's instructions. She remained completely aware of what was said during a reading, but most conversations passed from her memory after the person departed.

One case, however, defied Anne's ability to remain detached or to ever forget the events that transpired. Carolyn Miller, a resident of nearby Winter Park, called one Wednesday morning and asked for an appointment as soon as possible. Everybody always wanted to see Anne sooner rather than later, but Carolyn seemed especially anxious to discover if Anne could help locate a brother whom she hadn't seen since childhood. Ordinarily, Anne had no immediate openings, but a woman had called minutes earlier to cancel her appointment that same afternoon.

"If you can get here by two o'clock, I'll see you," Anne said.

Carolyn showed up at Avalon on time, but she didn't come alone.

"This is my friend Sarah," the willowy woman said. "She'd love to have a reading, too, if you can fit her in.

Anne smiled, but inside she winced. Saying no was always so difficult.

"There's someone scheduled right after you," she told Carolyn, "but if you don't mind waiting, I might be able to fit Sarah in after that."

The two friends shared a glance, then nodded excitedly. Anne asked Sarah to wait on the porch, then she led Carolyn to her office.

They sat across from each other with Foot Prince in his favorite spot at Anne's feet.

"We're going to take a moment just to enter into silence together, to be prayerful," she began. "And I'd like to hold a watch or something of yours that's imbued with your energy."

"I wear this all the time," Carolyn said as she removed a silver bracelet from her right wrist. "Will it do?"

Anne took the bracelet and held it in the palm of her hand. "This is fine."

She closed her eyes. After several deep breaths, she began with a prayer in the way Wilbur had taught her years earlier: "As we attune ourselves with that great Infinite Intelligence of the universe, that source of light and love, of wisdom and truth, we also invite the presence of our departed loved ones, as well as our guides and our teachers."

Carolyn rubbed her hands nervously as she listened.

"We ask them to draw very near to us as we ask for guidance," Anne continued. "We ask for insight, and for understanding to help us as we continue our journey through life. And today we ask a very special blessing for Carolyn, that there might always be light and love. And we give thanks for the presence of spirit in our lives and for the blessing that they bring. Amen."

"Amen," Carolyn echoed.

Anne sat in silence for a moment, her eyes still closed. Her shoulders and head began to sway ever so slowly in a tight, clockwise circle. Her lips turned up slightly as if she were experiencing a pleasant memory. When she opened her eyes, they had a dreamy quality, as did her voice when she spoke.

"I'm very conscious of the presence of several people."

Carolyn leaned forward.

"The first one to bring you a greeting is a woman who looks a lot like you. She would be a little bit shorter and heavier. I see gray hair, and the facial features are so very much the same. This woman passed over with some problem in the head, and it feels like there's a dark area here." Anne put her hand to the side of her head, just above the ear.

"This feels like a mother to me . . . I'm hearing the name Dorothy, but I don't think she was called that. I think she went by 'Dot.'"

Carolyn raised a hand to her face. "That's my mother! She died of a brain tumor, and everyone called her Dot."

Anne nodded slowly. "Yes, your mother's here, and I just feel so much love from her. I feel as if she's often near you."

"Is anyone with her?" Carolyn's voice was tense, but excited.

Anne closed her eyes. "Along with your mother I see a man who stands quite a bit taller and not real thin . . . I'd say more to the slender side. His forehead is quite full, his nose very prominent, and he has rather strong lines in the face."

She used her hands as she continued with the description. "The lines come down with sort of a strong, rectangular shape. I just see him reach out to you as if to embrace you. I feel this is a man who sometimes had a little trouble expressing his emotions. And yet, as I see him in the spirit world, he just feels like he wants to embrace you with love, and I don't know if he was that way when he was here. Does this make sense?"

"Yes." Carolyn's eyes were wide. "That sounds exactly like my grandfather on my father's side. You actually see him?"

"He's standing right beside you."

Carolyn shifted in her chair, as if to try and see the man. When she turned back, she grew more serious. "Do you see my brother—Jack?"

Anne closed her eyes and again began to sway ever so slightly. After almost a full minute she opened her eyes and shook her head. "I don't get the sense of any brothers or sisters in the spirit world. I do see the image of a house, though. It's in the Victorian style, but rather small. It's painted red with white trim around the door and windows."

Carolyn shook her head as if to shake away her disbelief. "That's the house where I was born. It's the last place I saw my brother."

"Well, for some reason, I see this house very clearly. There are toys on the porch and a large weeping willow in the front yard."

Carolyn nodded, her smile filled with wonder. "I remember that tree."

Anne had no trouble filling the rest of the reading with descriptions of the other spirits who arrived to greet her client. At the end of the hour, Carolyn put her bracelet back on her arm. She grasped Anne's hands and squeezed them. "Thank you so much for seeing me on such short notice. I'm sorry you weren't able to find my brother, but this has been truly incredible. By the way you described my mother and the others, I just know they were here."

Of course they were, Anne thought. *Why can't people believe that?*

The two walked to the porch where Sarah sat waiting. Beyond her, a tall man in gray slacks and a blue blazer, with thinning hair and thick eyebrows, was just getting out of a white sedan parked along the street.

"I believe my next appointment is here," Anne said. "If you don't mind waiting another hour, I'll give Sarah her reading after I've done his."

Carolyn reached out and touched her friend's arm. "It's worth the wait, believe me."

The man stepped onto the porch. He nodded politely at Carolyn and Sarah.

"You must be John," Anne said as she held the door for him. The man had scheduled the appointment months earlier.

Once inside, he explained that he'd traveled from New York solely for the reading.

Anne acknowledged his comment, but with Sarah still waiting outside, Anne didn't take the time for small talk. She showed John to his chair and asked to hold a piece of his jewelry. He handed her a Timex watch with a golden-metal band. She took it, then began with a prayer as she always did.

" . . . and today we ask a very special blessing for John," she concluded, "and we give thanks for the presence of Spirit in our lives and for the blessing that they bring. Amen."

"Amen," John repeated.

Anne remained seated with her eyes closed. She immediately saw several spirits, but she hesitated to tell John about them. Something wasn't right. The same woman and man from the last reading were still lingering about, and they were smiling. It was Carolyn's mother, Dorothy, and her grandfather. For some reason they hadn't gone away. Anne wondered if perhaps she'd failed to pass along all they wanted to say before she finished with Carolyn.

Anne silently acknowledged their presence, then continued trying to attune with spirits who might be there for John. As she swayed slightly, the vision of the red Victorian house appeared once again. Anne opened her eyes and smiled at John, knowing that he was waiting for her to say something.

What's going on? she wondered. Even with her eyes open, she could still see Carolyn's mother and grandfather standing off to the side, smiling and nodding. She didn't want to ignore them, but she didn't want John to know that she was experiencing an unusual event. She was grateful when the spirit of a middle-aged man she'd never seen before appeared by the bookshelves.

"I'm seeing a man in his 40s, and I'm hearing the name Henry," she said. "I sense a very gentle soul, very creative and very artistic. His features are sort of pointed, with a chiseled look. His hair is dark brown and parted here, to the side, but thinning here in the back." She ran her hand over the crown of her head.

"I get the feeling that he died rather unexpectedly, in some kind of accident."

"Wow," John said. "Henry was my brother-in-law—my wife's older brother. He was killed in a car accident five years ago, and he was an artist, just like you said."

"Well, he's here to greet you, and he asks that you send his love to his sister . . . Rosa, isn't it?"

John's eyes widened. "Yes! That's my wife's name. This is amazing."

Anne smiled and closed her eyes. The Victorian house from the previous reading flashed through her mind again. Dorothy still lingered, smiling. Anne shook her head as if to clear it and was relieved when she sensed something new to pass to John.

"I get the feeling that you're going to be returning to Florida again some time before the year is out. I can't tell whether it's for business or pleasure."

John shook his head. "I'm afraid you're wrong on that one. This is the only trip I have planned for Florida. I came here specifically for this reading because I heard you were the best."

"That's very kind, but I definitely sense that you'll be returning to Florida."

"No," he was adamant. "I have no other reason for coming back. I came here solely to see you. I was really hoping you could help me find my sister. I've spent years looking for her, and you're my last hope."

Anne rarely got chills when she gave a reading, but suddenly the hair on her arms stood on end. She instantly knew without any doubt why she was seeing the same people and the same Victorian house as in the previous reading. She closed her eyes and saw that Dorothy was not only smiling, she was now holding out her arms, as if in welcome.

Anne jumped to her feet, shoved her client's watch at him, and said, "Come with me."

John rose automatically, stunned by the sudden change in Anne's demeanor.

"What's going on?" he asked.

Anne looked at him as tears pooled in her eyes. "You've come all the way from New York to try to find your sister, and she's sitting on my porch."

John stood frozen, as if Anne were speaking a foreign language. Only when she grasped his arm did he move. The two women looked up when Anne and John appeared on the porch. Sarah glanced at her watch.

"Is it my turn already?" she asked.

Instead of answering, Anne looked directly at Carolyn. "You wanted to find your brother," she said, "and thanks to your mother's hard efforts, you've done just that."

She put her hand at the small of John's back and gently pushed him forward.

"Carolyn, this is your brother, Jack."

Carolyn's hand flew to her mouth as she rose to her feet. The two siblings stared for a moment, then rushed into each others' arms. They pulled back, stared some more, then both began talking and laughing at the same time. Their elation was so palpable that soon everyone on the porch was openly crying.

John wiped his eyes and turned to Anne. "I guess I'll be coming back to Florida, just like you said."

"How could this have happened?" Carolyn asked as she leaned her head against her brother's chest. "It's almost too much to believe."

Anne had experienced the presence of spirits all her life, but even she was amazed at how their mother had orchestrated Carolyn and John's reunion from the spirit world. Dorothy had known that her son had an appointment that day with a medium. Somehow—possibly with a little help from her spirit friends—Dorothy had caused Anne's earlier client to cancel the appointment before John's. She had planted the idea in her daughter's mind to call at just the right time to fill the empty slot. Then she had subconsciously urged Carolyn to bring her friend along so she'd have a reason to wait around.

Anne knew that what seemed like coincidence was often the work of Spirit. One very determined mother had gone to great lengths to bring her son and daughter together. Best of all, Dorothy was there to witness her children's joyful reunion.

Anne had learned from Wilbur to purge her mind of the strong emotions that arose during her work, but these particular memories she tucked away for safekeeping. In her private prayers that evening, Anne gave special thanks to God for her role in the day's events. She knew that she was only the instrument, but she never wanted to forget how Spirit had used her gifts to bring a family together.

Chapter 13

Wayne learned early in his training that becoming a priest and becoming a Jesuit priest were not one and the same. Priests who served a diocese were bound by celibacy, but they didn't take the vows of those who joined an order. Theological training for a diocesan priest extended four to five years after college, while Wayne's training as a Jesuit would take more than a dozen.

The main mission of the Society of Jesus was to educate young men to become leaders. Wayne's personal vision meshed perfectly with the Jesuits'. Georgetown University, where he dreamed of being a professor, turned out some of the nation's top leaders. He knew that earning a Ph.D. to teach there would add five more years of study to his already-lengthy career path. This realization only served to stimulate him further.

Still, by the time he left the novitiate, Wayne was ready for a program that would grant him a diploma. His younger brothers Omer and Lester had started college while he attended the Passionist seminary and Kansas State in Fort Hays. Les earned his bachelor's degree while Wayne studied at Wernersville. After six years of college-level work, Wayne had a head full of knowledge, but no gilded paper with his name in calligraphic script. Yes, the knowledge he'd acquired mattered far more than a mere document, but his parents had always stressed the importance of a college degree. Wayne wouldn't mind putting a couple of letters behind his name after all that time.

A three-year course of philosophy and liberal arts followed the novitiate. While many of Wayne's buddies chose Fordham University in New York for their philosophate, Wayne set his sights on St. Louis. Missouri was closer to his family than New York, but Wayne had a more practical reason for choosing the former: he'd decided to major in both philosophy and English literature. Walter Ong, one of the top Jesuit professors of English literature in the country, taught at St. Louis University.

The seminary was part of the campus. Wayne slept, ate, and studied philosophy and theology in the Jesuits' building. He attended literature, history, psychology, and other core courses with the rest of the student body. With several hundred of his fellow Jesuits enrolled at the school, the secular students were used to seeing the young seminarians in their classes. Wayne felt proud as he wandered the campus in his long black cassock.

Just as there had been no vacations at the novitiate, classes continued year-round for the philosophate students. Knowing Wayne wasn't free to travel home for the summer, his brother Omer decided to pay a visit to St. Louis. Omer arrived with his friend Robert in the middle of the week.

Wayne was glad to see his brother, but he had little time to socialize. Omer didn't want to waste the trip, so he followed his brother to the library. When Wayne joined his fellow Jesuits at a study table, Omer and Robert took seats nearby and looked around. It didn't take long for them to notice that St. Louis had no shortage of pretty coeds. Omer elbowed Robert and nodded in the direction of a particularly striking young brunette in a tight pink blouse. The two friends stared at the girl, willing her to look their way, but she and her friends never noticed the visitors. Instead, they focused their full attention on the black-frocked young men piously studying by the card catalog. The girls whispered among themselves and giggled as they ogled the priests in training. Frustrated and hungry, Omer and Robert got up and left.

Absorbed in his work, Wayne wasn't aware of the girls' attention. Still, he wasn't oblivious to the opposite sex. As the semester progressed, he took special note of a slender blonde who worked at the reference desk. Struck by how attractive she was, he started looking for her whenever he went to study. If the girl was on duty, he sought out opportunities to chat with her. Their conversations went no further than discussions about library issues, but he welcomed the diversion. He'd taken a vow of celibacy, but that didn't mean he couldn't enjoy a woman's good looks or her company.

After three years of continual study, Wayne earned a bachelor's degree in English and the equivalent of a master's degree in philosophy. Most of the seminarians moved on to the next phase of training, but Wayne had other plans. If he wanted to teach English at the university level, he'd need to specialize. He asked the Jesuits for permission to stay an extra year to earn a master's degree in English literature. Always supportive of anything that would further their mission, his superiors said yes.

The path he'd chosen was long, but Wayne had his vision to guide him. He was sure that nothing could deter him from the ultimate goal he'd set. Then one day at the end of the third year of his philosophate, he received a letter from Kansas. The postmark read Hays. He recognized the writing, but couldn't quite place it.

Wayne slit the envelope, removed the letter, and glanced at the bottom. It was signed by Dr. Anderson. Now he recognized the handwriting: the same script had adorned many a test and term paper back at Fort Hays Kansas State. Memories of the daily chats with his former philosophy professor passed through Wayne's mind. He smiled, pleased to hear from the department chairman.

His eyes rose to the date and salutation, then moved to the body of the letter.

"I'm preparing to retire at the end of the year," Dr. Anderson wrote.

Wayne was pleased but surprised that his teacher thought well enough of him to share his news after all these years. He continued reading, then stopped. He moved the page closer to his face, blinked, and reread the last sentence. His lips parted and his eyes grew wide as the words on the paper sank in.

"I would like to offer you the opportunity to be the chairman of the department of philosophy at Fort Hays Kansas State," the professor wrote.

Wayne's mind raced. Dr. Anderson had sent the letter to the seminary. Surely he knew that Wayne had joined the Jesuit order and was still a graduate student.

He reached for a nearby chair and lowered himself onto it. He stared at the letter, moved beyond words. He was years away from a doctorate—the level of education required for most full-professor positions and most certainly for all department chairs. Yet his former college professor wanted him now.

Wayne visualized his future plans. The picture of being ordained was clear in his mind. Even more perfectly focused was the image of the Georgetown campus with "Dr. Wayne A. Knoll" on the faculty roster.

Still . . . what an honor! Wayne couldn't dismiss the unique proposal outright and forced himself to think rationally.

His dream was to be a professor. He loved philosophy as much as English and would have no trouble teaching it. The current road he'd chosen stretched before him like an endless highway, and he had no guarantees that his vision would come to pass. He held an offer that would take him to the top seat in the philosophy department at an accredited college immediately, not 16 years in the future. It was an opportunity most academics would accept without hesitation.

He stared at his lap, still stunned by the unexpected turn of events. The white paper stood out in stark contrast with the black cassock that covered his legs. The dark cloth snapped him back to reality. Wayne closed his eyes and inhaled. He paused for a moment, then smiled as he let out his breath.

There was great wisdom in the familiar exercises of St. Ignatius. They'd taught him to listen to his feelings. The thought of accepting the proposal left him proud, but greatly unsettled. The offer in his hands represented a tremendous honor, but he had no need to spend another minute wondering what to do. He was committed to the Jesuits as well as to his vision, and nothing else felt more right.

Chapter 14

Anne knew better than most people that life in the spirit world wasn't one big vacation. Heaven wasn't a place where angels drifted aimlessly on clouds, listening to beautiful music. The clouds were real and the music was certainly heavenly, but the spirits themselves were actually quite busy. They had work to do, and much of it focused on helping the souls still existing in a physical body.

A spirit named Sally had been hovering around the Earth plane for years and never seemed to tire. Anne first met Sally when she spoke through Wilbur in a trance state. The spirit came to Wilbur through a close friend in Wisconsin—a Catholic priest who was also a medium. And when Wilbur moved to Cassadaga, Sally moved with him.

Anne figured that Sally was her mentor's exclusive guide, but Sally must have sensed a new assignment. One evening not long after she met Wilbur, Anne joined him and six others in his living room. She sat in a chair and listened quietly to the conversation. Suddenly, her head began to swirl. She gripped the arms of the chair to keep from falling, then lost all awareness of her surroundings.

When she opened her eyes, Wilbur was smiling. The others looked as dazed as Anne felt.

"Sally spoke through you," he said like a proud parent. The others described the sweet, slightly high-pitched voice with a Victorian speech pattern that Anne had heard through Wilbur countless times.

Anne had no recollection of anything she'd said, but shortly thereafter, Sally appeared to her while she was fully conscious. She described the spirit to Wilbur as a woman in her mid-20s with blue eyes and a very pretty face. She had long blonde hair that fell past her shoulders in natural ringlets. She wore a white, floor-length Victorian dress with full sleeves and a narrow waist.

Wilbur confirmed that the description matched his spirit guide's.

From that day forward, Anne felt Sally's presence often. She nearly always appeared at her side when Anne gave a reading, taking on the role of gatekeeper. Anne continued to have direct contact with the other entities who appeared, but Sally would line them up and help to filter their communication.

Anne thought Sally was simply a spirit guide, sent to help with her gifts. She had no idea that Sally would turn out to be a lifesaver. One afternoon, Anne was on her way to speak to a local women's club in central Florida about Spiritualism and mediumship. She was driving north on the interstate when Sally's voice spoke urgently in her head.

Get off the road immediately!

Anne knew not to question such a command and pulled over right away. Seconds later, a car came speeding down the highway, going the wrong direction in the lane where Anne had just been.

She was still thinking about her close call the next day when three women arrived at Avalon for back-to-back readings. The trio lived near each other in the Orlando area and had come in the same car. As Anne sat with the first woman in her office, she had an uncomfortable feeling.

"When you go home today, Sharon," Anne advised, "don't take Highway 4. There's danger if you do."

An hour later, while reading for the second woman, Anne had the same sense of foreboding.

"Joy, the three of you should go home today via Route 17. I sense trouble on Highway 4."

By the time the third woman entered the office, Anne's agitation had increased to the point of discomfort. She passed along to Janet the same warning she'd given to Sharon and Joy.

Janet looked at her watch. "I don't know . . . I told my sitter we'd be back by three, and we're already running late. If we take 17, I'll never make it on time."

"Wouldn't your babysitter wait if you were a little late?" Anne asked.

"I don't know." Janet shook her head. "Highway 4 is much faster."

Anne tried to push down her frustration. Prophecy was all about cause and effect. When she predicted an upcoming event, it simply meant that what she saw was in motion at the time. People had free will. They could always change their immediate future if they chose.

The next day when the headlines told of a fatal car crash on Highway 4, Anne knew that she'd done all she could.

Sharon and Joy survived the accident, but their friend Janet passed to the other side. Anne cried for the mother who never made it home to her children. The babysitter would surely have waited if she'd known it would save Janet's life.

Several days later, Sharon called to set Anne's mind at ease. "Joy and I feel simply awful that we didn't listen to you, but maybe it's for the best."

Anne scrunched her nose, not sure she heard correctly. "For the best?"

"Yes," Sharon said. "Janet had recently been diagnosed with stage-four cancer. It was only a matter of time."

Anne sat back, stunned. She hadn't detected any health issues during the reading—perhaps the warnings about the accident had overshadowed all else—but Sharon was right. It might well have been for the best. Janet was no doubt happy and pain free on the other side. Her family would surely grieve for her, but now none of them would have to endure the agony of a lingering illness.

In spite of her sadness, Anne couldn't help but wonder if Spirit had played a hand in the way things turned out.

⊕⊕⊕

Marsha Collins and Jane Heckman sat across from Anne with worried faces. The room had a heavy, clammy feel that had nothing to do with the humid Florida air. The last time the two women had seen their friend June, she'd been sitting at her desk smoking a Tareyton. Now no one had seen or heard from her in two days. She left behind a lighter and her cigarettes, and June never went anywhere without her smokes.

The three colleagues worked for the Leesburg court system. June, an attractive blonde, served as a secretary for the Lake County public defender.

"Can you really tell where someone is just by touching their belongings?"

Anne rolled June's lighter between her fingers. "I've had some success," she said modestly.

She thought back to one of her first missing-person cases that had made the news. Two sets of worried parents had shown up at her door. Their daughters, Darla Kaufman and Karen Simons, both 15 years old, had disappeared five days earlier. No one had seen them since they'd walked away from Jefferson Junior High School on Merritt Island. The police were actively searching for the girls, but the parents weren't satisfied with their efforts.

The Kaufmans and Simonses brought Anne purses, samples of the girls' handwriting, and some jewelry. Anne handled each of the items and instantly sensed that the girls were fine. She told the parents that Darla and Karen had run away because of a problem at school. They'd hitchhiked to Fort Lauderdale, helped by a man in a blue car. Although the girls split up once they reached southern Florida, Anne felt sure they'd be back safe and sound within days.

Her prediction proved accurate. Both girls returned as she said they would, and their stories confirmed every detail that Anne had provided.

Since then, Anne's phone often rang at odd hours. She never advertised her ability to solve crimes or locate missing persons, but somehow people found her. When Marsha and Jane called about their friend June Ritter, she told them to come right over.

Marsha had read about Anne in the *Orlando Sentinel's Florida Magazine* the previous Sunday. When June failed to show up at work two days in a row, the first person Marsha thought to call was Anne.

"Are you sensing anything now?" Marsha asked.

Anne frowned as she fondled the lighter. She was, indeed, sensing something, and it wasn't good.

Jane picked up on Anne's concern. "Has something happened to June?"

"Yes." Anne never held back, even if the news was bad. "I feel she's in grave danger."

She picked up paper and a pencil from the table at her side.

"This is Treasure Island Road," she said as she drew a vertical line. "It forks off State Road 44 here." She drew a *Y* and tapped her pencil.

"June's car is here, on the right side of the fork."

Anne sketched a few trees and outlined a circular lake beside the highway. She told the women to send the police immediately to the spot she'd described. She sensed that June was still alive, but wounded. They needed to find her before the sun went down, or it would be too late.

As Marsha and Jane hurried out the door, Anne warned them to have the police look closely. June's car couldn't be seen from the road.

The next morning, Anne retrieved the newspaper from her lawn. There, on the front page of the *Sentinel*, was the map she'd drawn for Marsha and Jane. She read the article and learned that the Leesburg police had followed her instructions but had found June's car on the left side of the fork, not the right. Anne pursed her lips. She'd clearly seen the car on the right side, and she realized that her dyslexia had caused her to reverse the image she'd seen in her mind. From that day forward, whenever she drew a map, she deliberately reversed left and right.

According to the news, the police hadn't yet located June. Anne had known the day before that the woman was close to death. She no longer felt the same sense of urgency.

The phone rang minutes later. It was Marsha.

"I'm sorry," Anne said with as much compassion as she could muster, "but I think your friend is dead."

Marsha gasped, then began to sob when Anne added that she felt sure that June had been murdered.

"I see a body in a shallow grave in very dark soil. It's near a clay pit about 30 miles southeast of the car."

When the police found June's body exactly as Anne described it, they sent two officers to Cassadaga. It was the first time the police had consulted her. Before, she'd always worked with the family and friends of missing persons. She invited the officers inside and watched as they glanced around her office with undisguised curiosity.

The men confirmed that by all appearances they were dealing with a homicide, and they asked if Anne could provide any further details to help with the case. Once again, she tuned in to the vibrations that had helped her thus far. The details flowed in a steady stream of disturbing images.

A threatening phone call had started the chain of events. June left her office in a hurry, without bothering to take her cigarettes. Anne sensed some kind of struggle in a shack or shed north of the abandoned car, followed by more movement. She sensed that June's injuries included a stab wound to her shoulder and a blow to the head.

The officers shared a knowing look, then asked Anne if she knew anything about the attacker.

She sat back and concentrated. "Yes, yes. It's a woman—a black woman."

One of the officers scribbled on a notepad.

"Her name is Marie . . . Marie Arring . . . Marie Arrington. She's the one who abducted June."

The other officer turned his head and spoke into a radio.

"I sense this Marie is a very strong woman, rather tough. But Miss Ritter put up quite a struggle."

"Was anyone else involved?"

"No," Anne said with her eyes half-closed. "She acted alone. I feel that she did this out of revenge somehow. There's something about her son, who is in jail . . . and June's boss, the public defender."

Armed with a name and a description, it didn't take long for the police to track down Marie Arrington. The story Anne told of revenge, struggle, and death proved true. Marie was later sentenced to prison just like her son. The charge was murder in the first degree.

Law-enforcement officials from local jurisdictions across the country all the way up to the FBI would consult with Anne in the years that followed, but she never took credit for her contributions. She felt very strongly that a psychic merely offered a few impressions that might help lead to an arrest. In her mind, it was the hard work of the men and women with the badges that solved the crimes.

Anne found it highly rewarding to help find missing persons, but her favorite work was guiding others on a new pathway in life. She felt honored to be used by Spirit to give encouragement or to help someone through a difficult time.

One such client gave his name as Michael Jarvis. He appeared highly agitated and distracted as he sat across from Anne in her office. Like many of her clients, Michael didn't tell Anne why he'd come; he simply said he wanted a reading. Anne had no problem with that. Spirit would tell her what she needed to know.

A few minutes into the session, Anne began to grow warm. She suddenly felt intensely claustrophobic, as if she were enclosed in a bubble. The heat continued to build until she had the horrific sensation of being consumed by fire.

She shook her head to clear the images, then described what she was experiencing. Upon hearing her words, Michael leaned forward, put his head in his hands, and began to cry.

The dreadful feeling of suffocation diminished and was replaced by the loving presence of Spirit.

"There are three men here to greet you. I'm hearing the names Virgil and Roger, but the third one isn't very clear. Do these names mean anything to you?"

She needn't have asked. At the mention of the names, Michael's head snapped up, his eyes intent.

"Yes. They mean a lot."

Anne nodded. "Virgil wants you to know that he and the others are fine. They seem to be saying that what happened wasn't . . . it wasn't your fault."

Michael choked back a sob. Foot Prince looked up, then put his chin on his paws.

"One of these men had a premonition that something was going to happen. Do you know what they're talking about?"

Michael nodded and explained, "I work at NASA. I'm an engineer. I was on the team in charge of the AS-204 spacecraft. You'd know it as *Apollo 1*."

Anne leaned back. She could still remember the headlines about the capsule going up in flames on the launchpad. The fire consumed all three astronauts before they could escape.

Anne had known nothing about Michael's involvement with NASA. For all she knew, he could have been a doctor or a lawyer. Now his story explained the frightening sensation of flames and claustrophobia she'd experienced moments before.

Michael shook his head. "The astronauts we lost were wonderful men: Ed White, Roger Chaffee, and Gus Grissom."

"Gus?" Anne said.

"Gus was his nickname. His real name was Virgil, just like you said."

Seeing Michael's pallor, Anne didn't need to be psychic to understand the reason for his visit. "And you felt somehow responsible for their deaths?"

He hung his head, unable to answer.

"But you heard what they said: It wasn't your fault."

"How can you know that?"

Anne put her hands together as if in prayer and leaned toward him. "They came here themselves to give you that message. They're still here, in fact, and they appear quite peaceful."

Michael looked around the office.

"They hold no malice toward you or anyone," Anne continued. "They want you to know that their lives didn't end on that launchpad, that life is eternal, and that what lies beyond this experience on the physical plane is wonderful beyond words."

The man who left Cassadaga that day was a different person from the one who arrived. Michael Jarvis returned to the camp many times and eventually became a Spiritualist. Anne never found out if he told his colleagues about his experiences during the reading, but over the next few months, a succession of clients from the aerospace industry booked appointments nearly one after another.

During this time, two men arrived one afternoon from Orlando. Anne glanced at the fishing gear mounted on their car rack. She noted their ball caps, plaid shirts, and rubber boots. They didn't look like her normal clients. In fact, they didn't look like fishermen either.

The two took their seats across from her. Anne settled into her chair and examined the men closely. One picked at his teeth with a fingernail. The other scanned the books on her shelves.

"How's the fishing?" she asked with a smile.

"Pretty good," said one.

"Not bad," said the other.

"Mm-hm." Anne waited a moment, but neither spoke.

"That's not really what you're about," she said pleasantly. "You're here to investigate me, although I don't know why."

The taller man in the John Deere cap shifted uncomfortably. The other, whose hat bore a Chevy logo, went on the offensive.

"You've been talking to a lot of employees at Martin Marietta. Why is that?"

It was true. Up to 90 percent of her recent clients worked for the large government contractor that supported the space program.

"They call me. I don't call them."

"Who's been passing you the things you tell them?"

"Who?"

"That's right. Who's your source?"

One side of Anne's mouth curled up. "Spirit is my source of information."

The men shared a look.

"You seem to know a lot of things you're not cleared for access to."

"I just repeat what the spirits tell me."

"Even classified information?"

Her eyebrows rose. "I don't know anything about that. Most of the things I share are rather ordinary, like the fact that your daughter's boyfriend rides a motorcycle, and you're not very pleased with him."

The man pulled back, startled by her words.

"And the fact that your mother-in-law is standing by your shoulder," she told the other. "She wants you to let her daughter take that class she's been talking about."

The men's disdainful look changed to surprised wonder.

"You're really good," the taller one said.

His partner scratched his head.

Several days later, Anne had a call from one of her Martin Marietta regulars, a member of upper management. He confirmed that the men who'd come for a reading were, indeed, investigators. She chuckled when she heard that they'd been impressed with her skills, but her delight turned to disappointment with the news that followed.

A flyer had appeared on bulletin boards throughout the company. Martin Marietta employees were put on notice: There would be no more visits to Cassadaga. . . . The medium B. Anne Gehman was officially off limits.

The sudden lack of clients from Cape Kennedy and Martin Marietta had little effect on Anne's workload. Her growing fame from speaking engagements and news articles kept her appointment book full to overflowing.

When a man called from Cocoa and wanted an appointment immediately, Anne told him she was booked. Normally, that would have been the end of it, but he was so insistent that she relented and squeezed him in. Later, as Robert Robeson sat across from her, his blue eyes the same color as the armchair where he sat, Anne couldn't help but smile back at her handsome new client. His thick eyebrows rose in a roguish way. His hair was full, and he wore it parted on one side, where a dark strip accentuated the striking gray of his sideburns. At 6'5", with broad shoulders and an equally broad chest, he'd had to duck when he stepped through Avalon's doorway.

"I appreciate your making time for me," Robert said as he crossed a long leg over his knee. "You're quite famous around here."

"Is that right?" Anne asked, and wondered why she was blushing.

"That's right. I heard about you in a barroom."

"Oh, my." She put a hand to her mouth, appalled, then noticed the twinkle in his eyes.

"I'm a member of the chamber of commerce over in Cocoa. We go to the Twilight Lounge after all our meetings. More than a few of my colleagues and their wives have been to see you, and they talk about you quite a bit."

"So you're familiar with mediumship?"

He gave a snort. "Only from what my friends have told me. Personally, I think it's all a bunch of nonsense. I only came here on a dare."

Normally, Anne would have bristled, but he flashed her such a disarming smile that she couldn't help but laugh.

"Well, let's see if we can't change your way of thinking, Mr. Robeson." She settled back in her chair.

"Please, call me Bob, but only if I can call you Anne."

To her embarrassment, she blushed again. "Shall we begin?" she asked a little too quickly.

The moment she closed her eyes, Anne saw a handsome older man, very large, with hair as thick as Bob's. She recognized him immediately, for the spirit had appeared to her several times in the last few days. She hadn't known who he was and had simply acknowledged his presence. Now she knew it was the elder Mr. Robeson who'd been visiting her in anticipation of his son's appointment. She described the man to Bob.

"You're telling me that you see my father?"

"I not only see him, but I hear him. He wants you to know that he's fine on the other side, and that he loves you."

Bob gave her a wary smile. "You probably say the same thing to everyone. That kind of message is rather generic, isn't it?"

"That's not how I work. If the messages from spirits are similar, that's simply because they focus on what you need to hear—what's most important."

He sniffed.

"You're quite the skeptic, aren't you?"

"I'm not even sure I believe in God, not to mention spirits and such."

"Well, I can tell you that your grandmother is here now as well. She's telling you that you need to forget all about that girl who broke off your engagement."

Bob's smug smile vanished. "How do you know about that? Did someone from Cocoa call you?"

"No, your grandmother . . . I'm hearing the name Maude. . . . She tells me that you've been rather depressed about the broken engagement, but things are going to be much better soon."

Anne described how Maude appeared with her right eye covered by glasses with a frosted lens. She told Bob that Maude had lost the eye when she fell down a stairway. Bob's cockiness diminished with each new revelation as Anne relayed detail after detail that she had no way of knowing. By the end of the reading, he looked ready to admit that his long-held beliefs might be wrong.

"I really wasn't expecting this at all, nor was I expecting someone like you. Do you mind if I come back?" he asked.

Anne lowered her eyes. "That would be fine."

He shook his head. "You're amazing. Everything you told me was completely accurate."

She toyed with a loose thread on her skirt. Normally, Anne held nothing back from her clients, but she hadn't actually told Bob *everything*. Somewhere in the middle of the reading, she had the unmistakable feeling that she was going to marry this man. But of course she couldn't tell him *that*. Some things just had to play out by themselves.

Just after four o'clock, right on schedule, the long green limousine rolled into Cassadaga. As soon as Anne glimpsed the shiny grille of Bob's fancy car, she got on the phone and called her friend Mary Rossi.

"Mary, he's back *again!* It's 80 miles to Cocoa, but he's been here every day."

"He likes you, Anne. What can I say?"

She brushed off the comment. "Quick! Run down here. You'll come with us to dinner again, won't you?"

Mary clucked her tongue. "You're 31 years old, Anne, and he's 37. Don't you think you're beyond the need for a chaperone? After three weeks, I think it's time you two spent an evening alone."

Anne knew that Mary was right, but Anne wasn't especially experienced with dating. Bob, on the other hand, knew exactly what to do. He said all of the right things and lavished her with attention. His confidence seemed to have no bounds—from the way he treated Anne to his many business dealings.

He called himself an investment broker. From what Anne could tell, he dabbled in a little of this and a little of that: real estate, sales, and investments, and he even owned a skating rink. That explained the limousine. According to Bob, a skating rink needed a touch of class. Most of the time he drove the limo himself, but it looked good sitting out front, and that was all that mattered.

Their backgrounds couldn't have been more different. Bob came from money. He'd grown up as an only child and had never lacked a thing. Anne had a hard time imagining such a life. His family had something to do with the Barden and Robeson Manufacturing Company, but Anne didn't ask for details; she was content just to listen to his stories.

One evening they went out to dinner as usual, but when they arrived back at Avalon, Bob flopped onto her sofa.

"I'm too tired to make the drive back to Cocoa. I'm going to sleep here tonight."

Anne stared at him, aghast. He stretched out and curled an arm under his head. She glanced warily out the window. Surely her neighbors would see the limo parked outside. She wanted to protest, but Bob's eyes were already closed. He hadn't asked, and she hadn't given him permission. Embarrassed beyond words, she slipped into her bedroom and shut the door tightly behind her.

Robert Robeson was a man who got what he wanted, and he wanted Anne Gehman. Just three months after they met, he strode into her house and swept her off her feet—literally.

"What are you doing?" She giggled as she wiggled her legs in the air.

"We're going to get married," Bob answered and headed for the door.

Anne only half thought he was kidding—it was just like Bob to do something so impulsive. Her mind raced as he carried her across the yard to his car. Until they met, she'd given up any thoughts of getting married. Her parents never said a word, but her brothers, sisters, nieces, and nephews were forever hassling her about being an old maid.

Spirit had told her the day she and Bob met that they were going to get married, but she had no idea it would happen so soon. She'd dreamed of a traditional wedding in a church with a long white dress and lots of guests, but Bob wasn't exactly traditional. He shifted her in his arms and she giggled again.

"We're really going to get married? Now?"

"Right now. I'm taking you to the courthouse."

We're getting married, Anne thought. *Just like Spirit said we would.*

Bob set her on the ground long enough to open the passenger door. She stared up at him, speechless.

"What's the matter?" he asked with a devilish grin. "Don't you want to be Mrs. Robert Robeson?"

She grinned back at him and got in the car.

Anne was forever telling her clients that people had free will—that they could change the future if they wanted to—but for some reason, as Bob closed the door, she didn't realize that she could say no.

Chapter 15

A person could only study for so long, and the Jesuits knew this. The novitiate and philosophate provided a strong foundation for the young priests in training, but after seven years of passive self-improvement, it was time to actively share what they'd learned.

Regency—the next period in Wayne's formation—was his chance to give back. He knew he would be sent to a Jesuit high school to help prepare the nation's future leaders. Rather than lament the interruption in his studies, Wayne, now in his late 20s, welcomed his next posting. It was far more than a much-needed break; it went beyond a mere diversion. He was finally going to have the opportunity to teach.

With his vision of becoming a Georgetown professor never far from his mind, he anxiously awaited word of where he'd be sent. Unlike his previous two assignments, Wayne had no say in the matter. No one asked for his desires, and he put in no request. There were Jesuit schools in 25 states. He had no real preference; any one of them would give him the opportunity to hone his skills.

On one of his final days in St. Louis, his superiors called Wayne into the seminary office. He knew what they wanted. Several of his classmates had already received their regency assignments.

The two priests welcomed him with friendly smiles, and one held out a piece of paper. Wayne felt a shiver of anticipation.

"We're sending you to Georgetown Prep."

Wayne blinked. Georgetown Preparatory School was a separate entity from the university. Other than the name, the only link between the two was their heritage: Both were founded the same year by Archbishop Carroll. The two institutions started out on the same plot of land, but the prep school was later rebuilt in Bethesda, Maryland, just outside of Washington. Still, the fact that Wayne would spend his regency teaching at "Georgetown" took his breath away. Was it sheer coincidence or a sure sign that he was following the right path? His mind sifted through the many conversations he'd had with his fellow Jesuits. He'd told some of them about his dream, but he'd never discussed it with his superiors.

Once the surprise of the school's name wore off, the reality of his new assignment sank in. Georgetown Prep was a wealthy school in a wealthy area. A worrisome thought passed through Wayne's mind: *Do I bat in that league?*

By this point he'd earned three degrees, but Wayne still saw himself at the wheel of a tractor.

The campus of Georgetown Prep, while small, resembled that of a college more than a high school. The classrooms, the athletic facilities, the dormitory where Wayne lived like the students, the beautiful chapel whose bells announced each hour, and the colonial-style administration building were spread across acres of lush lawn linked by tree-lined walkways and a nine-hole golf course.

Wayne arrived one week before the start of classes. He and two other new teachers were called to the main building. There, the headmaster, Father Michael Maher, greeted them and explained their duties. Once again, Wayne wondered how one man could be so lucky. His job for the next three years would be to teach the young sophomores religion, Latin, English literature, and writing.

The actuality of teaching proved even more wonderful than the anticipation. Dressed in a black robe with a slip-in collar, Wayne stood at the head of his classroom, thrilled every minute to share his love of learning with his students. St. Ignatius had taught that the acquisition of knowledge was not just an intellectual activity, but a sacred practice. Wayne had always felt this, and now he felt even more blessed to dedicate his daily work *ad majorem Dei gloriam:* for the greater glory of God.

Wayne teaching his students at Georgetown Prep.

During his initial meeting with Father Maher, the headmaster asked Wayne what extracurricular activity he wanted to be involved with. Wayne didn't need to think about his answer. He'd played football at Fort Hays Kansas State. He wasn't very good, but he'd had a lot of fun. If part of his duties involved coaching a sport, then football was his number one choice.

"Excellent," Father Maher said, smiling. "You can have the freshmen to start."

Wayne left the office, wondering if he'd made the right decision. Playing was one thing; coaching was another.

He stepped onto the front porch and spotted a couple of students who were on campus early to serve as orientation leaders. He walked over to the boys and greeted them, then casually said, "So tell me: how's the football team?"

Their laughter told him more than he wanted to know.

"Come on, it can't be that bad," he said, wondering what he'd gotten himself into.

The boys rolled their eyes.

"Have you noticed anyone in town wearing a Prep jacket?" one asked.

Wayne rarely got into town, but he shook his head nevertheless.

"That's because nobody wants anyone to know we're from 'Pansy Prep.'"

"Pansy Prep?" Wayne was appalled. From what he'd seen of his students so far, they were anything but effeminate.

"That's what the guys from the other schools call us. We haven't won a league game in almost ten years."

Wayne's eyes popped. At a boys' school, the football team was the symbol of masculinity.

"Even the JV players are losers," the other added.

"What about the freshman team?" Wayne asked, afraid to hear the answer.

The boys shook their head in unison.

The bells from The Chapel of Our Lady tolled as if in mourning.

Wayne was determined to turn the freshman football team around for the sake of the school. Knowing that learning wasn't limited strictly to classroom pursuits, he threw himself into studying the game. He researched tactics, plays, and the best coaching strategies. He took pages of notes and underlined the ideas that made the most sense, knowing that none of them would matter if he didn't have good material to work with.

Georgetown Prep wasn't a big place, so Wayne set out to personally recruit his players. He talked to those freshmen he knew were athletic. If he had a good feeling about a student, he didn't invite him to join the team—he *told* the boy: "You're coming out. Put on a uniform."

With his team assembled, it was time to get down to business. Wayne replaced his cassock with a T-shirt and shorts and surveyed the lineup. The boys weren't particularly big, nor were they fast, but Wayne wasn't worried. Everything he'd read convinced him that they could succeed with brains, not brawn—by being smart, not speedy.

He positioned two tackling dummies side by side on the practice field. He pulled his biggest player out of line and had him stand between the sleds, then he called forward one of his offensive linemen. The boy was small, but tough.

"There's your opponent," Wayne said, pointing at the much larger player.

The boy seemed to shrink beneath his shoulder pads.

"You don't have to overpower him," Wayne said. "We have four fast backs. All you have to do is hold him up so he can't tackle."

The boy gave him a questioning look.

"That's right. Just focus and keep him there for two seconds."

The boy did exactly as he was told. He held the bruiser in place while a running back whizzed past with the ball. The others gaped, then cheered. Wayne ran 20 plays in a row. The big guy never tackled a single player.

With brawn no longer an issue, Wayne moved on to speed.

"Listen up," he called. "The quarterback's signals will no longer be 'one-two-three-four.'"

The boys exchanged puzzled glances.

"He's going to call: '*Hut* one, *hut* two, *hut* three,'" Wayne announced. "If the ball's going to be snapped on the count of three, I want you to charge on 'hut,' not 'three.'"

He could tell by their faces that they still didn't get it, so he lined them up and ran them through the drill.

The quarterback called out the numbers. On the third "hut" the linemen charged ahead, a split second before the ball was snapped on "three."

"But Mr. Knoll," one of the boys said after the play, "isn't that cheating?"

Wayne had wondered that himself. In a sense, it might be construed that way, but to his way of thinking, the tactic was just plain smart.

What was theory on paper worked like magic on the field. The offense was penalized a few times for jumping the gun, but mostly they racked up points for having the fastest line in the league. The freshman team went undefeated that season, and their jackets came out of their lockers.

Just before the start of the second semester, the headmaster called Wayne to the main building. Father Maher congratulated him on his success with the football team, then asked if he'd coach basketball for the upcoming season. Wayne's only experience with the sport was shooting hoops with his brothers back in Victoria on the plot of land where his father kept their cows. As far as tactics, he knew next to nothing. Never one to shy from a task, however, Wayne told the rector he'd give it his best shot.

Studying strategy had helped him prepare for coaching football. It also helped that he'd played the game in high school and college. Unfortunately, when it came to basketball, he simply didn't understand the game and could find little written material to educate himself. After losing three games in a row, his frustration erupted. At halftime of the fourth game Wayne approached the referee and told him what he thought of the calls. When he finished berating the official, the man paused for a moment, then asked, "You haven't been coaching very long, have you?"

Wayne kept quiet after that.

In spite of his best efforts, none of the tactics he tried made any difference. His team didn't win a single game. At the end of the season, Wayne went to the rector.

"I'm not helping the boys here," he said. "You really should get someone else."

Father Maher agreed that Wayne was far better suited to coach football and asked him to try his hand with the junior varsity for the next year. Wayne accepted.

Once again, he personally recruited his team. He explained the strategies and taught them the same drills that had made the younger boys the pride of the school. The players had seen the way Coach Knoll turned around the freshman team. They worked extra hard during preseason practice in the hopes of claiming the same glory for themselves.

After the dismal failures on the basketball court, Wayne breathed a sigh of relief when his JV team won their first game. Week after week, the Prep team rolled over the competition. They played so well that Wayne began to field his second team more often.

One day during the lunch hour, one of his first-string defensive tackles came to Wayne's office. The beefy boy's face was grave as he stood in front of Wayne's desk.

"Mr. Knoll?"

"Yes, Jason?"

"Could you put me on the second team?"

"What?" Wayne did a double take. "You're on the first team, where you belong. You're a good tackle"

"I know," the boy said, "but if I go on the second team, I'll get to play more."

Wayne laughed and assured Jason that he'd have plenty of chances to play. He needed him with the first string for the final game of the season. They were slated to play Landon, an independent, nonsectarian boys' school in the heart of Washington.

Like the freshman team the year before, the junior varsity had enjoyed an undefeated season to date—but so had Landon. For 20 years the rival school had humiliated the boys from Bethesda. Landon didn't just beat Georgetown Prep; they trounced them.

The bus was as silent as a cathedral on the way to Landon's field. Wayne always insisted that the boys not talk on the ride, but in those final moments before the game, they wouldn't have spoken even if they were allowed to. After years without a single win, the last few months had been phenomenal. The thought of finishing the season without any losses was just too enticing; the opportunity to beat Landon was almost more than they could bear.

In the years that followed, Wayne would lie in bed at night and review that final game yard by yard and play by play. Georgetown Prep beat Landon by two touchdowns. The school's junior varsity had never before gone undefeated. It was the first time they'd beaten Landon in 20 years. And it was made all the more delicious by the fact that they did so on their rival's home turf.

The players and students were so exhilarated that they picked Wayne up and carried him to the bus on their shoulders. Once they were in their seats, he let them cut loose. The boys screamed, yelled, and pounded their feet on the floorboards all the way home. The fullback, responsible for the decisive touchdown at the end, sat in the back with tears streaming down his cheeks.

The driver, a maintenance man from the school staff, beamed as he turned the bus onto the grounds. The route to the field house took them past the chapel. Wayne leaned forward and asked the driver to stop. Then, without saying a word, he held up a finger and pointed at the statue of the Blessed Mother behind the small church.

The raucous shouting and the thunderous clatter of cleats came to an abrupt halt. The team trooped off the bus in total silence. They gathered around the statue, each knelt on one knee, and bowed their heads.

Wayne felt no need to lead his boys in prayer. He knew they'd each give thanks for the same gifts: the end of the semester, the end of the season, and the end of years of humiliation.

With his own gratitude expressed, he raised his head and said a heartfelt "Amen!"

"Amen!" rose the cheer in response.

The following year, Wayne would be voted Georgetown Prep's Teacher of the Year. It was an honor he'd treasure for the rest of his life. But his team honored him that fall football day with a memory he valued just as much: they raised their coach once again to their shoulders, marched him into the field house, and threw him into the pool.

Chapter 16

Anne smoothed the linen tablecloth and placed a silver fork beside the dinner plate. She added a smaller fork for salad, then ran her finger around the rim of the smooth, cool china. An image flitted through her mind, and she paused. She followed the memory back to DeLand, where she'd stood in front of a gift shop looking at the pretty dishes in the window. She could barely afford a paper plate at the time, let alone a full set of bone china like she owned now.

Her sterling flatware and fine dishes were but a few of the valuables that she and Bob had acquired. Their French-provincial-style apartment in Orlando was luxurious beyond anything she'd ever imagined when she shared the one-room cabin with Rosina and her father. Who would have thought back then that she'd be hobnobbing with industrialists and Ph.D.'s, going to the symphony regularly, and seeing her picture every time she opened a newspaper?

Thanks to Bob, their lives were full and exciting. If they hadn't married, she probably would have stayed in Cassadaga forever, but Bob was too gregarious to sit under the Spanish moss and wilt. It was he who suggested they move to Orlando. They kept Anne's little house, where she still returned to give readings or speak at the Spiritualist Assembly, but more and more their lives centered around the city.

These days, she spent most of her time at her pride and joy, the Spiritual Research Society. She and Bob had bought the former Presbyterian church on Conway Road just south of the executive airport. With its main hall, eight classrooms, library, bookstore, and office where Anne could give readings, the building fulfilled a vision she'd had eight years earlier of opening her own Spiritualist center.

At the beginning, the society's members numbered less than 100. Now, attendance at Anne's message services averaged almost 300 every Sunday. They went from one service a week to two, then three, then four. As pastor, Anne led the gatherings, even though she wasn't yet ordained.

The National Spiritualist Association of Churches granted her the charter, but Anne hadn't wanted to call it a church. To her, a church was a place where you went to be told something. She wanted it to be more than that—a place where people could go to share, to listen, and to be open to new ideas.

There were classes every week and workshops on the weekends. During a session on seeing auras, Anne noticed one couple that seemed particularly animated. The two talked back and forth excitedly as the group tried to detect the etheric bodies around their classmates. They stayed afterward and pulled Anne aside.

"My husband could see people's auras!" the woman said with awe in her voice.

Anne smiled at her enthusiasm. Many people reacted this way the first time they were able to perceive the glow of energy that extends outward from the physical body.

"That's wonderful," she said. "I'm happy you had that experience."

The woman shook her head. "You don't understand. Howard is blind! He normally can't see anything—not even shapes or shadows, but he actually sensed a glow and could pick out the different colors!"

The incident impelled Anne to conduct experiments at the center with Howard and other blind people. She gave them pieces of paper, fabric, and precious stones and asked them what they sensed. The more perceptive participants were able to differentiate the colors and materials through touch, attuned to the change in vibratory energy.

As its name implied, the Spiritual Research Society became a hub for investigation as well as innovation. Anne had two parapsychologists on her staff—men who'd spent their adult lives doing research in the field of metaphysics. The center had more advanced equipment than some of the local universities, including a faraday cage for testing psychic phenomena and a biofeedback machine—the first of its kind in the area.

Yes, Anne thought as she closed the dining room drapes, *Bob and I lead an exciting life. We have everything we need.* She glanced down at the table set for two. Everything except the one thing she wanted most.

She sank onto the upholstered chair. She was still trying to come to terms with Doctor Novak's news. He had sat her down after her latest miscarriage and in one short sentence put an end to her dreams. She had been raised in a family with seven children, but Anne would have none of her own.

An insistent buzz made her look up in surprise. She wasn't expecting anyone but Bob, and he certainly wouldn't ring the doorbell. She crossed the large living room and stopped in front of the door.

"Who is it?" she called.

"It's Henry."

"Henry!" she cried, opening the door with a welcoming smile. "What a wonderful surprise!"

A tall, good-looking man with graying brown hair that formed a widow's peak high on his forehead peered past her toward the dining-room table.

"Do you have room for one more?"

"For you, Henry? Always."

Henry Belk was always popping in unexpectedly. A member of the Belk family of Charlotte, North Carolina, whose department stores dotted the Southern landscape, Henry had the money and the time to travel at will. He also had a personal interest in mediumship and had started the Psychic Research Foundation. Its mission, like that of Anne's center, was to investigate paranormal phenomena.

Anne first met Henry when he came to Cassadaga for a reading. Jess Stearn, a prolific author, had written several sections about Anne in his book *Adventures into the Psychic.* Henry wanted to meet the pretty young phenomenon Stearn had described.

Anne had become quite famous from her classes, lectures, police work, and radio shows in Orlando and Daytona. Stearn's book made her even more so. It seemed as if every other week she was being interviewed on television. Reporters called frequently, asking her to make predictions. Her batting average was far better than most, and she earned the nickname "the Jeane Dixon of the South."

After Henry's reading, the two became fast friends. He was kind and caring, if a bit hard to get close to. He kept a houseboat in Ft. Lauderdale with a perpetual Christmas tree aboard. Every time Anne and Bob visited the boat, Henry had a gift for them.

This evening, Henry brushed past Anne and opened the oven. "Mmm . . . roast chicken. Smells good. Do you have any more potatoes?"

"I do," Anne said, laughing. She poured hot water over a bag of herbal tea as Henry leaned against the counter.

"I have an opportunity I want to discuss with you," he declared as he took the cup she offered.

"Okay," Anne said warily.

"I'm putting together a group of researchers for a trip around South America. We're going to look at different aspects of healing, psychic abilities, and mediumship in some fairly remote places. So far I have two parapsychologists and two medical doctors lined up. I could use a clairvoyant, and I was hoping you might want to be a part of it, too."

Anne brightened at the thought of a new adventure. It could be just the thing to help her out of the funk she'd been in since the doctor's latest news.

"How long will the trip last?" she asked.

"I'm thinking about a year."

"A year?" she put a hand to her chest.

"It's a big continent."

"I could never leave Bob for that long."

Henry waved casually. "We'll fly home now and then, but Bob can come, too, for the studies on healing."

Anne knew that Henry wasn't just being generous by inviting her husband. She'd recognized Bob's healing abilities shortly after they met. With her help, he'd become an excellent healer in his own right and regularly worked with people at the center.

"But I'd have to stop giving my classes and my readings."

"If it's money you're worried about, the Foundation will pay all of your expenses. And if you want to come home for a few months in the middle, that's okay, too. I don't plan on staying the whole time, myself."

"You're going, too?"

"Wouldn't miss it," he said as he drank the last of his tea.

Anne closed her eyes and concentrated. She began to sway just a bit as she tried to picture herself in the jungles of South America. The image was totally foreign, but at the same time it felt rather exciting. She opened her eyes.

"Let me talk to Bob about it."

The oven timer went off and Anne glanced at her watch. Bob was due home any time.

She opened the refrigerator and pulled out an extra potato. "You know," she said, turning to face Henry, "it would be really nice if we had a green vegetable to go with this."

"I'll go out and get something," Henry said, and pulled his keys from his pocket.

After he left, Anne wrapped the potato in foil, placed it in the oven, then cleaned up the dishes she'd dirtied so far. One hour later, Henry still hadn't returned.

She looked at the empty table. Bob was late as well, but that was nothing unusual. Lately, it seemed she was always waiting for him.

Finally, the front door opened. Bob walked in with a carefree smile on his face, but no apology on his lips. They waited another hour for Henry, but Bob was hungry and the chicken was long past done. They went ahead and ate without him.

Three days later, the doorbell rang. Anne wasn't expecting company.

"Who is it?" she called through the closed door.

"It's Henry."

She'd heard nothing from him since she sent him out for vegetables. She knew him well enough not to worry, but now that he was here, she wasn't going to let him off the hook for his disappearing act.

She opened the door, ready to tease him, but stopped cold at the sight. There stood Henry Belk with a blonde on one arm and a bag of frozen green beans in the other.

Henry never did anything halfway. Just as he'd finally shown up with the green beans, he was true to his word about the trip. He put together an aggressive itinerary that would take the research group counterclockwise around all of South America. They began in Bogotá, Colombia, where they held their first meeting with a priest who was alleged to be one of the best trance mediums in the country.

Anne felt a tingle of excitement as the group sat in a circle for a séance with the priest. The two parapsychologists and the doctors held notepads on their laps with pens poised to write. Anne sat quietly with Bob to her right and Henry to her left. All eyes were focused on the man in the white collar.

When the priest hadn't said a word after a few minutes, Anne leaned in closer. She'd seen Wilbur practice trance mediumship dozens of times, but it was never like this. The man's head was bobbing slightly, and tiny snorting noises were coming from his nose.

Anne shifted to her left. "Henry!" she whispered. "This is not Spirit!"

"What do you mean?" he whispered back. The others shot her an irritated look, as if she were talking in a library.

"That man isn't in a trance . . . he's snoring!"

The research team left Bogotá and headed for Quito.

Anne had been fascinated with Colombia, but Ecuador was even more exotic, with natives walking the downtown streets in brightly colored clothes. She found the people warm and approachable. Best of all, the women didn't fawn all over Bob like they did back in the States.

Henry had put together a challenging schedule. This was no luxury vacation. Often their research took them to isolated villages where water came from nearby streams, and the only energy came from the healers' hands.

Eighty miles north of the capital, in the heart of Ecuador's banana and sugar region, lay Santo Domingo de Los Colorados. The area was home to the *Tsáchila* people, nicknamed the *Indios Colorados* for the red vegetable dye they used in their hair. The natives were reputed to be shamanistic, making them prime targets for Henry's investigations.

After a wild journey that included a horseback ride, a canoe trip, and a hike through a thick forest, Anne and the group found themselves surrounded by bare-chested men and women with long ribbons in their hair and striped cloths around their waist. The chief approached Anne, having singled her out for reasons she didn't understand.

They'd brought along an interpreter, and after greeting the chief, Anne thanked him for allowing them to visit. They chatted for a few minutes, then Anne noticed the interpreter looking at her strangely. It took her a moment to realize that the native words she heard were not the interpreter's, but her own. Just as when she'd spoken to Eleni Papadopoulos in Greek without knowing the language, Anne and the Tsáchila chief carried on a conversation in his native tongue.

The tribespeople gathered in closer. The parapsychologists scribbled their notes as fast as their fingers could write. Anne didn't understand the individual words, but she knew the gist of what she was saying.

The chief explained that he'd prepared a demonstration of a traditional healing ceremony. That evening, as the sun went down, the researchers watched as the young Tsáchila men dug a hole in the ground. The hole was deep, and as wide across as a drain cover. A sickly older man, seemingly unable to walk on his own, was carried out and lowered into the hole. An assistant to the chief placed a sheet of mesh with twigs over the opening, then lit a fire atop it.

I wouldn't want to be in that hole, Anne thought as smoke billowed from the bright flames.

The Indians circled the flames and began to dance and chant. After the fire went out, the Ecuadorians removed the mesh. The Americans watched with interest, and no one was completely surprised when the old man climbed out of the hole on his own, looking well.

The researchers enjoyed a respite from the more isolated areas the following month when they continued on to Lima, Peru. Needing some time to herself, Anne decided to visit a museum near the hotel. Once inside, she felt strangely drawn to the Indian artifacts. As she stood in front of a display case filled with oddly shaped clay jars, she sensed someone standing beside her. Raising her eyes, she saw in the glass the clear reflection of an Indian woman with long black braids. Anne gasped in surprise: it was Honto, smiling back at her!

Anne's eyes filled with tears. She'd seldom seen her Indian guide since she was a young girl in Petoskey. She recalled a chat she'd had, years after leaving Michigan, when her good friend, the medium Arthur Myers, casually mentioned that his mother used to have an Indian guide in the spirit world named Honto.

"I know Honto!" Anne exclaimed.

Arthur related how one summer Honto spoke through his mother in trance and told him that she'd select someone to work through after his mother passed on. Anne learned that Arthur and his family spent their vacations along the lake in Petoskey where Anne grew up. The friends put the timelines together and discovered that Mrs. Myers's guide had become Anne's trusted childhood friend.

Anne had noticed then that Honto was different from the local Chippewas, and Arthur explained that Honto was from South America. Now a visitor in Honto's homeland, Anne walked away from the display case feeling her spirit friend beside her just as she had when they'd walked hand in hand through the Michigan woods. She left the museum and sat on a bench in the sunny courtyard, adrift in memories. An American couple walked out of the museum shortly after her and stopped at Anne's side.

"What happened to your friend?" the woman asked.

Anne looked beside her. The bench was empty.

"I've been here by myself," she said, feeling more alone than ever now that she no longer sensed Honto's presence.

"No," the man said, "we saw someone walking with you all the way through. She was an Indian woman with long black hair."

"Was she some kind of guide?" the woman asked.

Anne laughed aloud with delight. Yes, Honto was her guide all right. She was one of the best.

A few months of respite in Florida did Anne a world of good. She was able to spend time at the Spiritual Research Society and reconnect with her congregation. Best of all, she and Bob were able to convince his mother and their friends that they hadn't fallen off the face of the earth.

Now, surrounded by grass-thatched huts under a thick jungle canopy, Anne thought she might have landed on a different planet after all. They'd rejoined the research group in Brazil. Henry was anxious to learn more about psychic surgery, a practice shrouded in mystery but widely accepted in a country where Spiritism was hugely popular.

Spiritists followed the writings of Allan Kardec, a Frenchman who published his initial work, *The Spirits' Book,* in 1857. While there were many similarities between Spiritists and Spiritualists, the former espoused reincarnation, while the latter found no proof that spirits lived multiple lives.

Anne and the others rode two days by car to meet a well-known psychic surgeon. The man singled out Anne to stand beside him in a three-sided shack from which a line of people stretched well beyond the property line. Anne's training as a nurse caused her face to blanch as she watched the man perform one operation after another on a cold, hard table using an unsterilized kitchen knife and forceps with no anesthesia. His patients appeared to be asleep. After the procedures, they calmly rose from the table and walked away unassisted. Anne knew that there was no such thing as a miracle—that nothing could violate natural law—but even she found her beliefs stretched to the limit in the mountains of Brazil.

Anne was happy to get back to civilization and a decent restaurant later that week, but she wasn't especially hungry. It wasn't the gory sights she'd witnessed in the mountains that made her lose her appetite; she hadn't been feeling well for days. The group always drank bottled water and stayed away from unwashed fruit, but she wondered if some kind of bacteria had invaded her system.

When she started feeling poorly, she was especially glad to have a clean place to rest. Henry had promised that she would sleep every night in comfort throughout their yearlong trip. He hadn't told her, however, that she'd spend three of those nights in a mental hospital. When the director of a Spiritist psychiatric institution invited her to witness their operation from the inside, she was too curious to say no.

Anne came away from the visit impressed by the Brazilians' open-minded approach to mental health. The hospital offered traditional treatment with psychiatrists, but patients could also meet with mediums and healers. The cure rate was impressive, and Anne wondered how much better off Americans would be if U.S. doctors considered a different approach.

She found it hard to keep up with the group in the following days as her weakness and vomiting only grew worse. Finally, at Bob's urging, she told Henry that she was going home.

She arrived in Orlando, where Dr. Novak immediately admitted her to the hospital. He kept her overnight and put her through a battery of tests. It didn't take long for news to spread that the popular psychic medium was back in town. Anne sat propped on pillows in her hospital bed the next morning and opened the *Sentinel* to the social pages. The headline read: *Anne Gehman Picks up South American Bug,* proving that even after a long absence, she hadn't been forgotten.

Dr. Novak came into the room while she was finishing the article. She put the paper down and told him that she felt no better, even after a good night's rest.

He shook his head. "We did all of the lab work and can't find anything."

Rather than despair, Anne felt a flutter of hope. "Did you do a pregnancy test?"

He laid a hand on her arm. "No, Anne. We've been through all that before."

"Please," she said. "Do the test anyway."

"All right," he replied, "but I hate to get your hopes up."

Dr. Novak performed the test, but he had no other reason to keep her. He discharged her from the hospital, and she spent the remainder of the day resting at home.

The following morning, still nauseated and discouraged, Anne decided to go to her office. She couldn't begin to think about giving readings or leading classes until she felt better. Still, she thought it might help to be around the staff and her beloved center.

Pink message slips covered the top of her desk. She stared at the piles, too sick to return even one call. When the phone rang, she almost didn't answer it, but it wasn't in her nature to leave people waiting. She picked it up on the fourth ring.

"Anne? It's Dr. Novak. I like it when my patients prove me wrong."

She sucked in her breath. "What are you saying?"

"I'm saying, 'Congratulations . . . you're pregnant'!"

Anne screamed and dropped the phone. Her malaise vanished as she ran down the hall to share the big news.

Chapter 17

In the early 1960s, the Jesuits sent Wayne to Woodstock College, a small theological seminary outside Baltimore, Maryland. Later in the same decade, 100,000 long-haired youths would attend a festival in New York with the same name as Wayne's school. The hippies would remember the event as a celebration. Wayne would remember Woodstock as the most difficult period of his training.

After three years of regency at Georgetown Prep, readjusting to monastic life proved more painful than he imagined. In Bethesda, Wayne was always on the move, giving to others. When necessary, he'd had the use of the school car to get around the city streets nearby.

At the theologate, he once again became a passive student, living in a silent, contemplative environment with no means of personal transportation. Yes, the grounds were beautiful, with more than 100 acres of rolling hills and a river view. True, he would earn the equivalent of a third master's degree, this one in theology. But that didn't make the adjustment any less difficult after having been so actively engaged in the world.

The Jesuits' training model called for removing seminarians from the mainstream and placing them in a tranquil, secluded setting. The superiors would later admit that this was a mistake. They realized that no matter how beautiful the location, it wasn't good to subject the young men to rural isolation. They decided to move Woodstock College to lively New York City. Unfortunately, that wouldn't happen until years after Wayne completed the course.

In the meantime, he found it nearly impossible to focus. His class work seemed dull after the thrill of teaching and coaching. For the first time in his life, Wayne, now in his early 30s, had no motivation to open his books. He sat in his cell, staring at the bare walls and wrestling with his thoughts. Finally, he took his concerns to the seminary rector, Father Ed Sponga.

"I just can't study," he admitted with downcast eyes.

"I understand," the priest replied. "You're not the only one."

Wayne looked up, surprised.

"Just do the best you can," Father Sponga advised. "You won't flunk."

Wayne returned to class and did as he was told. He didn't fail, but for the first time in his life he didn't earn *A*'s.

The '60s were a period of turmoil for the country, and they were equally tumultuous for the Catholic Church. While Wayne prepared for his ordination, men were leaving the priesthood in droves. The Second Vatican Council brought about changes intended to close the gap between the Church and its followers. The students at Woodstock followed the new ideas with interest, but some on the staff were slow to catch up.

One professor was particularly set in his ways. Father Archibald Bennett was older than most and quite traditional in his thinking. Wayne and his fellow students sat in the classroom and listened with consternation to his outdated lectures. The course topic was crucial: how to counsel their future parishioners. The old priest explained that for every human situation, there was a Catholic law or regulation. He went down his yellowed list of *Thou shalts* and *Thou must nots* as if it were a restaurant menu with no substitutions allowed.

The students were confused. Why was there no discussion of psychology? How could they study moral theology without an understanding of the human mind and emotions?

Jesuits had a reputation for being activists, and the students decided to rebel. Each of them had taken a vow of obedience, but what could their superiors do? They already lived a life of solitary confinement.

When the time came for the next lecture, Wayne and the others remained in their cells. Father Bennett arrived at a classroom occupied by one lone student who didn't have the heart to stay away. The priest opened his book and taught the lesson as if the entire class were in front of him.

The next day, Father Bennett returned to the same empty room. Just like the previous day, he opened his book and began lecturing to the empty seats. One minute into the lesson, however, he broke down in tears, closed his book, and left.

The young priest who replaced him had a dual degree in moral theology and psychology. The 40 chairs remained filled for the rest of the course.

⊕⊕⊕

The civil-rights movement was a frequent topic of discussion among the theologians at Woodstock. All of them had been "out in the world"—a term they frequently used when recalling their regency years. Before their theologate experience, some had played an active role in the fight against racial discrimination.

Events in Birmingham, Alabama, earlier in the summer resulted in a surge of protests. More than 1,000 demonstrations took place in nearly 100 cities throughout the South. Now, word spread around Woodstock's campus that leaders of major religious and civil rights groups had planned a massive demonstration in the nation's capital that weekend.

"We should go," one of the brothers suggested.

"It's part of the Jesuits' heritage to fight for justice," another said.

Wayne was intrigued. "We could carry a banner for the school."

The idea quickly gathered momentum. A small delegation approached Father Sponga the next day. Without hesitation, the rector gave his total support.

On the morning of August 28, 1963, 70 men boarded the school's two ancient buses. Wayne had mastered the art of driving the old rattletraps and was elected to lead the way. With a full load of passengers, he pressed the pedal to the floor going downhill to make sure they made it over the next incline.

The decision to participate in the demonstration was so impulsive that no one had contacted the organizers to find out where to go. When they arrived in downtown Washington, Wayne followed the heaviest traffic. He parked the bus near a spot where large crowds were starting to gather. He and his brother Jesuits filed into the street and looked around them, wondering what to do next. Only one in every five people they saw was Caucasian, but they would have stood out in any case because of their identical black suits and white collars.

Wayne and his buddy Tom Parker had created a banner from an old bedsheet. Large black letters stood out starkly against the white background: "Woodstock College for Civil Rights."

"You men come up here," a marshal said, and signaled for the clerics to form up near the head of the march. The group in front of the Woodstock delegation moved out, and the marshal signaled that Wayne and his colleagues were next. The Jesuits were often referred to as the "long black line" representing the army of Christ. Wayne and Tom proudly led two long black lines of their own with their banner held aloft by two broomsticks.

Wayne simmered with excitement as they marched past the Washington Monument and continued along the reflecting pool. He'd never seen so many people in one place. The mass of bodies filled an area larger than his hometown back in Kansas.

When they reached the Lincoln Memorial, the marshals ushered the men to a spot in front of scaffolding that had been erected for the speakers. Wayne looked up and found himself standing just four steps below the podium. He stared in awe at the faces on the platform. Some he didn't recognize, but others he would know anywhere: Joan Baez, Sidney Poitier, and even Marlon Brando. His family would never believe it.

The big names were impressive, but Wayne was far more awed by the hundreds upon thousands of ordinary citizens gathered in front of him. They were crowded along the reflecting pond and beyond as far as he could see.

What an incredibly positive event, he thought. *What magnificent creative energy for good!* God's presence was undeniable.

He listened with rapt attention to the succession of speakers. He couldn't help but be moved by their fervor. When a black man with short-cropped hair stepped to the podium, a ripple of energy passed through the crowd. Wayne recognized the name when Dr. Martin Luther King, Jr., was announced, but he had never seen him nor heard him speak. At Georgetown Prep, Wayne had always been running from one place to the next and rarely watched TV. The students didn't have televisions in their cells at Woodstock College.

It was immediately obvious that the charismatic preacher had spent plenty of time in the pulpit—his delivery was captivating. The crowd hung on every word as the man spoke about his people's long struggle to banish inequality. It appeared as if Dr. King's remarks were drawing to a close, when a woman shouted, "Tell them about your dream, Martin! Tell them about the dream!"[1]

"That's Mahalia Jackson, the gospel singer," one of Wayne's classmates whispered in his ear.

Dr. King remained at the podium and began to tell the crowd about his vision for the future. Wayne listened, enthralled, to the rhythmic, rolling phrase "I have a dream," repeated with such passion and eloquence that the hairs on the back of his neck stood on end. He knew that he was witnessing history in the making.

The bus ride back to Woodstock was quiet as each of the Jesuits reflected on the powerful experience. Wayne had to force himself to concentrate on his driving. He parked the bus and walked into the theologate with images of the day still flashing before his eyes.

"Wayne," someone called out. "Your father's on the phone."

Puzzled, he turned toward the alcove where a community telephone sat on a small table.

He answered with trepidation. "Hello, Dad? Is everything all right?"

"Wayne! What are you doing?"

He looked at the receiver in bewilderment. What did his father think he was doing?

"I'm here at school, talking to you," he replied.

"No," his father said. "We saw you on the television. You were marching in that parade, carrying a banner."

Wayne smiled. He could never keep anything from his father.

His father expressed his concern. He'd seen plenty of demonstrations on television recently, and some were violent. Wayne assured his father that he was fine, then described the unforgettable day.

He returned to his cell and stared at his books, even less motivated to study than usual. Dr. King's speech echoed in his ears, making it difficult to think of anything else.

"I have a dream . . ."

Wayne knew all about the power of vision. It was his own vision that kept him going through this difficult stage of his training. He bowed his head and prayed that the millions who heard Dr. Martin Luther King's haunting words that day, whether in person as he had, or on their television screens in their homes, would do whatever they could to help turn one man's dream into reality.

Wayne faced the altar of the unfamiliar church. He knew none of the men on either side of him. They were all from the Missouri Province, but he could feel familiar eyes boring through the back of his gold chasuble and white robe. His mother and father sat on a pew just a few yards behind him flanked by Omer, Lester, Carroll, Devon, Iris, Janie, Terry, Larry, and their respective spouses and children.

His fellow second-year students from Woodstock were being ordained in Maryland, but Wayne felt it was asking too much for his family to travel so far. This way, they only had a three-hour drive to St. Mary's, Kansas, for the 10 A.M. ceremony.

To all in attendance, it seemed as if the church was bathed in an extraordinarily bright light as the officiating bishop commenced the Sacrament of Holy Orders.

"Are you willing to faithfully discharge the office of priesthood?" the bishop asked. "To celebrate the sacred mysteries of Christ, and to consecrate your lives to God in union with Christ the High Priest?"[2]

Wayne responded without reservation: "I am."

At the bishop's signal, Wayne got down on all fours along with the other candidates, then stretched out fully on his stomach. Lying prostrate as a symbol of his humility, he gave himself totally to God.

Blinking back his tears, Wayne returned to his knees and remained kneeling for the critical act of the ritual, the Laying on of Hands. The bishop silently placed his hands on Wayne's head, then invoked the Holy Spirit to come down upon him. Wayne shuddered from the enormity of the moment, fully aware that with this irreversible act, his very character was changed, setting him apart eternally for the sacred duties of the priesthood.

Wayne held out his hands as the bishop anointed them with consecrated oil.

"Know what you are doing, and imitate the mystery you celebrate," the bishop recited as Wayne then took the chalice and paten offered to him.

"Model your life on the mystery of the Lord's cross."[3]

Wayne realized that he was holding his breath as the bishop raised his hand and greeted him with the sign of peace. Mass proceeded as usual then, but it was anything but ordinary for Wayne as he tested his new title in his mind.

Father Knoll.

He soaked up the warm hugs and congratulations of his family after the ceremony, then traveled with them back to Victoria. His mother babbled the whole way, not bothering to hide her emotion as she relived every precious moment of the morning.

The ordination ceremony was a singular event for Wayne, but his pride reached its peak the following day. No one had asked him if he would say his first Mass at the Cathedral of the Plains; it was simply understood that he would. As he walked out the door of his childhood home on the way to vest for the service, Wayne turned to his mother.

"I've been gone a long time, Mom, and I don't remember everyone's name."

She reached out and adjusted the 32-year-old's collar. "Don't worry, son."

"Please don't put me on the spot," he said as he adjusted her adjustment. "Let me know who I'm talking to, okay?"

Less than an hour later, he gazed out at 300 faces. Family, friends, old school-yard chums, and every priest in the area had come to witness the special event. It was only with God's grace that Wayne was able to speak past the large lump lodged in his throat.

Step by step, he performed the rituals he'd assisted with as an altar boy in the same familiar sanctuary. The church had changed little over the years. The biggest difference was the noticeable absence of dear Brother Wendolyn. He'd passed away sometime back, leaving memories so strong that Wayne could almost sense the old monk standing there beside him.

At the conclusion of the Mass, Wayne moved to the front of the church. He greeted and shook the hands of those first to approach, then stiffened at the sight of a heavyset man with long, dark sideburns. The face was familiar, but Wayne couldn't place him.

"Good morning," Wayne said with a smile, while inside he burned with embarrassment.

Mother Knoll appeared like an angel at his side.

"Wayne, you remember Mr. Harvey, don't you? He used to run the movie theater."

"Of course I remember Mr. Harvey," Wayne said, squeezing the man's hand. "I'm glad you could come."

He thanked his mother with his eyes and greeted the next in line. Mother Knoll lingered nearby until the last person emerged from the church.

The party at the grammar school rivaled the best wedding reception in town, minus the dancing. A celebratory cake big enough for the happy crowd graced a folding table in the center of the room. Several more tables covered with colorful paper lined the walls. The local women had done all of the cooking. Platters overflowed with crisp fried chicken, tender roast beef, and creamy mashed potatoes and gravy.

When the reception broke up, the party continued at the Knoll house. Wayne had no trouble remembering the names of his family and closest friends, but Mother Knoll never wandered too far from his side. The decision to become a priest had been his alone—the answer to a calling. Jesuit training was among the most demanding of the Catholic orders, but seeing the pride and love on his mother's face that warm spring day, Wayne would have done it all over again just for her.

While Woodstock's rural setting was at first a disadvantage, its proximity to Washington proved to be a godsend during Wayne's final year. With nothing to lose and everything to gain, he approached the chairman of the theology department at Georgetown University, a fellow Jesuit priest.

"I'd like to teach a course dealing with the theological dimensions in literature," he said, formally proposing an idea that he'd been tossing around in his mind for some time. He held his breath. Literature was his passion, and teaching was his destiny. Georgetown University was the place where he dreamed of putting the two together.

It didn't take the chairman long to decide. Wayne's credentials were excellent, and the proposed class would add an interesting dimension to the department's regular course offerings.

Once a week, Wayne made the hour-long trip in the seminary car to teach his first college-level students. He'd visualized himself standing in a Georgetown classroom so many times that the reality, while heady and exhilarating, felt completely natural. The experience further cemented his desire to return and do the same rewarding work full-time.

As much as he would have loved to spend all of his days teaching, third-year seminarians at Woodstock were expected to put their pastoral skills to use. On weekends and holidays, the new priests were farmed out to local parishes. Now that he was ordained, he was able to administer the sacraments just like the diocesan priests he supported.

When Holy Week arrived, Wayne was assigned to a small church in a rural area west of Woodstock. The pastor was a gruff old German with a thick accent, but he welcomed the extra help. With all of the Easter activities, the church was busier than usual.

Wayne bustled about, happy to give back to the community.

On Good Friday, Wayne was tasked to hear confessions. With confessionals on both sides of the church, Wayne and the pastor took their seats in their respective stalls. The penitents were lined up one after another to receive their absolution. Wayne took a deep breath. He'd been going to confession ever since his first Holy Communion, but it still felt a bit strange to sit in the priest's position.

By early evening, the line had thinned. There was no one waiting to talk to Wayne, and the church grew very still. Suddenly, the silence was broken by the pastor's booming voice.

"You did *what?*"

Shocked, Wayne leaned forward and cocked his ear toward the wooden partition.

"Who do you think you are?" the older priest demanded from behind his partition. *"The town bull?"*

Wayne slowly parted the curtain.

A young man emerged from the far confessional and scurried from the church. His face was like a flashing neon sign, blinking every color of the rainbow. Wayne carefully pushed the curtain back into place, mortified.

He returned to the theologate determined never to embarrass a parishioner as the older priest had done. Still, he couldn't get the incident out of his mind. He tried not to think about the activities that had led the young stud to confess; Wayne's inner conflict had increased enough while at Woodstock.

The mystique of the priesthood and Jesuit life had diminished nationwide, due in no small part to the issue of celibacy. It was clear that the Jesuits recognized there were problems. They no longer accepted novices straight out of high school. They now encouraged young men to attend college, to date, and to have social experiences before deciding to accept a celibate life.

Wayne was committed to his vows and never considered breaking them. It was obvious, however, that others at the college were grappling with the same issue. Several of his classmates made the decision to leave, including one like Wayne who'd been ordained less than a year. The ultimate shock came when Woodstock's rector, Father Sponga, left mid-year to marry a former nun.

After years of schooling, Wayne had only one criticism about the Jesuit training: They didn't know how to help young men to deal with the question of celibacy. It was neither discussed in the classroom nor tackled in his textbooks. In all of his readings, he came across only one phrase in a musty spiritual manual that addressed the problem: "Let their chastity be like that of the angels," read the pious prose.

He stared at the page, then closed the manual in frustration.

How in God's name do we do that? he wondered. *We're not angels.*

Chapter 18

With a sweep of his arm, the Reverend Ralph Cutlip presented the newly ordained minister to her flock. Anne stood next to the podium and beamed, resplendent in her pink dress with its stand-up collar. More than 200 members of her congregation had come to witness the special event, and her parents sat proudly among the many familiar faces. The literature Anne sent them years earlier had sparked their interest in Spiritualism. Later, after seeing their daughter give messages on the platform at Cassadaga, they joined the church. Now they attended her services at the Spiritual Research Society whenever they could get to Orlando.

Anne's first time on the platform seemed like a lifetime ago. Who would have guessed when she stood with shaking legs at the front of Cassadaga's Colby Temple that she would one day be ordained and the pastor of her own church?

She'd learned so much in all those years, thanks mostly to Wilbur. The many books he insisted she read now lined the library of the center. It was he who encouraged her to take the Morris Pratt Institute's general and advanced courses. With that added preparation, she'd easily passed the oral board with the Reverend Arthur Myers and the Reverend Robert MacDonald, the president of the NSAC.

The National Spiritualist Association of Churches sent the Reverend Cutlip from Ohio to conduct the ceremony. As he concluded his remarks, Anne glanced at the happy scene in the front row. Her mother couldn't seem to decide where to focus her attention. One minute the elder Beatrice was listening to Ralph Cutlip, the next minute she was toying with the tiny fingers of her granddaughter, lying beside her in Bob's arms.

Little Rhonda was the answer to Anne's prayers. She'd wanted a girl so badly. The 500 guests who attended her fund-raising baby shower had paid $1 per ticket to guess the sex and birth date of Anne and Bob's child. Most had predicted that she'd have a boy. Anne had sensed from the beginning that the baby was a girl, but she hadn't dared to say it aloud.

Nobody won the prize for guessing the right date. Who could have predicted that Anne, now in her mid-30s, would carry the baby for ten long months? On September 27 at 11:12 P.M., Anne gave birth by caesarean section to Rhonda Anne Robeson. Several days later, the happy couple bundled their daughter in a pink blanket and took her home to meet Brigitte Marie, the toy poodle Bob had bought for Anne after Foot Prince passed away.

Brigitte Marie had jumped about with excitement, correctly sensing that Rhonda's arrival was a special occasion. The dog was just back from the groomer. She looked particularly festive with freshly painted pink nails, pink ribbons behind her ears, and her normally white curls dyed rosy from a quick rinse in beet juice.

By Anne's way of thinking, you could never have too much pink.

Anne pulled her car into the Lake Sumter Community College parking lot. Her day had already been full with readings and paperwork. It was hard to leave Rhonda again after dinner to drive all the way to Leesburg, but Anne felt it was important to carry on with her teaching.

Spiritualism had gone through its ups and downs since its founding. It enjoyed especially wide popularity after World War II, when so many men had died. Bereaved families longed to find a way to connect with their loved ones, and mediums offered them that connection. Lately, much to Anne's dismay, there seemed to be more than a few unscrupulous practitioners who called themselves mediums, but who were actually nothing more than con artists.

Their kind gave Spiritualism a bad name. They made the truly gifted mediums like Anne have to work even harder to let the world know that communication with the dead was a fact, scientifically proven by the phenomena of Spiritualism.

The administrators at Lake Sumter College had told her to expect a good turnout. Almost 100 students had preregistered for her class on practical parapsychology and meditation. Anne retrieved her handouts from the seat beside her and got out of the car. As she walked down the sidewalk toward the classroom building, she noticed a group milling about outside the entrance to the school.

They must be having some kind of special event, Anne thought.

As she got closer, she noticed that many of those gathered were carrying signs. She took a few more steps and peeked with curiosity. The words "Anne Gehman go home!" stared back at her from a large white banner.

At first her brain had trouble computing that she was seeing her own name. She did a double take, then read another sign: "Let not evil enter our community!"

When she realized that she and her class were the focus of the demonstration, Anne closed her eyes and took a deep breath. She'd always loved a challenge, and now, instead of sneaking inside, she smiled and addressed the crowd.

"I'm Anne Gehman," she said. "Who are all of you?"

She was only partially surprised to learn that most were ministers from local churches.

"Why don't you all join me in the classroom?" she said. "I'm a minister as well. I'd love to talk about this and understand what you're thinking."

The small auditorium was nearly packed, as she'd been told it would be, but there was room for a few more. The protestors chose seats in the back and sat frowning with crossed arms as Anne introduced herself to the rest of the students.

"I want to make it clear at the beginning that it is not my aim to convert any of you during the course of this class."

One of the ministers coughed loudly into his hand.

Anne ignored him and continued. "Spiritualism isn't a religion of conversion; it's a religion of conviction. I'm always pleased to share our understanding of God and the universe, and the knowledge of the other world that spirits bring to us through mediumship."

"Do you believe in Jesus Christ?" a man called out. "Do you believe that the only way into the kingdom of heaven is through our Lord Jesus?"

"I believe in the wonderful teachings of Jesus," Anne replied without missing a beat, "but we Spiritualists also believe in personal responsibility. A person must replace wrongdoings with right actions rather than counting on vicarious atonement."

The basic question initiated a debate that went on for most of the class. Instead of being intimidated, Anne felt inspired. She harkened back to her childhood, when her father would affirm her gifts using quotes from the Bible. The passages flooded back to her now and she quoted them freely after every volley of challenges from the back of the room.

"Wasn't it Jesus who said, 'Those things which I do, you can do also'?" she asked with a disarming smile. "He was referring to the gifts of spirit—of healing, clairvoyance, clairaudience, and speaking in tongues—you see?"

The ministers seemed to be running out of steam, when one of them held up a hand.

"You're going to be teaching people in this class to meditate, aren't you? Do you have something against prayer?"

"Not at all," she replied. "I like to say that prayer is talking to God, and meditation is listening to Him."

The room grew quiet. Anne glanced at the large round clock on the wall. They had used up all their time.

"I appreciate so many of you coming out this evening," she said. "We'll be meeting every week at this time for the rest of the semester. I invite all of you, not just those of you who registered, to come back and join us."

The students gathered their papers and filed from the auditorium. As usual, several hung back to ask Anne the questions they were too shy to pose in public. Anne recognized the last man in line as one of those who'd been carrying a placard.

"How did you enjoy the class?" she asked after shaking his hand.

"I'm really embarrassed for having come here to protest." He folded his cardboard sign and looked her in the eye. "You sound like a good Christian to me."

Half of the original group of protestors returned the following week. They continued to show up for the remainder of the sessions. On the last day, a man who had been one of the most hostile at the beginning stood up and addressed the group.

"I'm sorry for the attitude I brought here," he said. "This class has convinced me that to really understand Jesus and his teachings, you have to understand psychic phenomena and mediumship."

The drive back to Orlando didn't seem so long that night as Anne thought about the man's comment. It wasn't easy giving up her evenings with Bob and Rhonda. The teaching job paid little compared to what she earned giving readings, but the money was secondary. She'd been given her gifts for a purpose, and she was meant to share them with others. The man's words confirmed that she was making a difference, even if she had to do it one soul at a time.

Henry Belk set his fork on the plate. "How'd you like to take a trip?"

Anne fell back heavily against her chair. "Oh, Henry, not another one!" She'd barely recovered from the expedition in South America and her ten-month pregnancy.

"No, nothing like the last one," he said with a wave of his hand. "Just a short hop over to Arkansas."

Bob wiped his mouth with a napkin. "What's in Arkansas?"

"The International ESP Workshop. Harold Sherman holds it every year."

"Harold Sherman?" Anne perked up. "Isn't he an author?"

"Many times over."

Anne flashed back to Wilbur's house. Their first week together, he'd given her a stack of books to take home. She'd run her fingers over the spine of one with Harold Sherman's name on it. At the time she thought, *I'm going to meet this man someday.* Now, it seemed as if she'd been right.

She met Harold at the ESP conference, and the two of them hit it off immediately. He led her and Bob through the crowds and personally introduced them to all of the big names he'd invited. He held this event annually and included the likes of Raymond Moody, Robert Schuller, Gloria Swanson, Gerald Jampolsky, and Olga Worrall. Anne's attention had been so focused on her life in Florida that the names meant little to her. Bob was in his element, schmoozing with everybody who was anybody in the world of paranormal research.

Harold invited Anne to speak on the platform, and she happily agreed. When she saw that she was scheduled to follow a speaker named Edgar Mitchell, she faintly remembered hearing the name. He'd called her awhile back to see if she was interested in participating in some long-distance psychic experiments. At the time, Anne was giving readings every hour and doing research of her own. Feeling rather overwhelmed that day, she'd been a bit brusque and had told the man no. Only now did she learn that Ed Mitchell was the pilot of the Apollo 14 mission. The long-distance experiments she passed up had been conducted from the moon.

Harold invited Anne to speak at his workshop the following year. While there, she was introduced to an attendee named William Keeler, president and chief executive officer of Phillips Petroleum. Bob immediately sidled up to Bill to talk about the world of big business. Anne was far more interested in Bill Keeler's previous position as chief of the Cherokee Nation of Oklahoma. Native Americans had always been more sensitive to energy and Spirit than most others.

If Bob and Anne were impressed with Bill's credentials—albeit for different reasons—Bill was equally interested in Anne's. She'd recently assisted in solving a high-profile missing-persons case, and Bill had read about it in the paper.

"How did you know where to tell the police to look?" he asked after bringing up the case.

Anne shrugged modestly. "I just dowsed."

He raised his eyebrows. "You dowse for people? How do you do that?"

"I move my hand over a map and see if any images come to me."

"She's very good," Bob added.

"Have you ever dowsed for oil?" Bill asked. The expression on his face showed that the question was more than idle curiosity.

In fact, Anne had. Years before, a man named Harvey Grisham had come to her office in Cassadaga. He spread a map on a table and asked Anne to tell him if she sensed oil anywhere in the region shown. She held her hand out just as she did when searching for missing people and gave Mr. Grisham her impressions. He came back several times and told her that she'd been right. If Harvey earned any money from Anne's advice, he didn't share it with her. He simply paid Anne the normal fee for a reading and left.

Bob had been appalled by Anne's lack of business acumen. Sensing a potentially lucrative opportunity with Bill Keeler, he put an arm around Anne's waist and stepped closer to Bill. "Anne is amazingly gifted, and she'd be happy to give you a reading," he said.

Bill accepted the offer and brought along his wife and son. He later told a reporter from *Florida Tropic* magazine that Anne discussed things about him she couldn't have learned by researching his life. She came up with the real name of his grandmother, who was known to his family only by a nickname. Bill was amazed by her abilities, and he was equally impressed with her gentle, unassuming personality.

He approached Anne with a proposal: "I've been investigating the oil in southwest New Mexico. I've used dowsers in the past with some success, and I'd like to work with you to check out these new opportunities."

Anne accepted without pause. Dowsing for an oil company sounded like an interesting new twist on things.

"Bring me the maps," she said. "I'll sit down with them and see what I come up with."

Bill Keeler wasn't interested in simply poring over maps, though. After he gave Anne a chance to check the area out on paper, he sent his private jet to Orlando and whisked her out west.

Once on the ground, Anne asked if she could have some privacy. She intuitively sensed what she needed to do, but she didn't care to have anyone watch her. After Bill left and there was no one else around, Anne got down on all fours, then stretched out fully on her stomach. Lying prostrate with her forehead touching the bare soil, she gazed clairvoyantly into the earth. In her mind's eye she could see the different layers of rock and detected the movement of a thick, dark liquid.

She got to her feet and brushed the dirt from her clothes and hands. With nothing to guide her but instinct, she extended her arm and slowly began to raise and lower it.

"One thousand feet," she said with the first vertical pass of her arm.

"Two thousand feet," she said with the second.

Just after beginning the third pass, her arm stopped.

She made a mental note, then moved her arm once again. This time, she counted the passes in hundreds of feet. Her arm stopped at the sixth cycle.

When Bill returned, Anne announced that he'd find oil at a depth of 3,600 feet. He gave her a curious look, then held out several vials.

"These are samples of oil. They contain everything from commercial grade to sludge. Can you tell me which kind is down there?"

Anne handled each of the vials in turn. When she was finished, she picked out one of the first she'd touched and said, "It's this one." The vibrations from the vial perfectly matched the energy she'd sensed deep within the ground.

Bill Keeler was more than pleased to call Anne and tell her the number of barrels and the quality of the oil they'd retrieved from the well. The depth of the strike and the type of oil were exactly as she'd predicted. To celebrate her first big hit, Bill gave her one of the oversized bits from the drill they'd used. The hunk of metal was a nice souvenir, but even better was the hefty salary he paid Anne for her services.

Anne had never been too good with numbers. She didn't have a head for money like Bob did. She was more than happy to find the oil and let her husband handle the financial end of things. She knew that Bob used some of the proceeds to pay the mortgage for the Spiritual Research Society. Other than that, she wasn't quite sure what he did with it.

Anne and Bill continued their unique arrangement for the next five years. Every six to eight weeks, Bill would send his jet to Orlando. Many times Bob; his mother, Margaret; and little Rhonda would go along for the all-expenses-paid trips around the southwestern United States, to islands throughout the Caribbean, and to select locations in Central America. They stayed only at the best hotels, but thanks to Anne, Bill Keeler could afford it.

A good geologist could find oil one out of every ten tries. Anne's success rate was nine out of ten. When Harold Sherman asked Bill Keeler to write a foreword for his latest book, Bill did so with pleasure. In his tribute, he praised Anne's gifts, but he left out the details about their business dealings. After all, he was the president of a public corporation. The company's shareholders might not have been open to the real reason their stock kept rising.

Chapter 19

With few exceptions, the young men who began their schooling with Wayne at Wernersville followed the same training track. All attended the novitiate, philosophate, regency, and theologate. At the end of Wayne's three years at Woodstock College, he and his fellow Jesuits embarked on divergent paths for the first time.

As the new priests determined their life direction, the same phrase taught to the students at Georgetown Prep, *ad majorem Dei gloriam,* applied to them as well. Their choice of career mattered little, as long as it was for the greater glory of God. The Jesuit superiors normally supported whatever decisions the young clerics made, knowing that what benefited the individual benefited all.

Most left the theologate and went directly into teaching at a Jesuit high school. Many became missionaries, and a few became social workers. Some, like Wayne, chose to continue their studies and earn a doctorate.

Wayne didn't share his dream of being a university professor with his superiors. He simply informed them that he wanted a Ph.D. Father Provincial, the head of the Maryland Province, told Wayne that he could pick whichever university he wanted to attend. As long as he could gain admittance, the Jesuits would pay his tuition, room, and board and give him the five years he needed to complete the degree.

For Wayne, there was no question where to send his application. Ever since he stood on the President's porch at Old North on the Georgetown campus, he knew he would need a doctorate from the finest school in the country. In Wayne's mind, that meant only one place: Harvard University.

His academic record was stellar, but so was that of most students who applied. To gain an edge over the stiff competition, Wayne needed something unique. He found his answer in the form of Father Walter Ong. The brilliant English professor's presence on the faculty at St. Louis University was the main reason why Wayne had chosen that school for his philosophate studies. But Father Ong's reputation spread far beyond Missouri. He was one of the foremost scholars in his field and served as president of the Modern Language Association. He was also a Harvard graduate.

The letter of recommendation from Father Ong cemented the deal. Wayne was accepted into Harvard's Ph.D. program and transferred to the New England Province.

Changes in the Church in recent years had resulted in a relaxation of restrictions. No longer were Jesuits required to wear cassocks or live in communal residences while students. The choice was up to Wayne. The Jesuits operated two apartments near the Cambridge campus, but at 34 years old, he was ready for a taste of independence.

That freedom came in the form of a three-story town house in Cambridge, three blocks from the university. Wayne shared the top floor with two of his fellow Jesuits: Jim Marsh, who was working toward a Ph.D. in mathematics; and Bob Harrington, a future physician studying anatomy at the University of Massachusetts. The second floor of the town house was rented as well, but the first floor was occupied by the owner and his family.

Wayne had never been to Boston and knew little about the streets surrounding the campus. He had no trouble getting to know his new town, however. His landlord, Walter Sullivan, was the mayor of Cambridge.

Wayne took an immediate liking to the Sullivans. Walter and his wife, Marion, were as friendly and homespun as any of the folks back in Kansas. Wayne, Bob, and Jim appreciated the Sullivans' hospitality and wanted to show their appreciation. One Sunday, the three roommates issued them an invitation to come to the third floor for dinner.

Having lived in a communal residence since the age of 14, Wayne barely knew how to boil an egg. Jim and Bob had a bit more experience in the kitchen. They offered to do the cooking if Wayne would shop for the groceries. The three put their heads together and came up with a suitable menu for the mayor and his lady: they'd serve roast chicken, potatoes, and vegetables, then finish off the meal with warm chocolate brownies.

With grocery list in hand, Wayne pushed a metal cart through the store aisles. He had no idea what to look for when it came to produce. He picked out the greenest broccoli, then agonized over the different types of potatoes. After choosing a box of brownie mix, he moved to the poultry section. Feeling more pressure than during any exam, he scanned the refrigerated shelves lined with plastic-wrapped chickens. Suddenly, his eyes fell on a magnificent specimen. It was easily large enough to feed the party of five, and the price was unbelievable.

Wayne handed over his purchases to his roommates, relieved that the worst of his duties was over. He set the table, confident in his ability in that area, while Jim prepared the chicken for roasting and Bob washed the vegetables.

The predinner conversation was lively and entertaining. The Sullivans regaled the newcomers with stories about Cambridge that they never could have learned from a guidebook. At a signal from Jim, the group moved to the table. Wayne gave the blessing as the savory aroma of roasted chicken wafted from the plates.

While his roommates began to eat, Wayne turned to answer a question from the mayor. As the two men chatted, Marion Sullivan politely tapped Wayne's arm.

"Father Knoll, would you mind helping me? I'm having trouble cutting this chicken."

Wayne shifted in his chair and took the utensils she offered. His brows bunched as he sawed the knife gently back and forth, then resorted to greater force. Try as he might, the chicken refused to yield to the blade.

Jim Marsh later remarked that the scene reminded him of a Greco-Roman wrestling match. Bob Harrington joked that once he became a doctor, he hoped he'd cut better with his scalpels than Wayne did with a butter knife. Only after Wayne pulled the wrapper out of the garbage and showed it to his roommates did he learn of his mistake. He'd bought a stewing chicken that was so old it was only good for soup. Roasting the chicken had turned the bargain-basement bird into a tough old buzzard.

Wayne was appalled. Rather than impress the mayor and his wife, he'd sent them home with nothing to eat but vegetables and brownies. He smiled pleasantly when he ran into the Sullivans in the ensuing days, but inwardly he cringed, remembering the disastrous dinner. The evening had one silver lining: Mrs. Sullivan became convinced that the three men upstairs were unable to feed themselves. Every week thereafter, she left a care package on the back steps for the poor starving priests.

At St. Louis University, Wayne's studies had included the theological classes required for philosophate students mixed with regular campus courses. At Harvard, Wayne had no religious class work. He enrolled strictly in courses for the Ph.D. program in English and American literature. He found the work stimulating beyond anything he'd previously experienced. Most of his fellow students were on par with those at Georgetown, but each class had one or two scholars who were certifiably brilliant.

As a graduate student, Wayne had the opportunity to teach at Harvard as well. One of his full professors taught a class in modern American literature to a large group of undergraduates once a week. Wayne led a smaller section of the course as a teaching assistant for the remaining two weekly meetings. He was awed by his students' intellect, energy, and gifts, which often extended beyond the classroom: For example, Miss Brown was not only highly sensitive to the nuances of the literature Wayne reviewed, but she played her flute in the Boston symphony orchestra. Mr. Simmons was an international expert in samurai swords. Others displayed similarly impressive talents that left Wayne proud to be in their presence.

With the combination of his own studies and the chance to teach, Wayne's years at Harvard would have been idyllic were it not for the timing. The conflict in Vietnam reached a peak in the late

'60s, and Harvard wasn't immune from the unrest that erupted on college campuses across the country.

Members of the activist group Students for a Democratic Society came to Cambridge by the busload. In April 1969, the unshaven radicals, many of them not even Harvard students, swarmed the campus. They took over the university administration building for two weeks, virtually shutting down the school for the first time in its history.

For the most part, Wayne stood back and watched the protests with a wary eye. He, like his roommates and many others, simply wanted peace. He joined a march for that purpose and walked from Harvard into downtown Boston. Along the way, the SDS stepped in, waving their flagrant banners and changing the flavor of the demonstration in the eyes of the public and the media.

One afternoon, while working out at the gym, a solitary young man in blue shorts and a Harvard T-shirt caught Wayne's eye. He watched as his fellow student loaded a barbell with the largest weights at each end. Wayne knew from experience that the total load exceeded 200 pounds. He cringed as the man approached the bar with knees locked and tested it. Wayne wanted to say something, but he stood back. The man leaned over a second time, legs still straight, and appeared ready to jerk the bar.

Unable to remain quiet any longer, Wayne approached the stranger. "I know it's none of my business, but if you lift that much weight with your knees locked, you're going to throw out your back."

The man stood up and looked Wayne in the eye. "That's exactly what I'm thinking of doing."

"Why would you deliberately do that?" Wayne asked.

"I just got my draft notice," said the student and he lowered his eyes to the bar.

Wayne's shoulders sagged as the meaning of the words sank in.

"Can we just talk about this?" he asked. Wayne had found that individualism was so stressed at Harvard that students often felt they were completely on their own. People rarely intruded into the privacy of others.

"Why not? I nearly killed myself earlier," the young man admitted.

"There are far better options than maiming yourself or taking your own life," Wayne said as his counseling experience kicked into high gear.

The man shook his head. "If this were the second world war, I'd volunteer, but in this one, I don't see them as the enemy. I can't in good conscience aim a gun at a Vietnamese with intent to kill."

"Would you want to pursue the avenue of becoming a conscientious objector?" Wayne asked.

The student glanced up. "I don't know. Tell me about it."

Wayne put the man in touch with the Jesuits, who were helping others with similar doubts.

Some Jesuits took a more active role in the protests than others. One Jesuit priest, Father Daniel Berrigan, became so well known for his antiwar activism at Cornell University that he had to go underground. Wayne didn't consider himself an activist. He only wanted to see a peaceful resolution of the conflict—both the combat abroad and the strife among his fellow citizens. To that end, one afternoon, with the total support of the Harvard faculty, Wayne donned his vestments. As students walked by on their way to class, he and several other priests said Mass for peace in the middle of Harvard Yard.

Wayne's classes were strictly secular, but he used his weekends to give back to the Church. Every Sunday, he said Mass at different parishes throughout Boston. He deeply valued the opportunity to write his own sermons and connect with a congregation through his love of words. The pastors were grateful for the assistance and always gave Wayne a small stipend for his services.

Rather than turn the money in to the province treasurer, Wayne set it aside in his room. The dollars accumulated little by little, until one day he took the entire bundle and went to a used-car lot. Living in the bustling Boston area in a pleasant rented room had introduced him to the delicious taste of independence. A car would allow him to venture even farther afield.

A navy blue Mercury Cougar caught Wayne's eye. He ran his hand over the shiny hood and hesitated. The money he'd earned belonged to the Jesuits. If he wanted to buy a car, he needed to ask their permission first.

As he climbed into the driver's seat, Wayne wondered how many other men in their 30s had never owned their own car. He gripped the wheel in both hands and pictured himself driving to New Hampshire with his friends or getting to the downtown parishes without having to rely on public transportation.

An eager salesman handed Wayne the key. When he cranked the starter and the V-8 engine roared to life, all thoughts of asking for permission disappeared. He handed over the cash and drove off the lot. Later, when friends questioned where Wayne got the car, he simply smiled and didn't say a word.

As the newness of his purchase wore off, shame moved in to take the place of pleasure. Even a drive to the beautiful White Mountains did little to assuage the guilt that tugged at his conscience every time he drove the car. As a Jesuit, Wayne had taken formal vows of poverty, obedience, and chastity. He'd said those vows in a chapel in the presence of God. In buying the car, he'd broken not one, but two, of his vows. He'd always considered himself completely committed to the Jesuits, but now he saw his actions as a crack in his convictions.

Wayne began to question whether he was as dedicated as he should be. It didn't help to know that 80 percent of the novices who'd started their training with him at Wernersville had already left the order due to their own inner struggles. To salve his conscience, he eventually sold the car and bought one for his father. It made him feel good to see his dad so happy, but even that didn't completely eradicate his guilt. In truth, he should have given the proceeds from the sale to the community treasury.

The basic problem remained, nagging at him like a burr in his shoe as he once again walked around campus. At least half of his classmates were women. He talked and joked with them just like any other graduate student. He wasn't really tempted to stray, yet the longing never went away.

Wayne couldn't help but wonder: if he'd so easily broken two of his vows, how long would it be before he fell in regards to the third?

⊕⊕⊕

In Wayne's final year at Harvard, his thoughts moved more and more to his future. As much as he was ready to begin his life as a professor, one final step in his Jesuit formation remained: the stage known as the tertianship. As its name implied, it was the third and final year of self-reflection and application of the Spiritual Exercises that he'd begun as a novice. The experience was intended to bring his training full circle.

After five stimulating years in Cambridge, Wayne couldn't picture himself returning to the isolation of a rural monastery. He proposed to his provincial superiors that he be allowed to spend his tertianship in a location where he could picture himself far more easily: at a seminary in Florence, Italy.

When word arrived that his request had been approved, Wayne was ecstatic. He made arrangements to enroll in Italian classes in Milan over the summer. He shared his excitement with his fellow graduate students who were busy preparing for their own futures. Most of Wayne's associates shared his aspiration to teach at the university level.

One friend, David, complained how difficult it was for Ph.D. candidates to get a teaching offer. "It's hard not to get discouraged," David said.

"What do you mean?" Wayne asked. He'd recently taken the momentous step of inquiring at Georgetown about an opening.

"I have yet to get a single interview," his friend said.

When David explained the extent of his efforts, Wayne bit his tongue. The last thing he wanted to do was to make his friend feel bad. David had sent out more than 200 letters; Wayne had sent only one.

It was neither arrogance nor cockiness that kept Wayne from applying for a professorship elsewhere. Georgetown University was the only place he wanted to be. Even while he taught the gifted undergraduate students at Harvard, he never considered staying there permanently. As much as he loved the intellectual stimulation, he found that the competitive nature of the school took away any sense of community. Worse yet, the issue of religious values never came up in the classroom, the assumption being that the spiritual dimension of life was private. Wayne knew that this was not the case at Georgetown. He was committed to the Jesuit mission and wanted to teach at a Jesuit university where he could assist students both intellectually and spiritually. And only Georgetown University would do.

In the days that followed Wayne's conversation with David, he couldn't help but wonder if perhaps he'd been foolish. He knew that he was taking a risk by applying to only one school, and he had no fallback plan. His heart was so set on Georgetown that he never allowed himself to think about what he'd do if he wasn't accepted.

One sparkling Tuesday afternoon, Wayne headed back to his room after class. He walked slowly, taking his time and enjoying the warm sunshine. A robin sat in a tree in front of the three-story town house and whistled a greeting as Wayne stopped to pick up the mail.

He sifted through a handful of flyers, then stopped. The golden seal of Georgetown University stared back at him from the corner of a crisp, white envelope. With trembling hands, he opened the letter.

There would be no need for an interview. The faculty was well familiar with his skills from his days teaching the course on theological dimensions in literature. The board understood that he was unable to start until the following year due to his tertianship, and they were willing to wait. Wayne barely dared to believe what he was reading. He skipped to the bottom line, and his heart threatened to burst from the acute surge of happiness: Georgetown University was pleased to offer Father Wayne A. Knoll, S.J., a teaching position in the department of English in the College of Arts and Sciences.

He didn't know whom to tell first. He could call his family back in Kansas, or maybe Father Ong in St. Louis. He glanced up at the town house. His roommates were probably home. As fellow Jesuits, they'd understand the enormity of his news. They'd also understand why, instead of going upstairs to share his happiness, he went straight to the chapel, got down on his knees, and gave his thanks first to God.

Chapter 20

Anne stood at the kitchen counter slicing chicken breasts for a casserole. She never knew these days if Bob was going to come home for dinner or not. Casseroles were easy to reheat.

She heard laughter and moved to the window. Rhonda and her little friends seemed to be having a good time playing in the yard. Anne shook her head. Rhonda was still too young to notice how little time her father spent with his family—but Anne noticed. In her heart, she knew that she and Bob wouldn't have a lifetime together, but she wasn't willing to give up on her marriage.

She returned to the cutting board and scraped the last of the chicken into a pan. *This would be better if I had some fresh mushrooms to add to it,* she thought.

Moments later, Rhonda dashed in from outside and stopped beside her mother. "Mom, do we have any mushrooms?" Then the four-year-old cocked her head and added, "What are mushrooms?"

Anne looked down at her daughter and beamed. The apple hadn't fallen too far from the tree. Rhonda was forever surprising her by saying things she had no way of knowing. Anne was convinced that everyone had psychic and mediumistic abilities to some extent, but Rhonda's were already far more developed than the norm. It was just like music and art: most people could sing and draw, but not everyone was a Caruso or a Monet. Anne knew that with the proper encouragement and guidance, Rhonda's gifts would unfold naturally.

With her dark brown hair and hazel eyes, looking at Rhonda was like peering in a mirror. Anne gazed at her daughter's face and thought about the recent investigations she'd conducted with Harold Sherman. Until giving birth, Anne had believed in reincarnation. Once she had a child of her own, she began to question her beliefs. How could any parent look into the eyes of their son or daughter and think that their child had belonged to someone else in a prior lifetime? The whole concept now seemed like an insult to motherhood.

Harold was sure that reincarnation was a myth, but Anne wasn't totally convinced. While there were some Spiritualists who openly admitted their belief in multiple lives, the official word from the NSAC was that spirits spent only one lifetime on the physical plane. The Declaration of Principles and all of Spiritualism's teachings were derived from communication with those in the spirit world. No spirits who had communicated with Anne ever claimed to have occupied more than one physical body.

Anne and Harold decided to conduct their own informal research. They discussed the possibility of publishing their findings, but mostly the two were simply curious. For the better part of the next year, Anne traveled at her own expense to meet with purported experts in the field. She ventured to South and Central America and as far east as England and Scotland, where she sat on the receiving end of dozens of past-life readings.

Thanks to her background, Anne was open to ideas outside the mainstream, but the more readings she attended, the more skeptical she became. She took detailed notes during each session. Afterward, she added the names and descriptions to a growing list of people whose lives she had allegedly lived in the past.

As she correlated the data, Anne found very little that matched. Had she truly experienced other physical manifestations, the experts should have all detected the same past lives. Twice she was told that she'd lived as Mary, Queen of Scots. That might have been significant had Anne not found several others who claimed the same past life. Once she was told she'd been Cleopatra, but Antony's sweetheart turned out to be one of the more popular bodies occupied by those who believed in such things.

One of Anne's reasons for believing in reincarnation was that she often had the sense that she'd once been a young French maid named Camille. None of the many past-life readers ever mentioned such a girl. Then one day Wilbur described to Anne a little French girl in a maid's uniform from the spirit world. He heard the name "Camille" and told Anne the girl came around her often.

Wilbur's revelation took away any remaining beliefs Anne had that she'd lived in other times and places. The images and sensations that she thought were memories were simply the touch of a living spirit. She ultimately sided with Spiritualism's idea that only those concepts for which we have proof should be believed. As long as humans occupied a physical body, there were some things we would never understand about the universe.

Even after coming to her own conclusions, Anne couldn't resist giving her theories one final test. She'd heard about an American woman named Margaret Cummings who could detect past lives. Anne flew to Massachusetts for the sole purpose of having a reading. Margaret turned out to be a petite woman with a face full of wrinkles and a head of white hair. She greeted Anne at the door of her modest Boston brownstone and invited her inside. The two shared a cup of tea, then Margaret got down to business.

Hunched in a hard wooden chair with a slatted back, Margaret closed her eyes, then began to shake her head. "You know, honey," she said, now looking at Anne and waggling a finger, "you were a very bad girl in one life."

Anne leaned away, taken aback by Margaret's schoolmarm manner.

"That's right. You were a prostitute."

Anne forced herself to swallow her laughter. She wondered if the sweet little woman even knew what prostitution was. When Margaret launched into a detailed description of Anne's tawdry activities in her so-called past lifetime, Anne turned as red as the tasseled pillows on the couch where she sat. The prim old lady knew more about life than her appearance indicated.

When Margaret ran out of details, she scanned the ceiling as if searching for cobwebs. "Ah," she said, finally nodding her head, "in your next lifetime you were very good and made up for everything."

Relieved, Anne sat forward. "I did?"

"That's right," Margaret said. "You were a nun."

If the year of investigation did nothing else, it gave Anne some good stories to share. From that day forward, when people asked her if she believed in past lives, Anne would tell them about Margaret and joke: "I went from being a prostitute to a nun and came back a happy medium."

Rhonda provided Anne with more happiness than she'd known a person could enjoy. But Anne's marriage to Bob went from good to bad to worse. He always treated Anne nicely, and she never stopped caring for him, but when she could no longer deny the reality of their marriage, she locked her bedroom door.

Through her oil dowsing with Bill Keeler, Anne had earned a small fortune. She'd always been told that psychic gifts couldn't be used for personal gain, but in this case she reasoned that her good fortune came because many others could benefit greatly from the oil she found. The money from Bill paid for the apartment complex in which she and Bob lived, a horse ranch, a herd of cattle, and several orange groves.

Bob would ask for her impressions about one investment over another, but that was the extent of her involvement in their hold-ings. He was forever moving funds and putting money into schemes about which Anne had little understanding. Her life was busy with the center, her classes, readings, public appearances, and research. She didn't have time for financial matters; that was more in line with Bob's skills.

Trusting Bob proved to be a major mistake. She'd known for some time that there were troubles, but she had no idea how bad things were until he began to sell off their property. His green limo had long ago been repossessed when she found paperwork for a Porsche in the name of a woman she didn't recognize—along with hotel bills and dinner receipts for Broadway shows. When she later came across proof of payment for nursing-school tuition, she didn't have the nerve to ask which student her husband was sponsoring.

Anne may have turned a blind eye to Bob's activities, but her mother-in-law missed nothing. Margaret spent half of each year at her home in New York and the other half at a small place in Orlando. She adored her granddaughter and spent much of her time playing with Rhonda and chatting with Anne in their home.

One morning, Anne and Margaret sat together at the table in Anne's kitchen sipping cups of hot tea. After 11 years with her daughter-in-law, Margaret didn't have to be a psychic to know that something was wrong. When asked, Anne admitted that Bob hadn't been home in a couple of nights. That wasn't so unusual, but when she last saw him, he'd dropped the bombshell that they were out of money.

Margaret shook her head. "I don't know how you live with him."

The words had the effect of a slap in the face. Her mother-in-law had spoken aloud what Anne had been thinking for some time now. Before the day was over, she made an appointment with a lawyer. The next morning, still with no sign of Bob, Anne filled out the papers and initiated a divorce.

In spite of their problems, the decision devastated Anne. She believed in "till death do us part" and had wanted the storybook marriage every woman dreamed of. In spite of his faults, she loved Bob, with his effervescent charm and love of life. He'd always been a fun playmate, but a companion he was not. The day after seeing the lawyer, Anne retreated to her office, unwilling to share with anyone the news that her marriage was over.

A court reporter from the *Sentinel* had no problem spreading the word.

News of Anne's divorce and bankruptcy filled a large section of the next day's front page. The oversized headline blared: "Psychic Fails to Foresee Own Future." Mortified, Anne shoved the newspaper in her purse and rushed to the front door. On the sidewalk outside the center, a mob of photographers and reporters circled like a flock of vultures.

Anne scurried back to her office and cowered there until well into the evening, but she could only hide for so long. Eventually she had to answer the question that everyone was asking: *How could a psychic not have known that her own marriage wouldn't work out?*

To Anne, the answer was simple. She was no different from anyone else. Psychics and mediums didn't go through life floating on a cloud either here or in the hereafter. Every person existed in a physical body for their spiritual growth. As her failed marriage illustrated, Anne had to experience the same problems and challenges that everyone else did in order to learn life's lessons.

She endured the painful period with her head held high. She was well aware of the gossip and chatter behind her back, but the support of close friends and Rhonda's love helped her move above the petty comments.

For his part, Bob didn't contest the divorce. He did, however, suffer a severe heart attack just days before the final proceedings. Three cardiologists took Anne aside and informed her that her ex-husband's heart was so damaged that he wouldn't live beyond six months.

She and Bob were bankrupt, but they still had their home. Unable to send a dying man into the street, Anne invited him to stay. Bob had been sleeping in the spare bedroom for the past five years, so there was little to do to prepare for his return. When he was discharged from the hospital ten days later, Anne continued to care for him as if they were still man and wife.

"I think it's time you leave," she said one year later—when Bob was still going strong.

He moved out later that week and lived for years.

Anne's research into reincarnation had shown her that she only had one chance to get things right while living on the physical plane. Faced with a young daughter and a growing stack of bills, Bob's departure meant the start of a whole new life.

Chapter 21

Three male students, their arms laden with books, halted mid-stride and pivoted clockwise with near-choreographed precision. The object of their distraction, a leggy redhead in skintight jeans, continued in the opposite direction, seemingly unaware of having nearly caused a pileup on the school's sidewalk. From his perch under the arched entrance to Healy Hall, Wayne surveyed the scene with a wry smile.

The previous summer, while studying at the Berlitz school in Milan, he'd witnessed a similar incident just after crossing the Piazza del Duomo. He was passing through the Galleria Vittorio Emanuele, a magnificent covered arcade of elegant shops just beyond the cathedral. The walkway was crowded with Italian businessmen rushing to work. Suddenly, the flow of human traffic came to a dead stop. Like a gondola parting the waters of a Venetian canal, a stunningly beautiful Italian woman came strolling against the current of swiveling male heads.

Wayne learned a great deal about Italian art, history, and culture during his tertianship in Florence. Some things, however, like a man's instinctive reaction to a good-looking woman, were universal.

There had been no women students at Georgetown when Wayne first toured the campus 20 years earlier. Now, his long black cassock seemed almost medieval in contrast with the unsettlingly short skirts the female freshmen flaunted from their front-row seats in his classroom. As a new professor, he'd been required to sign a contract stating that he wouldn't become intimately involved with any of his students. His signature had seemed somewhat superfluous, considering the vow he'd taken years before in the presence of God.

He descended the steps and walked toward the new library. In designing the building, the architects intended to create a modern version of Healy Hall. They'd failed miserably. The gray slab exterior lacked any sense of warmth or aesthetic appeal. Nevertheless, a door down a quiet hallway on the first floor held a placard stating that the room within belonged to Dr. Wayne A. Knoll, S.J. Cozy or not, the office represented Wayne's dream come true.

The reality of sharing his love of literature with his students far exceeded the vision that had guided him throughout his years of training. To the credit of the university and the English department, Wayne was able to teach the subjects he felt most passionate about. As a consequence, he saw his passion reflected in his students' faces when he lectured, in their class discussions and papers, and in the way they visited his office or stopped him around campus just to chat.

He entered his office and set his stack of books on the corner of his desk. He was about to sit down when a rap on the door made him stop and turn around. He recognized Sarah Stewart from Texts and Contexts, his favorite freshman course. The attractive young student with her long, straight blonde hair and tight-fitting sweaters was hard to forget. Now Sarah stood in Wayne's doorway with a sheaf of papers in her hand and a provocative smile on her lips.

She lowered her head so she had to look up at him when she spoke. "Father Knoll, I was hoping you could help me."

Years earlier, Omer had complained that his brother was oblivious to the female students' attentions at St. Louis University. Now in his mid-40s, Wayne could no longer claim such ignorance, nor could he deny that he was attracted to some of his students. He was a priest, but that didn't stop him from having normal feelings like any man. It didn't help that some of his students, even knowing that he'd taken vows, openly came on to him.

"How may I help you, Sarah?" he asked, almost afraid to hear her reply.

He'd seen from her body language that she had something other than her essay in mind, but Wayne was completely unprepared when Sarah launched herself toward him. She flung her arms around his neck, then gave a little jump and wrapped her legs around his hips.

At a total loss for words, Wayne gave her a fatherly hug. Then, smiling dumbly, he stepped back, forcing her to stand.

Sarah didn't seem the slightest bit flustered. She straightened her skirt, waggled her fingers in a friendly wave, and left.

Unable to concentrate, Wayne turned off the lights and went straight to the Jesuit residence. The priests and lay brothers who worked at Georgetown lived in an old, red-brick building in the center of campus. Each man had a private two-room suite, the nicest setting Wayne had ever enjoyed. The building also housed a dining room, a communal social area, a large chapel, and several smaller chapels where the priests could say Mass in private.

Wayne visited the chapel every morning, but that evening, unnerved by the incident in his office, he paid a special visit to the altar. He'd made a promise to the school on paper, now he made a promise to himself and to God that he wouldn't take advantage of a student, no matter how badly he wanted to.

And as much as it pained Wayne to admit it, he wanted to.

To Wayne, the Jesuits were a brotherhood in the truest sense of the word. The men who lived in the residence hall at Georgetown University were a family. They provided him with companionship and stimulating conversation. Most had been through the same training, and all shared the same beliefs and love of humankind.

The men would gather in the evenings in the residence snack bar to enjoy a soft drink, coffee, or beer and a chat. Their discussions, while often lofty and philosophical, were punctuated with hearty laughter. Wayne always looked forward to discussing politics with Father Bob Drinan, dean of Georgetown's law school. Father Drinan made history by becoming the first Roman Catholic priest to be elected to Congress. He represented the state of Massachusetts for two terms before the Pope asked him to step down.

Some of Wayne's most treasured moments came in conversation with the dean of the College of Arts and Sciences, Father Royden B. Davis, a bespectacled man with a round face and wide, welcoming smile. In spite of his high-ranking position, Father Davis was as humble and unassuming as he was hardworking. On the evenings when the dean's duties kept him late in his office, Wayne stopped by to lift the older man's spirits as much as his own. When time allowed, Wayne and Dean Davis attended the theater or concerts.

While living in the Jesuit residence, Wayne had no need for a car. Most of his activities centered around the campus, where he could walk to the gym for a workout, get lost among the special collections in the library, or enjoy a first-rate student production at the university playhouse. Events and museums off campus were easily accessible by public transportation.

His mobility was severely impeded one evening, however, during an impromptu game of basketball. Wayne ran down the court with the ball, but one of his students was guarding him closely. Wayne went up for a shot, then came down on his opponent's instep. He heard an awful sound and felt a searing pain. The student's foot was fine, but Wayne had torn a ligament.

Georgetown University's hospital offered some of the finest care in the country. The doctors patched Wayne's leg and sealed it in a plaster cast. He hobbled back to the residence on crutches, where he received a welcome dose of sympathy from his brothers, along with their prayers for a speedy recovery.

Perhaps it was the newness of the cast that caused him to awaken in the middle of the night shortly after his injury. He sat up and immediately knew that there was a problem far more life-threatening than a torn ligament. The unmistakable smell of smoke filled his room, sending him hopping into the hallway.

"Fire! Fire!" he shouted as loud as he was able.

Frustrated by his inability to run down the halls and pound on the doors, he continued to shout as men began to stumble from their rooms. Several of the floors housed students, and roused by Wayne's cries, they helped the elderly Jesuits on the top floor escape to safety.

Wayne stood on the street looking up at his corner window. The heaviest smoke seemed to be coming from an area beneath his room and over just a bit. Within five minutes, trucks from the campus fire department arrived. By then flames were visible, and Wayne watched with awe as one of the young firefighters rushed directly at the blaze with his hose.

Thanks to everyone's quick reactions, no one was injured and the building was saved. Wayne learned that a painter had left an open can of paint thinner on the ground floor. He returned to find the rooms that had been his home for the past five years blackened by smoke and uninhabitable.

While the building was under renovation, the Jesuits moved to a hotel rented by the university a short distance from the campus. Each day as he traveled back and forth to his office and classes, Wayne couldn't help but notice the couples of all ages walking hand in hand on the city streets or sharing intimate meals at the local restaurants.

In spite of his vows, in spite of the promise he made in his first year of teaching, Wayne's doubts about his ability to remain celibate had reached a crisis point. It was no longer merely difficult, but downright painful, to have a life that didn't allow him to love a woman, to be loved by a woman, and to experience physical intimacy. It was only a matter of time before he fell, Wayne knew, and a priest didn't mess with his vows.

Torn by emotions that wouldn't give him rest, Wayne turned to the one man he trusted above all others: Father Davis. He confided that he didn't know if he could go on as a priest. There was no woman in particular, he assured his friend, rather a relentless longing that threatened to consume him.

Father Davis advised Wayne to get away from the university. In the silence of a prolonged retreat, he was told to do as Jesuits had done for centuries and turn his problem over to God.

Wayne chose a retreat center run by the Dominicans on the outskirts of Washington. There, over a period of seven days, he returned to the Spiritual Exercises of St. Ignatius. Through prayer and self-reflection, and in the quiet of meditation, it became very clear to Wayne what he needed to do.

He returned to his hotel room on Massachusetts Avenue and sat on the edge of his bed. The renovation of the residence would be complete within a year, but Wayne knew now that he wouldn't be moving back in with the others. He'd had no idea when he fled from the burning building that it would be the last night he slept in a Jesuit residence.

There would be formalities and papers to sign, but Wayne needed to talk to Father Davis before all else. He found the dean in his office.

He cleared his throat, then said, "I've come to a decision."

The older priest frowned. "And?"

The answer was clear from the look on Wayne's face, but still he needed to say it aloud. The words seemed to stick in his mouth, but he forced them out.

"I'm leaving the Society."

His friend sagged as if he'd been struck. "But why?" the dean asked, even though they'd discussed the issue at length before Wayne left for his retreat.

Wayne hung his head. "I just desperately need human love."

It was as simple as that, and as difficult.

Royden B. Davis stared back at Wayne, his eyes tearful and full of sorrow like those of a grieving parent. "But Wayne," he said, almost pleading, "*I* love you."

Wayne appreciated his friend's sentiments more than he could ever express. He loved Father Davis and all of his brothers in the Society of Jesus.

But it wasn't enough.

Chapter 22

Anne pulled off the highway and checked her map. She'd never much liked driving, and the roads around Washington, D.C., made no sense at all. At times she questioned her sanity in moving to such a busy area, but it had seemed like a good decision at the time. She wanted a place far from Florida, somewhere she could continue her work without struggling to get by.

A number of her former clients used to drive to Orlando from northern Virginia. When they told Anne that she'd have no trouble lining up readings in their area, she gave the idea serious thought. She recalled her visit to Georgetown in the '60s to speak at the Church of Two Worlds. When Pastor Burroughs predicted that she'd one day live in Washington, she'd laughed. It was now the '80s, and the laugh was on her as she pored over the map while cars whipped past.

Luckily, her clients were right. The area was ripe with open-minded citizens hungry to learn more about other dimensions. She sublet an office from an insurance company in Fairfax, where the owners allowed her to replace the ugly flooring with cheery pink carpet. She didn't bother with a sign or advertising. From the first day she started giving readings, word of mouth kept her appointment book full.

She and Rhonda settled into a three-story town house in Springfield, not far from the office. The entrance was on the middle level, with a large finished room on the ground floor. Anne immediately turned the area into a library, where she set up chairs and continued her classes in Spiritualism that had been so popular in Florida.

The same year she moved to Washington, Anne made her annual trek to Lily Dale. There, she stumbled upon an offer that was too good to pass up. One of the quaint Victorian houses with an unimpeded view of Cassadaga Lake was being offered at an unheard-of price. Anne had been saving her pennies since the divorce, and the little house seemed to be calling her name.

She'd been invited to speak at the Spiritualist camp many times since she was 17, and now she was in her 40s. On each visit, she stayed at the Leolyn Inn or the Maplewood. She'd only been in Washington a short time, but it was long enough to know that having her own little getaway in the rolling hills of western New York would be worth twice what the owners were asking.

The reason for the low price became immediately obvious once she stepped inside. The owners' children had run amok, hosting parties and using drugs in the cottage. Anne was able to look past the destruction and see the house's potential, with its multiple bedrooms for guests, a roomy parlor, and a delightful enclosed porch overlooking the lake.

She closed the deal and immediately set about cleaning up the mess. Gallons of elbow grease and fresh paint transformed the little white cottage over the course of that first summer. When the job was finished, there was no need to hang a sign out front. The pink porch, pink window frames, and cheery pink trim let the Lily Dale locals know which house belonged to the medium Anne Gehman.

Pulling her car back onto the busy Washington beltway, she longed for Lily Dale's narrow lanes where pedestrians outnumbered the cars. Within half an hour, though, the congestion eased and she began to relax. Driving north on Highway 270, the strip malls and residential neighborhoods were soon replaced with scenic farmland much like Anne's native Michigan.

Her destination that morning was a farm of sorts, but one so famous that most needed a ticket to tour it: the former farmhouse of President Dwight Eisenhower and his wife, Mamie. Anne had received a personal invitation from Priscilla Baker, chief of public affairs for the National Park Service, to visit the Eisenhower National Historic Site. The farm sat adjacent to the Gettysburg battlefield in southeastern Pennsylvania.

Mrs. Baker had learned of Anne's work through a chance encounter with a member of the American Society of Psychical Research. Priscilla felt that a medium would be just the person to investigate reports from several park rangers about unexplained goings-on at the Eisenhower farm. No one at Gettysburg had specifically requested a medium's services, but Priscilla thought it might be interesting to see if Anne could determine the cause of what the rangers had been sensing.

Anne knew little about the Eisenhower farm, other than what Priscilla told her over the phone. Ike and Mamie bought the 189-acre property in 1950 as a retirement home. Their retirement was delayed when the general was sent to Europe and later elected President. During his presidency, the Eisenhowers used the farm as a weekend retreat where they entertained family, friends, and leaders from around the world. When the President suffered a heart attack in 1955, he recuperated at the farm, earning it the nickname "the Temporary White House."[1]

General Eisenhower died in 1969, and Mamie lived at the farm until her death ten years later. The Eisenhowers had donated the property to the National Park Service years earlier, and the farm opened for tours in 1980.

The park historian and two rangers—one male and one female—met Anne upon her arrival. They were joined by Becky Lyons, the park tech who had originally contacted Priscilla Baker with stories of ghosts at Gettysburg. The park superintendent wanted nothing to do with a medium on the premises and kept his distance. He hadn't invited Anne and scoffed at the stories his rangers told of strange rustling noises, unusual smells, and blinking lights.

Anne walked in the front door of the large white home and immediately stopped. She turned to the historian and said, "I'm hearing a name. It's rather faint, but it sounds like *Clinton.*"

The historian's head gave a little jerk and one side of his mouth curled up. "The man who built the original home here was Quentin Armstrong, but that's not public knowledge."

"Quentin," Anne repeated, then nodded. "Yes, that's it. Quentin."

The group moved into the living room and Anne turned to the rangers. "Tell me what's been going on."

Twenty-six-year-old Mark Harris was a seasonal employee who worked at Gettysburg nine months out of the year. He spent most of his time at the battlefield, but once every two to three weeks he ended up at the Eisenhower farm. He told Anne that one day in early December, he was on duty in the house while only a couple of visitors took the tour. The visitors were both on the first floor when he heard the swish-swish of a taffeta dress moving down the hallway upstairs. He mentioned it to the other ranger on duty, who confirmed that he heard it as well.

"There were also a few times when we smelled cigarette smoke, but smoking isn't allowed in the house," Mark added.

The historian confirmed that both Mamie and Ike were heavy smokers.

Mark glanced toward the staircase. "Some of the rangers talk about seeing lights blinking on and off, but I haven't seen that myself."

"I have," Leslie Coker, the female ranger, chimed in. "And I've heard that sound just like Mark described it. If you believe in ghosts, it makes sense, because Mrs. Eisenhower loved to wear taffeta."

Mark nodded. "I'll swear till the day I die that I heard that swishing."

Anne smiled at their sincerity. "Well, I'm sensing a woman here, and I'm getting the name of Rose. Rose Wood."

"That was the Eisenhowers' housekeeper," the historian said.

"Yes, Rose is here, and she says that she's around much of the time because she loved it here so much. She also tells me that Mrs. Eisenhower visits on occasion."

The group looked at Anne wide-eyed, as if unsure as to how to react to such unusual news.

"May we go upstairs?" Anne asked.

The rangers led the way, with Becky Lyons and the historian trailing close behind.

"This was Mrs. Eisenhower's bedroom, wasn't it?" Anne asked as she stepped into a cozy room.

"That's right," replied the historian.

Anne sat on a chair and closed her eyes. Instantly, she sensed a female presence. She would have recognized the former First Lady from photos, but she knew intuitively that Mamie Eisenhower had decided to appear.

"Mrs. Eisenhower is here," she reported. "She's wearing a very elegant dressing gown that flares out here at the bottom, and a pair of fancy slippers with low heels."

Becky Lyons and the two rangers glanced at each other as the historian confirmed that the description matched the way Mamie would have dressed around the house.

Anne concentrated on the images she was sensing. Mrs. Eisenhower was pacing back and forth in front of her as if she were worried about something. The lights in the room flickered as Anne sent a mental message to Mamie, asking her to communicate her concerns. The reply came back loud and clear.

"She tells me there's talk of digging up some land to put in a parking lot, and she doesn't want that to happen."

"There *has* been talk of a parking lot," Becky said.

"And now she's showing me an area near what looks like some kind of well where a woman is buried. She doesn't want the grave to be disturbed for the parking lot."

Becky and the historian conferred for a moment. Neither knew anything about a burial on the property.

"Well, just remember that. It may be significant later."

Anne concentrated on the message. "Now she's sharing something about a problem with the stairs. . . . They're not the stairs we just came up, but a smaller set. Does that make sense to anyone?"

Ranger Harris explained that the normal sequence for a tour was for the visitors to come in through the front door and circulate through the first-floor rooms. All traffic flowed to the second floor by way of the main staircase. After touring the rooms upstairs, visitors went down a smaller set of back stairs and exited through a door off the kitchen.

"Well, Mamie wants someone to take a look at those stairs, because they're in need of repair. I get the sense that the reason she's been making her presence known here is that she's very concerned that someone will get hurt if those stairs aren't fixed."

Once Mamie's messages were delivered, Anne no longer sensed her presence. The group continued the tour of the house and finished in the library. As they walked into the room, Anne clearly saw Ike sitting at his desk, smiling as if he were there to greet her. She sensed the presence of a black man at Ike's side and felt he was an aide or valet.

According to the historian, the President's aide had been a black man, as Anne described.

"I hope what I told you was helpful," Anne said as the five stepped outside.

Mark Harris spoke up. "There's been some activity at my house, too."

All heads turned toward the young ranger. He explained that he rented a room in one side of a nearby farmhouse that had been built around 1810 and had been turned into a duplex. The house had a reputation for being haunted, although he hadn't personally seen anything unusual. Anne agreed to take a look.

Mark didn't tell her about the woman who had appeared at the foot of his neighbor's bed. Nor did he mention that a friend who spent the night saw a woman at the top of the staircase matching the same description his neighbor had given.

The house sat along Taneytown Road on the way to the battlefield. Anne took no more than four steps inside and announced, "This home was used as a field hospital at one time."

Mark looked up in surprise. He hadn't mentioned anything about the house's history to Anne, but she was absolutely correct. Historical records showed that wounded soldiers had been brought there for treatment.

"Can you take me to the old fireplace?" Anne asked.

Mark led her to the living room, but Anne shook her head. "No, this fireplace is old, but there's one here that's older."

Mark recalled that there was a fireplace in the unfinished basement. He never went down there because the ceiling was too low for his 5'11" frame, and the dirt floor was messy. The five guests descended the basement stairway and crowded into the dim, musty space. Anne turned in a circle, then described the presence of a young woman. She sensed that the spirit had no connection with the field hospital, so she didn't know why she lingered about the house.

"She's rather tall for a woman, and has long, brown hair pulled back to here." Anne held her hands high on her head. "She's wearing a floor-length dress with puffy sleeves and a full skirt."

"That sounds exactly like the woman my friend and my neighbor described," Mark said. "So this house really is haunted?"

Anne shook her head. She hated when people talked about ghosts or haunted houses. The words carried such a negative connotation, especially since the film *The Amityville Horror* had come out a few years back. When people couldn't explain something, they made it out to be frightening or bad. She always tried to correct the misconception by explaining that spirits were benign, but negative energy could linger in a place where something unpleasant had happened to someone. The residual energy from a negative event such as a murder and the energy of the spirit of the deceased were totally separate.

Once she assured Mark that the woman wasn't there to harm anyone, the group left the house and moved on to the Gettysburg battlefield.

"Let's stop here," Mark said as they passed one of his favorite spots.

The others stood back and observed as Anne slowly walked through the grass. After a few minutes, she turned to face them.

"I'm getting the sense that someone important was killed here . . . someone higher in rank than most of the soldiers. I think he was from the north. He was standing where I am now when a Confederate soldier shot him from that rock . . . there." She pointed to a large stone across the road. "I'm hearing the name Cox . . . no, Cross."

Mark was stunned. He shared a look with the historian, then told Anne the history of Colonel Edward Cross, a brigade commander in the Second Army Corps. Cross had previously been the regimental commander of the 5th New Hampshire Volunteers and was shot by a Confederate soldier, exactly as Anne had described.

Mark led Anne to a monument to the New Hampshire regiment not far from where she stood. "Did you see this before?" he asked her.

"I've never been here," she said.

Mark shook his head. The story of Colonel Cross was one of his favorites. Legend had it that the colonel had a premonition of his death. If what Anne said was true, he'd come back now to talk about it.

"And you actually see him?" Mark asked.

"No, but standing here, I can sense what happened."

She went on to give several other names that popped into her mind. The historian wrote them down as she spoke, but none of them meant anything to anyone in the group.

"Are you saying those poor soldiers are still lingering around the battlefield?" Becky Lyons asked.

"No, not at all," Anne was adamant. "Once you've passed on, you don't linger for long."

She explained that in times of high emotion, an area becomes charged with that energy. She didn't remember much of what she'd learned about Gettysburg in school, but she knew that any battle was full of fear and other negative emotions.

"That energy is strongly implanted here. I get the impression of the fighting, and I sense the soldiers' names; but I don't see them walking through the fields as if they don't have anyplace to go."

Anne returned to Washington as amazed by the events of the day as those in the group that hosted her. Two weeks after her visit, Becky Lyons called with a report. The historian had checked the archives. Each of the names Anne had reported belonged to actual soldiers who had died at the Battle of Gettysburg.

Following Anne's advice, engineers checked out the back stairs at the Eisenhower farmhouse. They found them weak and hazardous, and repaired them before anyone was injured.

Rangers Mark Harris and Leslie Coker signed up for Anne's classes and made the two-hour drive once a week to Springfield to learn more about mediumship.

As for the burial in the Eisenhowers' backyard, Becky called one year later with an update. A park worker had discovered a document that described how a gardener had unearthed some human remains sometime in the '60s while digging near the well behind the farmhouse. He immediately took his concerns to Mrs. Eisenhower. According to the report, Mamie told the gardener to put things back as he had found them and not disturb the grave further. Until this point, no one had known anything about a body being buried on the grounds of the farm. Anne had no way of knowing this either. She'd simply related the details as Mamie Eisenhower had passed them on to her.

Anne's fellow dinner guests listened with interest as she recounted the details of her trip to the famous farm. This kind of evidential report was precisely the sort of thing the members of the American Society of Psychical Research were interested in. She'd traveled to New York City to address the group, and her lecture was well received. The dinner she attended afterward was pleasant enough, but she was plagued with an uneasy feeling.

"I'm sorry," she said, "but you'll have to excuse me."

She returned to her room and picked up the phone. She had a flight back to Washington the following morning, but she clearly sensed that she was needed in Florida. She bought a ticket for the next day on a flight going from Washington to Orlando.

That night she awakened from a sound sleep to the sound of her father's voice.

"Beatrice Anne!" he called out. "Beatrice Anne!"

His voice was full of enthusiasm, as if he had something he couldn't wait to tell her. She sat up and saw a bright light at the foot of the bed. Within it was the form of her papa. He smiled back at her and held out his arms as if he wanted to hug her, then he moved to the side of the bed and disappeared.

Anne fell back asleep but she was awakened before daybreak by the phone. A neighbor of her parents was on the line, having tracked her down to deliver the news that Anne dreaded yet somehow expected: her father had passed away in the night.

Thankfully, Anne had already booked her reservation, and she boarded the flight to Florida later that day. At the little house near Paisley, Anne hugged her mother and tried to console her. They all knew he had to go sometime, but at 97, her father had rarely been sick. In fact, Anne's mama told her, he'd been out surveying land the day before he passed.

Beatrice told her daughter that John had gone to bed, but got up about an hour later to go to the bathroom. When he climbed back under the sheets, he wanted to lie there and talk. He chatted on about their children—how much he loved each one and how proud he was of all of them. Then, according to her mother, he smiled, closed his eyes, and never opened them again.

Anne cried with her mother, but her tears weren't for her father. She knew better than most that he was now in a much better place. She grieved only because she'd miss him. Her heart ached that she hadn't gotten to speak with him before he passed, but she had the comfort of knowing that he'd stopped at her bedside to pay her one final visit.

When Anne's friend Nicki Brintzenhofe called and invited her to a lecture at the National Cathedral, Anne was glad for an excuse to do something special. Earlier that day, she and Rhonda had gone to a drugstore where they'd stopped at a Father's Day display. Anne was busy reading through several cards, wondering which one her father would like best, when Rhonda put a hand on her arm and said, "But Mama, he's gone."

Of course she'd known that. He'd been gone for quite some time, but she still had her moments. She stood in the store and cried, wondering if a person ever got over the loss of a parent.

Now she sat beside Nicki, glad her friend was at the wheel. She was feeling better after the emotional morning, but she still didn't care to drive around downtown D.C.

They headed north on Interstate 395, then took Route 27 past the Pentagon. A short distance beyond, Anne stared at the neat rows of white gravestones aligned with military precision at Arlington National Cemetery. They continued on between the high-rises of Roslyn, then joined the heavy traffic crossing the Potomac River on Key Bridge.

Anne glanced up at the cluster of buildings that seemed to hang at the far edge of the river. She knew the distinctive spires belonged to Georgetown University, but she'd never visited the campus.

Georgetown University.

"Nicki," she said, voicing a thought that occurred to her as if from nowhere, "there's a man up there I'm going to meet."

"Up where?" Nicki asked, turning her head only long enough to glance curiously at Anne.

"Up there—at Georgetown. I just saw this image."

"Ooh," Nicki said. "Describe him."

Anne's eyes narrowed. "He's about average height, rather muscular and athletic . . ."

"Mm-hm."

"And he's very intelligent and spiritual . . . a lot like my dad, actually."

"Interesting." Nicki stopped at the traffic light at the end of the bridge. "What's he into?"

"Well, I get the feeling he likes the classics . . . and languages and philosophy . . . and literature and theology."

"Wow," Nicki said. "He sounds like quite the intellectual. Can you tell what he does?"

Anne glanced up at the towers as they made the turn onto M Street. She leaned back against the headrest and rolled her eyes. "He's probably a priest."

The two girlfriends laughed all the way to the cathedral.

Chapter 23

"Don't leave the priesthood until you have tenure," one of Wayne's colleagues advised.

Wayne had been a junior professor at Georgetown for six years. His future as a permanent member of the faculty rested on the decision of a board that would meet in his seventh year. Tenure was granted to those members of the faculty who demonstrated a strong record of research, teaching, and service. His colleague worried that since Georgetown was a Jesuit university, Wayne's decision to leave the priesthood might have a negative impact on the board.

Wayne appreciated his friend's concern, but he couldn't wait another year. That would be dishonest.

He had his own doubts about how things would work out, but he recalled his Aunt Anna's advice from long ago: "The Holy Spirit will provide." Now those words echoed in his ears as he moved forward with his decision.

Leaving the priesthood and leaving the Jesuit order were two different events. Shortly after talking with Father Davis, Wayne filled out the paperwork to initiate both processes. It would take years to receive his dispensation from the Vatican. The Jesuits were far more efficient.

Little time passed before Wayne was called into an office and asked to sign a document from the Maryland Province. Like a man married for 20-plus years who finds himself divorced with the stroke of a judge's pen, Wayne signed a piece of paper and was officially dismissed from the Society of Jesus. The day was so gut-wrenching that he would suppress the details for years.

The Jesuits knew that Wayne's decision was the result of prayer, and they held no ill feelings toward him. They understood how difficult his transition would be. Once he signed the final papers, Father Davis and Wayne's other superiors at Georgetown told him to take his time moving out. He could remain among the community as long as he needed.

Wayne was in no hurry. He needed to find a place to live and to furnish it, and he needed a car. While the thought of a new path was exciting, he had to admit that it was also somewhat scary. For his entire life he'd had all of his needs taken care of by either his parents or the Jesuits. He was 44 years old and had never lived on his own.

Wayne's transition was transparent to his students. From his first days as a professor, he always had a choice about how to dress. Some days he wore the long cassock, other days the black suit with white collar, and occasionally he wore a regular suit. When he started going to class in secular attire, no one questioned him.

He chose not to tell his students that he was no longer a priest. With his family, he had no choice. He planned to tell his brothers and sisters over the phone, but he knew that he'd have to talk to his parents in person. His father would be supportive no matter what he did, but Mother Knoll was fiercely proud of her son the priest. Wayne held no illusions that she would take the news well.

A month passed while he got used to the idea that he was no longer a priest. He turned a second page in the calendar while adjusting to the idea a little more. He remained in the hotel as if nothing had changed and talked to no one in his family. Finally, just before the start of the fall semester, he booked a flight to Victoria.

Iris Knoll chose the same weekend to go home to Kansas. Wayne didn't know whether to be happy or upset when he saw his little sister at the house. She would surely be as shocked as his parents.

His palms were sweaty as he joined his mother, father, and Iris in the dining room. The last time he'd visited was Christmas; and the long table had been crowded with all of his brothers and sisters, their spouses, and their children. The big old house seemed deadly quiet now, in spite of his parents' happy chatter.

Wayne cleared his throat. It was mid-afternoon and he wanted to get the painful announcement over with.

"I, uh—" he paused to clear his throat again.

Iris eyed him with suspicion. Everyone in the family knew that anytime Wayne started making that noise in his throat, he was nervous about something.

His parents seemed to sense the change in his manner as well, and they grew suddenly serious.

"There's something I need to tell you," he said, then plunged into the talk he'd toyed with over the past two months. He spoke haltingly until the words he'd rehearsed in his mind gathered their own momentum. Just as he did during his lectures in the classroom, he gave a little background and set the scene, selectively arranging the events of the past few years as he built to the inevitable, painful climax. Finally, the moment he had avoided for months was upon him, and he could delay no longer.

"And so," he cleared his throat yet again, "I felt I had no choice but to—" he coughed into his hand, "—to seek dispensation from the priesthood."

He could tell by their stunned faces that they'd heard what he said, but not one of the three said a word. His mind raced to find a way to fill in the silence, but he'd used up all of his words.

Suddenly, his mother let out a guttural wail that split the air like an unexpected crack of thunder. Wayne watched, mortified, as she rose shakily from her chair and stumbled down the hall as if she were going to be sick. She disappeared into her first-floor bedroom and shut the door behind her.

His father, as Wayne had expected, merely shook his head.

Iris, tough like their usually strong mother, looked Wayne in the eye and said, "You'd better get your butt in there and talk to her."

Wayne traced his mother's steps and tapped softly on the door. Hearing no reply, he peered inside. She was lying on her side with an arm across her face. He moved to the bedside and peered down at her.

"I'm so sorry, Mom," he said, his chest full as if his heart had swollen to twice its size, "but I'll always be a priest in the eyes of God."

She moved her arm. "Then you've already done this?"

He nodded. If he'd discussed it with her first, it would have been even harder.

She seemed incapable of saying more, so he stumbled on, repeating the words from his earlier speech and rearranging the sentences. The ending still came out the same. When he could think of nothing else to say, he retreated from the bedroom and pulled the door softly closed.

His father and Iris still sat at the table.

"It's not going very well," Wayne said in answer to his sister's questioning eyes.

He took his seat again and the three talked quietly, alternately casting glances toward the bedroom. When Mother Knoll failed to appear, Iris stood.

"I'll try to talk to her."

Iris knew her parents better than Wayne. He might have been alive longer than she had, but he'd been gone longer. She knew how much it meant to her mother that Wayne was a priest. Other than her parents' marriage, Wayne's ordination ceremony was the highlight of her mother's life. Mother Knoll was old-Catholic, and once Wayne took the Sacrament of Holy Orders, he became something far greater than the boy she'd given birth to.

If Iris was going to get her mother to come around, she had to get her to see Wayne once again as her son, and not a priest. Iris stood in the spot vacated by Wayne and looked down at the bed.

"Mom," she said, "you know Wayne doesn't do anything on an impulse. I'm sure he's talked to God about this."

Mother Knoll said nothing.

"This must have been a big decision for him."

Still silence.

"I think this has been bothering him for a long time. You know he's been sick an awful lot this past year or two, and Wayne never gets sick."

Her mother glanced up. Sensing a crack, Iris pushed on. "He's gotten all those colds and the flu. I think it's because he wasn't happy doing what he was doing. He probably didn't even realize himself that's why he was getting sick."

Mother Knoll stared at the far wall.

"Mom," she said, knowing the time had come, "you can either have a dead priest or a live son."

The two women locked eyes.

"You've let God have Wayne all these years . . ." Iris let her voice trail off.

Her mother held out her arms, and Iris kneeled and leaned into them. When they pulled apart, Mother Knoll finally spoke.

"You go on now and just leave me alone."

Iris nodded and slipped quietly from the room.

When their mother didn't appear at dinnertime, Iris put together some things from the fridge. Wayne ate little. He and his father spent the rest of the evening in front of the television. The mood was grim.

Wayne came downstairs the next morning after a fitful night's sleep, unsure of what he'd find. His heart sped up at the sight of his mother sitting at the kitchen table.

She looked up, patted the seat beside her, and said, "Now, Wayne, you sit down here and tell me all about this."

He cleared his throat and pinched the bridge of his nose to keep his tears from welling—no longer a priest, but his mother's son once again.

⊕⊕⊕

With the worst behind him, Wayne returned to Georgetown. One of his colleagues had heard that he was looking for a place to live and recommended an apartment complex outside the Washington beltway. Vienna wasn't far, but he'd need a car to get back and forth to the campus.

Until leaving the priesthood, Wayne's teaching salary went directly into the common treasury. Now he made arrangements to receive his first paycheck. Until that money arrived, the treasurer gave him $8,000 as a kind of severance pay. Wayne looked at the check and realized that the money had to cover not only a car, but his rent and furnishings.

As if sensing his thoughts, the treasurer told him to go to the storeroom on the top floor of the old residence building. Wayne could take anything he needed to furnish his new home. Later, when he walked around the musty attic and surveyed the dusty furniture, nothing seemed suitable for a man who was starting a new life. Rather than insult the Jesuits' generosity, he carried out a couple of well-worn Oriental rugs.

He spent the first fraction of his check at a local used-car lot. The beat-up Toyota with its drab gray paint job was a far cry from the sporty Cougar he'd owned at Harvard. The sedan's driver's seat was loose and sat at an angle, but unlike the Mercury, the Toyota came with no guilt.

The apartment his friend recommended turned out to be just what Wayne needed: cheap and convenient. The roomy two-bedroom place was within walking distance of a major shopping center. Months after leaving the Jesuit order, Wayne signed the lease and finally moved out on his own.

He arrived at his new home on a Friday afternoon. He left his suitcases on the floor and walked to a nearby hardware store. In the lawn-and-garden department, he found exactly what he needed. The redwood picnic bench was far cheaper than a couch and light enough to carry home by himself. It looked lonely in the empty living room until he rolled out one of the Jesuits' old rugs.

At the grocery store, Wayne pushed a cart through the aisles, overwhelmed by all of the choices. Everyone around him seemed to know exactly what they wanted, but he'd never cooked for himself and found the task a bit daunting. Finally, he took the easy way out and loaded his cart with cans.

He returned to his apartment just as the sun was setting. He stacked the cans in the empty cabinets, but set one aside for his dinner. When he tried to read the cooking instructions, the darkening kitchen made it difficult to see the writing, so he reached up and flipped the light switch—but nothing happened. Frowning, he moved the toggle up and down several times with the same lack of result. He crossed the kitchen and tried the switch on the opposite wall, but the overhead light remained off.

As the last of the daylight disappeared, Wayne walked from room to room testing the switches. The windowless bathroom in the back was a black cave.

He knocked on a neighbor's door and asked to use the phone. He felt too embarrassed to explain his problem to a stranger. Iris was an expert when it came to homey things. He dialed her number from memory and waited impatiently as it rang.

"Iris?" he said when she answered. "It's Wayne. I've moved into an apartment, and I can't figure out how to get the lights to come on."

"What do you mean?" Iris's scratchy voice squawked.

"Is there a special box or something?"

There was a brief silence, then his sister began, "Wayne . . ."

The tone of her voice did not bode well.

"What?"

"Did you call to set it up?"

Wayne pictured the light switch. "Set up what?"

Iris made a snorting noise in the back of her throat, then said, "Holy cripes, Wayne. You mean you didn't set up your electric? How dumb can you be?"

"Iris," he complained, "I've never done this before."

She sniffed. "Well, you'd think with all those degrees . . ."

Wayne said good-bye to his sister and called the electric company. After the fourth ring, a recorded voice announced that the business office was closed until Monday. He hung up the phone, returned to his apartment, and lowered himself onto the hard redwood bench.

In the emptiness of the living room, even the silence had an echo. He thought of the Jesuits at the residence, enjoying the warmth of each other's company and collegial conversation. It had been his own choice to give up that life, but only because he felt he *had* no choice. Now he was free to search for a companion to share his life with—to have and to hold and to love. It was that thought that he concentrated on.

He had no way of knowing whether there was a woman out there for him, and if there was, how long it would take to find her. He found great consolation in having classrooms full of students to brighten his days. In the meantime, Wayne spent his first weekend on his own completely in the dark.

Chapter 24

Anne set the brake, sat back, and took a deep breath. She'd made it to the parking lot of the Key Bridge Marriott, but Simon could drive from there. As she waited for her friend to join her, she glanced across the Potomac. The sight of the Georgetown campus made her think of the vision she'd had a couple of years earlier. She would have completely forgotten the incident, but every time she ran into Nicki, her friend asked, "Have you met your priest yet?"

Anne hadn't met a priest or anyone else, and that was fine with her. She led a full life with Rhonda, her classes, and her clients. The NSAC had recently granted her a charter to start her own church. The group of Spiritualists would continue to meet at the Burke Community Center until they found a more suitable venue, but the charter gave them an official organization.

A short, balding man emerged from the Marriott lobby and waggled his fingers at Anne. She got out of the car and greeted her longtime friend Simon Parker with a warm hug. He'd flown in from Lily Dale for a conference. When he called and invited Anne to join him for dinner, she agreed—as long as he drove into the city.

Simon took the wheel and followed Anne's directions downtown. The circuitous route took twice as long as Anne had anticipated, but nothing was easy to get to in Washington. They never did find the restaurant Simon had in mind, but a little Thai place near Dupont Circle turned out to be just fine.

After a tasty meal and time spent catching up on news of their mutual friends, the two got back in the car for the return trip to the hotel.

"Do you mind driving again?" Anne asked.

"Not at all, as long as you know the way."

Anne gave a nervous laugh and told him to take a right at the next corner.

They needed to get to Georgetown, where the Key Bridge would take them back to Roslyn. Anne recognized a few landmarks at first, but after several more turns, nothing looked familiar.

"What's that over there?" Simon asked. "Are we near Georgetown?"

Anne squinted to read the lettering on a sign.

"Oh my."

"What is it?"

"We're up near American University. I'm afraid I've taken us a bit out of the way."

Simon didn't seem to mind the detour, but as Anne tried to direct him where she felt they needed to go, they seemed to keep circling the same block. Every time they made a turn, they ended up in front of the same brownstone building.

Simon pulled the car into an empty space next to a fire hydrant and gently asked, "Do you mind if I look at the map?"

Anne wrinkled her nose as she handed it to him. "I'm afraid I've never been very good with directions."

He checked the street signs and ran his finger over the grid.

"Are we okay to park here?" Anne asked, looking at the hydrant.

"We'll just be a minute."

She peered nervously into the darkness.

A moment later Simon looked up from the map and chuckled. "We are a bit out of our way, aren't we?"

She gave a sheepish grin.

Half an hour later, they arrived back at the hotel. Anne apologized for her poor navigation, thanked Simon for the dinner, and said good night. She managed to find her way home and went straight to bed.

The next morning, the phone rang as she fixed her first cup of tea. She answered on the second ring.

"Miss Gehman? This is Detective Davis with the Washington, D.C., police department."

She flashed back to the previous evening. "Is something wrong, Detective?"

"Yes, ma'am, we have a bit of a problem. I understand you've done some work with the Queens police department in New York."

"That's right," she said, relieved that the call wasn't about her driving the night before. The officer's words, however, brought a flood of images instantly to mind. The case to which Detective Davis referred had been closed for over a year, but she could never forget her work with Joe Pepe. Nor, Anne was sure, would Joe ever forget her.

When 13-year-old Carla Sanders failed to return to her home outside Queens, her parents were willing to do anything to find her. They contacted Anne and had her flown to New York. Detective Pepe was doing a favor for a friend on the force when he picked Anne up at the airport. It wasn't even his case.

Anne was unaware that the chief of detectives had told his men not to pay any attention to the medium. When Joe sat down with her at the station, he humored her with friendly conversation, but Anne wanted to get down to business. She asked the detective if he had anything that belonged to the girl. Joe rooted around in his buddy's desk and found a large yellow envelope. Inside was a piece of Carla's clothing, and he handed it over. As soon as Anne touched the cloth, she knew that the girl had been murdered.

She described how an older boy had lured Carla into a house under the pretense of showing her some kittens. Anne clearly smelled a musty room and saw green walls, brown carpeting, and a metal bed with chipped white paint where the boy had taken the girl. When Carla refused the boy's sexual advances and screamed, he panicked.

Anne told Detective Pepe that the boy had strangled Carla, then stabbed her. She saw him loading the teen into a car with the help of his father and driving to some woods. Anne was sure the police would find the body in a spot that had water in some places but not in others. She sensed something big and round nearby, heard a roaring sound, and saw the image of people skating.

Anne could tell that Detective Pepe was skeptical, but she was pleased when he tried to walk her through the crime scene in her mind.

"Where are you?" he asked in a thick Queens accent.

"I'm right there with her," Anne said, keeping her eyes closed.

"Then can you go outside and look at the address of the house you see?"

The question caught Anne off guard. It hadn't occurred to her to do so, but she told him she'd try. She concentrated so hard that she began to sweat.

"I see five numbers," she said after a long pause. She gave them to Detective Pepe and added, "They may not be in the right order, but I'm fairly certain those are the right ones."

"Have you ever been to Queens before?" he asked.

"Never."

He shook his head. She had no way of knowing that street numbers in Queens were almost always a sequence of five numbers.

"All right, then," Joe said. "How about going to the corner and giving me the name of the street."

Anne traveled to the end of the street in her mind.

"I'm at the corner, but there's no sign."

He sent her to the other corner.

"There's no sign here either," she said, "but I see a big orange light."

The next day, the detective in charge of the case and the department's captain took Anne in a helicopter to survey the area. With all of the noise and vibration, she found it impossible to orient herself. Back on the ground, Anne got in a car with an inspector who drove her to the neighborhood of a young man they were watching.

When they got to the suspect's street, she pointed to a house.

"That's where the girl was murdered," she said with confidence.

The inspector looked at her, surprised. The suspect lived next door to the house she had singled out. The numbers on that house matched the five she'd seemingly pulled out of thin air the day before. The two went to the corner and discovered that there was no street sign, just as Anne had said. There was no sign at the other end of the street either, but there was a big orange light atop a fire alarm.

Anne noticed a young man coming out of the house she'd pointed to. "Look! That's him. That's the murderer!"

The detectives in charge of the case learned that the house Anne had singled out belonged to the suspect's grandmother. They got a search warrant and talked to the older woman. She confirmed that her cat had delivered a litter of kittens the same week that the victim disappeared. She then led police to a musty bedroom with green walls, brown carpeting, and a bed matching the description that Anne had given.

Joe Pepe got an irate phone call from the detectives on the case. They were convinced that he'd told Anne where the suspect lived.

"I didn't even know you had a suspect," Joe complained.

Because Anne had claimed to see the boy's father helping dispose of a body, the police interviewed the man. When they asked to see his car, he admitted that he'd had it crushed.

Anne tried to stay out of the detectives' way. She could tell that most of them thought she was some kind of sorceress. One lieutenant in particular had no confidence in psychics or mediums. He asked Detective Pepe to make up two photo arrays, with one containing a picture of the suspect. Joe placed the photo of the suspect in the number one position of the second array. The lieutenant told him to make it more difficult and move the photo to the fifth position.

When Detective Pepe called Anne in to his lieutenant's office to identify the murderer from a photo array, she didn't see the young man in any of the photos and said so.

"Try the second set," the lieutenant said.

Detective Pepe handed Anne six more photos. All of the men were of similar height and weight, but Anne immediately recognized the boy who had killed Carla.

"He's photo number five."

"No, that's not him," the lieutenant said. "Look again."

Detective Pepe stood off to the side, stone-faced.

"Lieutenant," Anne said, "you're a nonbeliever. The suspect's photo was originally in the number one position, but you had Detective Pepe move him to number five."

The two men exchanged a look as she turned and walked out of the room.

Joe Pepe followed Anne and apologized. He asked her to have a seat, curious now if she could do more than find missing people. He worked in the central robbery division and asked for her help with an armored-car robbery he'd been unable to solve.

Anne asked if he had any money bags from the crime that she could handle. He didn't, but he produced a photo of the vehicle that had been transporting the loot.

Once again, Anne hit pay dirt.

She described guards loading bags of money into a car with no backseat. The car was so weighted down that the auto's body was touching the back wheels.

"There's so much money!" she said. "It's so heavy they can't move it all."

Detective Pepe once again shook his head in wonder. Most people would think that money was light. Anne had no way of knowing that this booty was from a bus company's fares—a total of two and a half tons in coins.

Joe led her to a map of the city on the squad room wall. She moved her hand in a circle in front of it then pointed to where police would find the money. She heard the perpetrators speaking in a foreign language. She gave the names Juan and Toy, then corrected the latter to Tom, for no one went by the name of Toy.

"You need to be careful," she warned. "One of them is going to be shot three times in the stomach over money." She added that she couldn't tell which one would be shot because she saw him lying facedown.

Detective Pepe scribbled notes as she spoke. He wasn't quite sure what to make of such detailed information, but she'd been so accurate about the murder case that he could no longer dismiss her words outright.

"You're going to make an arrest in this case," she told him. "You have to find a girl whose name is either Lisa or Lydia. She has some kind of sister relationship to one of the guards. If you put the slightest pressure on her, she'll tell you everything you need to know."

Detective Pepe went looking for one of the armored car's guards—a Hispanic man named Juan. They found him at the Golden Gloves and questioned him. As Joe and his partner left the gym, the air suddenly erupted with gunfire. In all, six shots whizzed past. When it was over, a man lay dead, facedown on the pavement not 25 feet behind them, shot three times in the stomach.

The scene wasn't exactly as Anne had predicted. The dead man was the victim of a drug deal gone bad and had nothing to do with Joe's case. But Anne had seen a man being shot, and that was close enough for Detective Pepe. A week later, he knocked on Juan's door. A young girl answered and identified herself as Lisetta, Juan's sister-in-law.

Remembering Anne's premonition that a Lisa or Lydia would break under pressure, he pushed the girl against the wall.

"You're under arrest," he said. "You know all about the robbery of an armored car, and I'm taking you in as an accessory."

"I didn't do it!" Lisetta cried. "It was Juan and Toy!"

Lisetta drove the detectives to the spot where her brother-in-law and the other guard had taken the money. It was one block from the location Anne had picked from the map. They searched the area, but the robbers had already taken the coins to Atlantic City and laundered them for 70 cents on the dollar.

"I'm the most skeptical person you're ever going to meet," Joe later told Anne, "but you have some kind of very special power."

Unfortunately, Anne could see the future, but she couldn't change the past. One year after Carla Sanders disappeared, her skull was discovered by two game wardens in a large, round storm drain. The drain was in a swamp where children sometimes skated in winter. The roaring Anne had heard when she first handled the victim's clothing came from the traffic on the nearby interstate.

Joe Pepe later retired from the police force and became a private investigator. The former skeptic would call Anne as often as he could to help with his toughest cases, but he had to be careful; his paying clients didn't always go for all that psychic stuff.

As she reflected on these events, the voice on the phone pulled Anne back to the present. "We have a little boy from Washington who's missing," Detective Davis said. "We feel fairly certain that he's been abducted, and we're hoping you can help us find him."

Anne invited the officer to come to her house immediately. She advised him to bring a map of the area where the boy was last seen, along with a photo of the child and his family.

Detective Davis wasted no time. Anne answered the bell and found a large black man in dress slacks and a blue blazer waiting on her front step. He greeted her and held out a badge, then handed over the items she'd requested.

Anne took the detective to her kitchen where she spread the map on the table.

"This is Washington," she said, surprised.

"Yes, ma'am. We think he may still be in the area."

She studied the photos, then held her hand over the map just as she did when dowsing. She immediately experienced an image so fresh that she thought she might be reliving one of her own memories. When the vision failed to go away, she turned to Detective Davis.

"I know where he is."

The man blinked in surprise at the confidence in her voice.

"If you'll take me in your car," she said, "I can show you the exact place."

The image that had flashed in her mind was the area where she and Simon had gotten lost the night before. They'd circled the same block several times, not knowing there was a critical reason for Anne's confusion.

"It's up near American University," she told the detective as they pulled away from her town house. "I can't tell you exactly how to get there, but I'll know it when I see it."

Detective Davis followed her instructions. Half an hour later, Anne pointed at a high-rise. "That's part of the university, right?"

"Yes, ma'am."

"Turn left just up there."

She recognized a corner liquor store and a travel agency, then pointed at the fire hydrant where she and Simon had stopped to get their bearings. "There! Pull over right there."

He stopped the car in front of a three-story building that housed a shoe store on the ground floor.

The face from the photo the detective had brought appeared very clearly to Anne in front of the building that she'd noticed the night before.

"He's in there right now—on the second floor."

Detective Davis looked from Anne to the building and back at her again. He hesitated for a moment, then reached for the handset on his dashboard.

When he finished his radio call, he turned to Anne. "We have units on the way. I'd like to take you home first in case things get out of hand."

Back at her town house, Anne paced the living room, unable to concentrate until the phone finally rang. When it did, the news was good.

The police had found the little boy unharmed, exactly where Anne said he would be. He'd been abducted by a family member who was packing a suitcase when the police arrived. Anne realized that the child had been in the house while she and Simon were circling the block. At the time, she'd been embarrassed by her ineptitude with a map. As it turned out, somebody else was doing the navigating that night.

Sixteen-year-old Rhonda came home from school and slumped onto the couch beside her mother. She'd broken up with her first love and had been moping around the house for a week.

"Mom," she said, her lower lip quivering, "am I ever going to meet anyone who's right for me?"

Anne stroked her daughter's hair and tried not to smile.

"Let's see," she said, and closed her eyes. "Yes, in fact, I see a young man with red hair, and I feel you're going to meet him very soon."

"Really?"

"I see him very clearly."

Two weeks later Rhonda came home, her previous despair a distant memory.

"Mom, I met him," she said, her eyes gleaming, "and he has red hair just like you said!"

"What's his name?"

"Christopher St. Amant," she said with a dreamy smile. "Isn't that the most beautiful name in the world?"

Rhonda was such a pretty girl that Anne understood why boys would be drawn to her. When Anne was her age, people had commented on her good looks as well, but she'd rarely dated. She'd been too busy trying to support herself with three jobs.

Little had changed. She was now giving readings on weekdays at her office; teaching classes in Fairfax, Springfield, and Annandale in the evenings; and leading church services in Burke on Sundays. She was actively involved in the community. If Anne was grateful to Bob Robeson for something other than Rhonda, it was the fact that he'd helped her become more outgoing and independent. After moving to northern Virginia, she'd joined the arts council and was active with the membership committee for the Fairfax symphony.

That evening she was going on a date herself as a guest of Pat and Bob Smith. Pat was a friend and former client from Florida. The couple had invited Anne to join them for dinner with two friends, Jim and Betty Wright. Anne worried that she'd feel like a fifth wheel without a partner of her own, but Pat assured her that conversation wouldn't be a problem. After all, Jim Wright was the Speaker of the House of Representatives.

Anne looked forward to the evening, but she didn't know if she could keep up with the high-powered political talk she expected. She needn't have worried. The Wrights were as down-to-earth as any couple Anne had ever met. It felt strange to sit in an elegant restaurant across the table from a man whose smiling face and bushy white eyebrows regularly graced the front page of the *Washington*

Post, but Jim put her at ease from the start. He and Betty seemed far more interested in discussing her work as a medium than affairs on Capitol Hill.

Anne was surprised but pleased the next week when Betty called and asked to get together. A short while later, both Jim and Betty showed up for Anne's class on the philosophy of Spiritualism, which she now held at her church sanctuary.

To some of those in the large room full of students, the man in casual attire may have looked and sounded just like any Texan transplanted to northern Virginia. Others may have recognized the Speaker, but Anne didn't tell her students that one of their classmates was second in line to the President.

She stood before the rows of chairs, focused equally on all those present, and began her lecture on psychometry. She was halfway through the explanation about the energy of inanimate objects when she heard a man from the spirit world talking to her. Anne paused, dumbstruck. She'd know that voice with its distinctive New England accent anywhere, as would anyone who'd ever heard John F. Kennedy deliver a speech.

She listened to the words, aware that the students were waiting for her to continue. The voice most definitely belonged to JFK, and he had a message for his friend Jim Wright.

Anne glanced at the Speaker and decided to be discreet.

"I'm sorry for the interruption, but I'm hearing the voice of a spirit." She looked at the Speaker and said, "Jim, your colleague John is here, and he wants to say hello."

The congressman's eyes widened, but instead of looking confused, his face brightened into a large grin. He nodded vigorously and whispered in Betty's ear.

When the class let out, Jim took Anne aside at the back of the room. He told her that he'd known immediately she was referring to Jack Kennedy. For some reason, he'd dreamed of the man the past four nights in a row. When Anne passed along the greeting from John, there was no question in the Speaker's mind to whom she was referring.

On the way home that evening, Anne paid no attention to how fast she was driving as she pondered the special visit from Spirit.

She was halfway down a hill on Prosperity Drive when the same deep voice with the New England accent spoke to her again: *Slow down or you're going to be stopped.*

She hit the brakes just in time to coast past a patrol car hidden behind a bush where the road started back uphill.

The next week, Jim Wright came to the class straight from his office. He hadn't been trying to disguise his identity, but now the dark business suit he wore and the black limousine that dropped him off out front clearly tipped off his fellow students that he wasn't your run-of-the-mill cowboy.

The Speaker had never asked Anne to conceal who he was, but she hadn't wanted to make it an issue. With his high-profile arrival, however, she felt free to tell the world that JFK had sent a greeting to her famous student and had done her a favor as well. She'd been unable to save the young President years earlier when she'd foreseen his death, but on a lonely back road in northern Virginia, John F. Kennedy had saved her from getting a ticket.

Chapter 25

Wayne crossed the campus on his way from the faculty dining room to Old North. The English department had long ago moved from the modern library into the more historic building. A flash of motion caught his eye, and he turned to see a colleague from the philosophy department flagging him down.

"Good to see you, Bill," Wayne said as the two shook hands. "How have you been?"

"Excellent, Wayne. I wanted to tell you that I finally finished my book."

Wayne pumped his friend's hand yet again. "Congratulations! That's quite an achievement."

"Yes," the man said, then he gave a wry laugh. "Ten years of work, and I'm not sure that ten people will ever read it."

The two exchanged a knowing look. "Publish or perish" was a well-known expression in the world of academia. Professors were expected to author books in their area of expertise, but some subjects were so esoteric that the readership was often quite limited.

Wayne continued on to his office, acutely aware of his lack of published papers. He was the first to admit that he should have written more over the years, but he'd never found the will to sequester himself with a keyboard for months on end behind closed doors. His heart lay in teaching—in reaching his students and making a difference in their lives.

Fourteen years earlier, the same issue—his lack of publishing, not the fact that he'd left the priesthood—nearly cost him tenure. The board met during Wayne's seventh year on the faculty. Because he hadn't done much writing, the vote ended in a tie. The chairman of the English department argued that Wayne's abilities in the classroom far outweighed any lack of published papers. "Professor Knoll could teach the telephone book," the chairman said. In the end, the tie was broken in Wayne's favor by the college administration.

The line of students vying for a spot in his classes each semester proved that Wayne was doing something right. Early in their freshman year, English majors would hear about Professor Knoll's passion for literature and his penchant for anecdotes that kept students hanging on his words. Rather than simply lecture about Hemingway, he would bring *Death in the Afternoon* to life, grabbing a marker and diagramming a bullfight on a blackboard like a football coach explaining plays to his team. His class on American expatriate writers and another on Faulkner were so popular that usually only senior English majors were able to get in.

Wayne often worked his love of nature and the mysteries of the world into his class lectures. It was no secret to his students that he'd bought nearly ten acres of undeveloped land near Shenandoah National Park. The property lay on the western slope of Old Rag Mountain, just a few kilometers from one of the most popular day hikes in the park. One senior, a member of the outdoor-education program, suggested that Professor Knoll lead a camping retreat to his property. Wayne thought it would be a great way for his students to actually experience what Faulkner felt when writing *The Bear*.

The mountain property was Wayne's second big investment. After several years of paying rent for his apartment in Vienna, he realized how much money he was losing. Still hoping to have a family of his own one day, he invested in a large brick home next to a farm in rural Clifton, Virginia. The extra bedrooms upstairs and the efficiency apartment in the basement with a private entrance represented an opportunity for added income that he chose not to ignore. He found two bachelors to rent the bedrooms and leased the efficiency to a single woman in her late 30s.

Elisa Aelin-Fleener worked as a writer, producer, and director for the American Red Cross. With her curly dark hair, people often thought she was Greek, not Jewish. She'd recently broken off a seven-year relationship and was still grieving the loss of her father when she answered Wayne's ad. She took an immediate liking to her fatherly landlord. She found him warm and kind, and with his pastoral background, he seemed like just the right person to talk to as she worked through her troubles.

Elisa and Wayne spent many an hour in his large living room. They not only discussed each other's personal lives, but also deeper issues of philosophy and theology that helped Elisa better understand her Jewish roots. More than landlord and tenant, counselor and client, the two became friends. They enjoyed the same love of jazz music, and Elisa would often go into Wayne's stereo room and blast Kenny G throughout the house. Several times she invited Wayne to cookouts with her friends, and introduced him to women she thought he might like.

Wayne appreciated Elisa's matchmaking attempts, but his experiences with dating over the years hadn't proved fruitful. For a long while he struggled not to become discouraged, until a friend advised him that he was more likely to meet a woman by sheer happenstance than from his own efforts. He decided that he wasn't going to be desperate. He was doing the work he loved and he had a comfortable home, good friends, and a little piece of paradise in the mountains.

Knowing that he couldn't control his future, Wayne placed it in God's hands. He'd be thrilled if he found a woman with whom to share his days, but if he didn't, he would go to God as the single man he was. His stoic philosophy got him through the nights, but the inescapable fact remained: he'd left the priesthood for a life of love and intimacy, and at 58 years old, he was still on his own.

Chapter 26

Anne watched, relieved, as Rhonda left to drive her boyfriend to the airport. She'd been appalled when Rhonda asked if Chris could stay at their house while on leave from the Army. Yes, he was the red-haired young man Anne had seen in her daughter's future; and he was now a mature military policeman, while Rhonda was a freshman in college. They'd been sweethearts since high school and were planning their wedding.

That didn't mean he could sleep under the same roof as her daughter.

Rhonda was upset at her mother for being so maddeningly old-fashioned. Chris had been badly injured in a jeep accident while on duty in Germany. The open fracture of his femur almost cost him his leg. His family no longer lived in Virginia, and he had no place to stay while visiting her during his convalescence.

Ultimately, Anne relented. She set up a bed for Chris in the basement. She was sorry about his injury, but smug in the knowledge that his walker made it difficult for him to maneuver the stairs. Anne slept soundly, knowing that Rhonda was safe in her bedroom, two flights above her boyfriend.

One afternoon shortly after Chris went back to Germany, Rhonda walked into the kitchen while Anne was preparing dinner. She set her textbooks on the table and leaned against the counter.

"Are you feeling any better today?" Rhonda asked her mother.

"Not really," Anne replied. Her upper legs and lower back had been giving her problems lately, and she didn't know why. She'd seen several doctors, but none could determine the cause of her pain.

"At this rate, I'll end up with a walker like Chris."

At the sound of her boyfriend's name, Rhonda stiffened.

"Mom," she said, reaching into her purse, "there's something I need to show you."

Anne took the salmon-colored card Rhonda offered her and studied it closely. She recognized Rhonda's picture, but little else.

"What is this? And why does it say 'Rhonda St. Amant'?"

"It's my dependent I.D. card," Rhonda said softly.

Anne smiled. "That's very good. It almost looks real. Where did you have this made?"

Rhonda met her mother's eyes. "It's not a joke, Mom. Chris and I got married while he was here."

The room seemed to swirl around Anne, but she didn't have the luxury of slipping into trance. Instead, she remained fully in the present, trying to make sense of the unexpected news. Anne had been as excited as her daughter about her impending wedding, helping plan a fancy ceremony with Rhonda and her five bridesmaids in beautiful dresses.

"But why?" she asked, barely able to breathe. "What was your hurry?"

"Chris is coming up for orders soon, and if we waited too long, we wouldn't get stationed together."

Rhonda had been talking about joining the Army ever since Chris enlisted. Anne knew she wasn't really serious and dismissed her explanation with a wave of her hand.

"So you just went to the courthouse and got married?"

Even as she said the words, Anne knew they didn't carry much weight. She and Rhonda's father had done the same thing after a far shorter courtship.

Rhonda explained that Chris would soon undergo further surgery on his leg. Neither of them wanted a wedding with him in a wheelchair.

"When exactly did you do this?" Anne asked, trying not to show the depth of her disappointment.

"About a week after he got here."

She gaped at her daughter and ran through Chris's visit in her mind. "Do you mean that the whole time he was sleeping in the basement, the two of you were married?"

Rhonda nodded glumly.

Anne didn't know whether to cry or laugh. Life truly did have a circular rhythm. Just like Rhonda, she and Bob didn't tell anyone that they'd gone to the courthouse. Shortly after they were married, Anne decided to drive her mother to visit family in Michigan. Bob didn't want to be without her and went along.

Her mother had always wanted to go to Canada, so while up north the three traveled to Toronto, Ontario, Montreal, and back to Florida via New York and Washington. It became a honeymoon of sorts, but one not much different from Rhonda's. Every time the threesome stopped at a hotel, Anne would crawl under the sheets with her mama while her new husband slept in the next bed.

She chose not to share the story with Rhonda.*

Anne found it hard to concentrate in the ensuing days as she got used to the idea that her little girl was now a married woman. She also wasn't particularly happy that her new son-in-law was a soldier. While she found it honorable that he was serving his country, Anne had always been a pacifist. If people could only understand that they were on this earth to learn to love each other, there would be no need for guns and bombs.

Thus, she was completely unprepared two weeks later when Rhonda dropped her second bombshell: She'd joined the Army just like Chris and was shipping out within days. After completing her training, she and Chris would be stationed together 3,000 miles away at Fort Lewis in Washington State.

Anne was heartbroken. She'd never taken Rhonda's talk of enlisting seriously. In dire need of consolation, she phoned her mother.

"Mama," she cried into the receiver, "Rhonda is going to be a soldier!"

She braced for her mother's reaction, knowing it would be the same as her own. Instead, there was a pause, then the older Beatrice calmly asked, "What will she be doing?"

"She's going to be a medic or some such thing."

Her mother made a small humming noise. "Now Beatrice Anne,

everything will be all right. Rhonda will be doing God's work—giving healing just like you."

Anne stared at the phone, the wind taken out of her sails. When her mother put it that way, there was little more to say.

⊕⊕⊕

Anne sat at the table and watched her neighbor put the last of the groceries in the cabinets. Colleen had been a great help over the past year. Anne's back and legs had been giving her such problems that she simply couldn't get around like she used to. With Rhonda clear across the country now at Fort Lewis, she had no choice but to accept her neighbor's assistance.

"Is there anything else I can do for you today?" Colleen asked.

"No, thank you," she replied. "You've been wonderful, as always."

Colleen Gallaher didn't mind running errands for Anne or helping her around the house. It was the least she could do for her friend who was so obviously hurting. She'd seen Anne taking the five steps out front one at a time lately, clutching the railing for support. Like Anne, she found it distressing that none of the doctors could do anything about the near-constant pain in her back and legs, nor could Anne heal herself.

"You need to get home and take care of that beautiful little Connor," Anne said.

Colleen's eyes lit up, but she gave a wave of her hand. "Don't worry. Rob's got him."

Anne felt a motherly connection with Colleen's baby. She and Colleen had become quite close during her pregnancy, and Anne had been honored when Colleen asked her to be present for Connor's birth, but things hadn't exactly gone as planned. In the birthing room, Anne's energy became so linked with Colleen's that Anne suffered labor pains of her own. She sat down several times on the couch, doubled over with cramps, until she finally had to leave.

"So what's next for you?" Colleen asked.

Anne twisted her mouth. "I heard about a holistic institute in Puerto Rico that sounds promising. I'd have to put my work on hold, but I'm willing to drink wheat juice for a month and do whatever else they want if it means stopping this pain."

"I just wish there were something I could do."

"Believe me," Anne said as she held onto the table and stood. "You're doing more than enough."

Colleen frowned and stepped forward. "Don't get up. I can see myself out."

"It's all right. I'm going to the spa," she said. "The heat seems to help . . . for a while."

Anne sat on the wooden bench and leaned her head against the wall. The hot steam stung her nostrils and clung to her skin like a wet robe.

The door to the sauna opened. Anne sensed that someone had entered, but at first she couldn't see anything through the white mist. A figure moved closer and sat on the bench next to hers.

She could now see that the new arrival was a woman a bit younger than she, with dark, curly hair. She reminded Anne of some of the Greek women from Tarpon Springs who used to come to Cassadaga for readings.

"Hi," the woman said with a friendly nod.

"Good evening," Anne replied.

"God, this feels so good, doesn't it?"

"It's very relaxing," Anne replied.

"I haven't seen you here before. Do you work during the day?"

Anne didn't usually chat with people in the sauna, but the younger woman seemed to be in a talkative mood.

"Yes," she replied, "and some evenings . . . and weekends."

"Really? What do you do?"

"I'm a psychic medium. I do spiritual counseling and teach," Anne said.

The woman's eyes widened. "Really? That's cool."

The two chatted until the heat got too much for them. They stepped into the locker room and continued the conversation.

"I'm really interested in your work," the woman said. "Would you be willing to give me a reading?"

"I'd be happy to." Anne adjusted her towel. "Let me get you my card."

They both turned to their lockers and pulled out their purses.

"I'm Anne Gehman. My number's on here." She handed over the pink card. "I used to be in Fairfax, but I work out of my home in Springfield now."

"That's great. I live out in Clifton, so you're not too far from me."

The younger woman handed Anne a card with a large red cross embossed in the corner and said, "I'll give you a call real soon, Anne. It's been great talking with you." They shook hands.

"I'm Elisa, by the way. My name's on the card in case you forget: Elisa Aelin-Fleener."

Traffic was particularly heavy, even for northern Virginia. Elisa thought she'd left enough time to get to Springfield, but now she was running late. The light up ahead had already been yellow for several seconds when she pressed the accelerator to the floor. Her car shot through the intersection and she winced at the red light overhead. She didn't normally drive so carelessly, but she was in a hurry to get to her reading.

She turned off Old Keene Mill Road into a pleasant housing development. She pulled into a spot in front of a three-story town house whose number matched the one on Anne Gehman's business card.

Anne greeted her at the door and led her to a sitting room decorated in soft shades of pink and blue. They chatted for a few minutes, then Anne got down to business.

"I'm going to begin as I always do, with a prayer. And I'd like to hold a watch or a piece of jewelry that's imbued with your energy."

"Is this okay?" Elisa asked.

Anne took the watch Elisa handed her and held it in her palm. "This is fine."

Anne closed her eyes and said, "As we attune ourselves with that great Infinite Intelligence of the universe, that source of light and love, of wisdom and truth, we also invite the presence of our departed loved ones as well as our guides and our teachers."

Elisa watched and listened, spellbound. She'd heard about mediumship, but she'd never had a reading. Anne didn't fit her vision of a wild-eyed palm reader with a flowing dress and crystal ball. Instead, she impressed her now, as she had at the spa, with her grace, poise, and gentle nature.

"I'm very conscious of the presence of a man," Anne said. "He looks much like you through here." She drew her hands across her cheeks. "I get the feeling this is a father figure."

Elisa stiffened. Both of her parents were dead, and if mediumship were real, she was hoping for some kind of sign that her mother and father were not gone for good.

Anne concentrated, then frowned. "Did you run a red light recently?"

Elisa's mouth fell open. "On the way here."

Anne nodded. "Your father says you need to be more careful when you drive."

Elisa's throat constricted. *How could she have known that?* Was it really true that death wasn't the end? Had her father actually been with her on the way to Anne's house? Was he there with her now, just as Anne said?

"I'm getting the sense that your mother is on the other side as well," Anne said. "I'm seeing a woman next to your father now, and it feels very much like a mother."

Elisa nodded, unable to speak.

"She wants you to know that she likes the picture your sister hung in her stairway."

Elisa struggled to think. "I don't know anything about a picture."

Anne smiled. "Just remember that. It may mean something to you later."

An hour slipped past as Anne talked and Elisa listened, wide-eyed. She laughed when Anne told her that she'd marry a teacher in the Pacific Northwest. It was nice to think there was someone out there waiting for her after her recent breakup, but Elisa didn't know anyone in that part of the country and had no plans to go there.

When the reading concluded, Elisa stayed and chatted with Anne until she began to worry that she was overstaying her welcome. She reluctantly stood and got ready to go, but not before signing up for Anne's class and arranging to meet for lunch the following week. The things Anne had shared with her had exposed her to a whole new reality. Elisa wanted to get to know Anne better, both professionally and personally.

She walked to her car and reflected on the amazing encounter. She was glad they'd met at the spa and would see each other again. Anne was fascinating, and so pleasant to be with. She was one of those rare people you could sit and talk to for hours. Elisa smiled as she got behind the wheel. Anne was just like someone else she knew: her landlord, Wayne Knoll.

Chapter 27

Elisa and Anne sat across from each other in a cheery café. Elisa had been looking forward to telling her new friend about the accuracy of her first reading. She'd called her sister immediately after her appointment to find out if she'd hung a picture in her stairway, as Anne had said. Her sister confirmed that she'd found an old photo of her mother while cleaning out a closet. It was one of her favorites, so she'd had it enlarged and framed, then hung it in the stairway. When her sister asked how Elisa had known about the picture, Elisa told her that their mother had sent a message through a medium. Elisa's sister was stunned. To Anne, it was business as usual.

"It's wonderful that your mother was able to come through for you so clearly," Anne said as she took a sip of tea.

Elisa nodded. The knowledge that her parents were watching over her and heard her when she spoke to them made it far easier to tolerate their physical absence. Anne had been completely accurate about several major issues in her life, except one. Elisa knew no teachers in the Pacific Northwest, let alone one she was going to marry.

"I may not have met Mr. Right yet," she told Anne, "but I know someone that you have to meet."

"Oh, boy," Anne rolled her eyes and laughed. "Here we go again." Friends were always trying to fix her up.

"No," Elisa was insistent. "I honestly think he's your soul mate."

Elisa described her landlord Wayne as a kind, intelligent, good-looking man about the same age as Anne. She told her that he was a professor at Georgetown, and that he'd once been a priest. Anne flashed immediately to the vision she'd seen when crossing Key

Bridge with her friend Nicki. She'd never imagined that the man would be a romantic interest. The thought seemed so far-fetched as to be laughable.

Anne really wasn't interested in meeting anyone, let alone someone whose spiritual beliefs might clash strongly with her own. She'd played the dating game on and off through the years, but after her failed marriage, she was quite content to remain single for the rest of her life.

In spite of Anne's protests, Elisa didn't seem to want to let the issue drop. Anne finally relented and agreed to let her friend's landlord call her. After all, she figured, a phone call couldn't hurt.

Elisa stood in Wayne's kitchen, arms on her hips. It had been a full week since she'd knocked on his door to tell him about her friend. He hadn't seemed too excited when she insisted that he and Anne meet. She'd left Anne's number on the back of a matchbook, but saw no sign of it now on his counter.

"You haven't called her yet?"

He shrugged his shoulders.

"You have to call her," Elisa insisted. "I'm telling you: this woman is your soul mate."

"Mm-hm."

Elisa shook her head in frustration. She'd told Wayne that Anne was a medium and he'd seemed intrigued by the idea. She also told him how pretty she was, and how sweet. Elisa couldn't understand why Wayne wasn't rushing to the telephone. The man was no longer a priest, but he certainly lived like one.

"Look, here's her number again." Elisa wrote the seven digits on a scrap of paper. "Call her," she insisted as she finished her coffee and left.

The following Saturday, Elisa was back in Wayne's kitchen. The two repeated the dialogue like actors in a matinee that was playing two weekends in a row.

"Have you called her?" she asked.

"Not yet," he said with indifference.

Elisa's eyes flared. "Wayne, I am not leaving your kitchen until you call her."

Wayne liked when Elisa stopped by, but he didn't care to repeat the conversation again the following weekend. To get her off his back, he picked up the phone and punched in the numbers as she recited them from memory.

He felt relief when a recorded voice answered his call. At least now he'd done his duty and could forget about this woman whom Elisa was so insistent about.

He locked eyes with his tenant and cleared his throat. "Hello, Anne, this is Wayne Knoll. I know that Elisa has suggested that we meet, so I'm just calling to say hello."

He left his telephone number and hung up.

"Thanks, Wayne." Elisa smiled triumphantly. "You're going to be glad you made that call."

Wayne closed the door behind her and picked up the book he'd been reading. He returned to the living room and settled on the couch, sure that he would never hear from Elisa's friend.

Anne dropped her luggage inside the door and rubbed her thighs and back. The month in Puerto Rico had been relaxing, and she'd lost a few pounds from the diet, but the treatment had done nothing to ease her pain. The number of doctors she'd consulted was beginning to add up, as were the diagnoses. Not surprisingly, Anne always seemed to suffer from whatever the doctors specialized in.

The light on her answering machine blinked continuously. Two orange dashes indicated that the tape was full. She pushed the Play button and a woman's voice spoke.

"Anne, this is Sharon. Remember when your guide Sally came through last month and told me about some jewelry I'd misplaced? I didn't even know it was missing, but she told me to look in a suitcase that I'd packed for my trip to Tahoe. I thought you'd like to know that I found the jewelry inside it, just like Sally said. I'd already unpacked that bag and was going to return it to the store because it wasn't big enough, so I just wanted to say thanks to both of you."

Anne smiled and put a kettle of water on the stove as the messages continued to play. There were two from Rhonda, several from friends and church members, and countless others from people who wanted readings. She sat at the kitchen table and made a list of the calls she had to return. Most were from women, until a pleasant male voice turned her head.

"Hello, Anne, this is Wayne Knoll."

She didn't recognize the name until he mentioned her friend, Elisa. Anne shook her head and added his number to the long list. He sounded nice enough, but she had too much catching up to do to think about meeting someone new. She'd acknowledge his call when she got around to it, if only to please Elisa.

Wayne set his luggage on the floor and leafed through his mail. The trip to Kansas had been draining. Saying good-bye to one's father had to be one of the most difficult of life's many trials. It would take some time to get used to the idea that Adam Knoll, the strong man who had raised a family of nine children, was no longer around.

Wayne glanced at the answering machine. An orange "1" blinked back at him.

He didn't recognize the woman's voice nor her name until she mentioned Elisa. He cocked his head, surprised that Anne Gehman had returned his call. He hadn't expected to hear from her at all, and after several weeks went by, he'd forgotten about her completely.

He sighed and looked at his suitcases. It was hard coming home to an empty house after being in Victoria. His childhood home was always so full of love and activity, even in the midst of the sadness surrounding his father's death.

The display on the answering machine now read "0." He stared at the phone. Anne sounded nice enough and had gone to the trouble of returning his call. Figuring he had nothing to lose, he reached for the receiver and cleared his throat.

Chapter 28

Anne sat at the upstairs window and peered down at the street. Rhonda's former bedroom was the best spot from which to get a glimpse of her date before she actually had to face him. If she didn't like what she saw, she simply wouldn't answer the door.

She could just make out her own reflection in the glass and touched a hand to her hair. As much as she hated blind dates, she'd taken care to make sure she looked nice. Her soft curls framed her face just the way she liked, but these days there was almost as much gray hair as brown.

Why am I doing this? she wondered. *What have I done?*

The phone rang in her bedroom across the hall. She wrinkled her nose and glanced at the street. With a shake of her head, she left her perch and went to answer it. The caller was one of the board members from her church. Anne had no time for business and quickly ended the call. Just as she replaced the receiver in the cradle, the doorbell rang. Her hands curled into frustrated fists. Once visitors passed the stoop, they were too close to the house for a view from Rhonda's bedroom, and the front door had no windows. She'd have to take her chances with Wayne.

She started down the steps and was halfway to the foyer when her father's voice spoke to her as clearly as if he were waiting at the landing: *He's here now.*

Anne stopped. The fact that her father had spoken to her wasn't so unusual. She heard from his spirit every few weeks. It was always special when he visited, but this time it was the way he said the words that got her attention. His tone was such that Anne had the distinct impression her papa had already checked out her date—perhaps he'd even been involved in bringing it about. At the very least, she sensed that her father approved of the man waiting for her on the front steps.

She continued slowly to the foot of the stairs, praying that she could get through the evening without showing how badly she hurt. The pain in her back and legs increased with each passing day. She straightened her dress and took a deep breath. Unable to keep her date waiting any longer, she opened the door.

The first thing that struck her were his eyes, followed closely by his smile. There was a rugged manliness to his looks, but at the same time a gentle kindness.

She held out her hand. "Hello, I'm Anne."

Wayne hoped his palm was dry; his mouth certainly was. He had no trouble smiling as he returned Anne's handshake. Elisa had said Anne was pretty, but she was more than that . . . she was beautiful.

"I'm Wayne Knoll," he said. "It's a pleasure to meet you."

Anne invited him inside, and they exchanged pleasantries while enjoying some hors d'oeuvres that she'd prepared. They talked about Elisa and how they'd each come to know her, then moved on to discussing each other's family and hometown. They laughed at the stories of growing up with so many brothers and sisters and marveled over how they'd both left home at the age of 14.

Before the small talk could falter, Wayne suggested they move on to dinner. He drove her to Duangrat's, a Thai restaurant he enjoyed in Falls Church. He noticed as they crossed the parking lot that Anne seemed to be in some pain. When he asked her about it, she briefly described her troubles and the doctors' inability to diagnose the cause. Wayne had the feeling that she was downplaying her discomfort and found her self-discipline impressive.

They sat at a quiet table in a corner. Wayne stole furtive glances at Anne as she studied the menu. The bright red walls of the dining room seemed harsh in contrast with her soft pink dress and delicate features. She was so feminine . . . so poised . . . almost queenly in her bearing.

Anne ordered Panang chicken, then Wayne asked for the same thing, but with beef. She studied her date as he talked with the server. It was no wonder her father approved of him; he and Wayne shared the same type of energy.

They chatted comfortably while waiting for their food to arrive. Wayne hesitated to discuss anything too heavy or deep, but Anne's questions showed that she wasn't shy when it came to sharing her philosophy.

Wayne had never heard of Spiritualism and was intrigued to learn that Anne was the pastor of her own Spiritualist church. He listened as she described the building not far from where they sat where she led Sunday services and taught classes. He'd never met a medium and listened with great interest as she described her work.

The Catholic Church had no official position on mediumship; some priests were enlightened and others were suspicious. He was fascinated as she talked about her psychic abilities as if they were the most natural thing in the world.

She's so spiritual, he thought.

Anne had never spoken at such length with a priest. She understood that Wayne had left the priesthood, but it was obvious that his faith was still an essential part of his life. She'd worried that he might be rather rigid and that his Catholic beliefs would conflict with her own. From what she'd heard so far, his God was no different from hers.

Wayne talked with great enthusiasm about his students and his work as a professor. Anne listened, amazed, as he detailed the long years of schooling and the personal drive that had led him to Georgetown. She'd had no idea that the Jesuits' training was so intense. Now, even though he'd left the order, he had nothing but good things to say about it. She intuitively sensed how difficult it must have been for him to leave. He was clearly a sensitive man, and quite committed to helping others.

He's so spiritual, she thought.

The time passed far too quickly for both of them. They could have talked for hours more and would have done so were it not for the empty tables around them and the anxious smile from the manager waiting to turn out the lights.

Wayne drove Anne back to her town house and helped her up the steps to the front door. She thanked him for his assistance as well as for the lovely evening. He assured her that the pleasure was his; then he leaned in and gently touched his lips to hers.

"May I call you again?" he asked, his eyes hopeful.

"I'd like that very much," she replied with a shy smile.

Wayne sat in the hard pew and silently repeated the familiar words as the priest celebrated the sacred sacrament of the Eucharist.

"This is my Body . . ."

When Wayne had called Anne and suggested they meet again, he never imagined that she would ask him to take her to Mass.

Anne had been quite excited about going to the evening service in Olney, Maryland, to see Father John Lubey. Wayne had never heard of the man.

Father Lubey was known as "the healing priest." He discovered his abilities when a woman who was crippled by arthritis and confined to a wheelchair came to him for a special prayer and blessing one Sunday after Mass. Two weeks later, she walked into his church unassisted and pain free. Doctors had no explanation for the x-rays that showed her previously disintegrated hip to be perfectly sound.

Father Lubey's reputation as a healer spread quickly. He took no credit for his abilities. Instead, he claimed that every priest was a healer, but that God had called him to this special ministry.[1] Anne had seen him once before when she took a group of students from her classes to his church. Now, as her pain grew more severe by the day, her reasons for wanting to see the healing priest were far more personal.

Anne waited impatiently for the Mass to end and glanced around the large church. Her face brightened when she noticed her neighbor Colleen sitting in a pew with little Connor beside her in his car seat. Anne knew that Colleen was Catholic, and the two had talked about the special service with Father Lubey. She looked forward to introducing Wayne when the service was over.

She noticed a shift in energy and turned her attention back to the priest. Father Lubey had finished the Mass and now invited those in need of healing to come to the altar. Anne turned to Wayne as she struggled to her feet.

"Will you come, too?"

"Sure," Wayne agreed. He had never heard of the so-called slaying of the spirit and was fascinated to experience something new in a Catholic church.

They joined a crowd at the altar. Father Lubey warned those gathered that they might fall backward "in the peace of sleeping in the Spirit." One by one he moved through the line performing his healing ritual, and one by one the people toppled backward like dominoes. Spotters caught them as they fell and gently laid them on the floor.

The priest stopped in front of Wayne and laid his hands on Wayne's head. He said a prayer and gave him a blessing.

"Now, just let go," Father Lubey said.

Wayne fell backward, but returned to his feet within seconds. Later, he admitted to Anne that he had fallen on purpose because he felt it was expected.

When Anne's turn came, the healing priest stepped in front of her and laid his hands atop her head. He said a prayer and she repeated it along with him, wanting desperately to be relieved of her pain.

"Now, just let go," Father Lubey said.

Anne fell backward into the waiting arms of a catcher, but hers was no act. Everything around her disappeared in a swirl of purple.

It was one thing for Wayne to watch all of the strangers swooning, but he was taken aback at the sight of his date lying motionless on the floor. Like him, many of those who had fallen quickly got to their feet, but Anne remained as still as if she were dead. Wayne gathered her in his arms and carried her back to the pew. She didn't move a muscle.

My God, what have I gotten into? he wondered as he sat beside her. At the front of the church, Father Lubey continued with his ritual as Wayne glanced back and forth from his watch to the slack features of Anne's face. Finally, after 45 long minutes, she opened her eyes.

"Are you okay?" he asked anxiously.

She smiled and stretched. "Oh, yes. Wasn't that wonderful?"

"I'm not sure. What did you experience?"

She described the purple colors followed simply by blissful sleep.

"How's your pain?" he asked.

She moved about on the seat and grimaced. "It's still there, but let's give it time."

"Are you okay to go out to eat?"

Anne assured him that she was fine. They left their pew, but stopped at the back of the church to talk with Colleen.

"You look so happy," her friend whispered.

Anne glanced at Wayne and smiled.

On the way to dinner, Anne chattered excitedly about the experience with Father Lubey. Wayne was still a bit stunned by the unusual evening in a Catholic church. Only after they arrived at the restaurant did he regain his equilibrium. He'd chosen a rather upscale place, and they'd both dressed for the occasion. He wore a light blue sport jacket, and as if they'd coordinated their outfits, Anne had chosen a long, flowing dress of the same shade. When the waitress commented on what a good-looking couple they made, both of them smiled.

They enjoyed a delicious meal, complemented by more of the easy conversation they'd shared on their first date. Only when they got back in the car did Wayne feel awkward.

"I'm not quite sure which way to go," he said as he looked at the unfamiliar road signs.

Anne didn't know the area either.

He pulled onto the main road and started back the way they'd come from the church in Olney. When they came to a four-way intersection, neither knew if they should turn left or right. The wrong decision would take them to Baltimore, the opposite direction from where they needed to go.

"I'm going to pull into this Exxon station and get directions," Wayne said as he turned off the road.

Anne's eyes grew wide. "I don't believe it," she said loudly and stomped her feet on the floorboards with childlike excitement. When he was out of sight, she threw her head back and laughed, thrilled to have found a man who could ask for directions without hesitation. She'd known from their first date that Wayne was a remarkable person, but in that seemingly inconsequential instant she realized that she could honestly love him.

Inside the gas station, Wayne and the attendant figured out the best route to get him and Anne back to Virginia. As he returned to the car, he stopped and looked at her through the window. The grin on her face matched the way he felt within.

Their second date hadn't turned out exactly as he'd planned; Anne had spent almost half of it unconscious. But even more unexpected was the thought that had planted itself firmly in Wayne's mind over the preceding hours: he was going to ask Anne out again, and then—at some time, he didn't know how, nor did he know when—he was going to ask her to marry him.

Chapter 29

Traffic was heavy on Route 66 as Wayne and Anne left the city and headed west. At the speed they were crawling, they wouldn't get to the Shenandoah Valley until autumn. Wayne was looking forward to showing Anne his property and had waited until spring for her to see it in all its glory.

The countryside around Old Rag Mountain would be even more lush in a few weeks, but he wasn't sure Anne would be able to maneuver the trails by then. The healing with Father Lubey two months earlier hadn't changed a thing. Her pain was getting worse by the day.

He tapped his fingers restlessly on the wheel.

"Don't worry, Wayno, we'll start to move just up ahead."

Three lanes of cars stretched before them in what seemed like an endless sea of traffic, yet Wayne brightened at Anne's words. If she said they'd be moving soon, then they surely would.

He'd learned that lesson shortly after they met, when Jane Henderson, a friend of Anne's living in North Carolina, suffered a stroke. Jane asked Anne to come to her home to give her hands-on healing. Because Anne didn't like to drive, she asked Wayne to take her. He agreed to go if she could wait until he finished teaching on Friday afternoon.

The end of the work week was the worst possible time to head south on Interstate 95 outside of Washington. Traffic was heavy at the start, but slowed to a stop-and-go crawl before reaching Fredericksburg. Wayne knew they had hours yet to go and quickly grew impatient.

Anne patted his arm and said, "Wayne, it'll be all right. There's a tractor trailer at exit 33B that's blocking two lanes while the driver fixes a tire. There's only one lane open, but once we get past that, it'll be all clear."

He looked at her strangely. The exit she'd named was miles ahead. The radio had been turned off since they got in the car, so she had no way of knowing what was causing the congestion.

With the bumper-to-bumper traffic it took them more than an hour to get to exit 33B. There they merged with the rest of the cars into the far left lane and squeezed past a tractor trailer with a flat tire, exactly as Anne had described.

Wayne had heard plenty of stories about Anne's abilities by now, but hearing them and seeing for himself were two different things. He was so impressed with her prescience that he pulled into a convenience store on the way home and bought ten lottery tickets for Anne to fill out. She had to explain to him later when the numbers she'd chosen weren't even close to winning that her gifts never seemed to work for personal gain.

Now, just as she'd predicted, the traffic heading west toward the mountains began to ease. It thinned with every passing mile until they were back up to speed.

"You've told me so many stories about your readings and your crime solving," Wayne said to Anne. "What was the most memorable incident you recall?"

"Oh, my," she stared at the road ahead. "I don't know. I appreciate all of them as gifts from Spirit, but none seems more special than another."

"You surely do have a gift from God," Wayne said. "But were there any that made even you sit back and say, 'Wow'?"

She thought a moment longer, then said, "There was one. It was back in Cassadaga when I helped reunite a brother and sister who had been looking for each other for years."

Anne recounted the story of the back-to-back readings that had been orchestrated by the clients' mother in the spirit world. Anne's voice cracked as she told about the cancelled appointment that was filled by just the right person. By the time she got to the part about the siblings' teary reunion on her porch, Anne was crying just as hard as she had back then.

"It was just so beautiful, Wayne." She wiped at her eyes and affirmed, "That was definitely a 'Wow' moment."

"These experiences are all so new to me," he said. "You've opened up a whole different dimension of reality I never knew existed, yet it's entirely consistent with my beliefs."

They continued to chat until they arrived at the outskirts of Shenandoah National Park. The ride had taken just over two hours, but surrounded now by the tall trees and thick foliage, they seemed a world away from Washington.

Wayne turned down a small blacktop road past a sign pointing toward Whiteoak Canyon Trail. He pulled over at an unassuming dirt driveway blocked by a chain between two posts.

"This is it," he told Anne with an excited smile. "I'll be right back."

He hopped out of the car, unhooked one end of the chain, and got back behind the wheel. The tires crunched on the dirt, and they climbed steeply as they moved away from the paved road.

The trail deteriorated into two narrow tracks running between the trees until they arrived at a clearing. Wayne would have normally hiked to this point from the blacktop, but he didn't think Anne could handle the climb in her current condition. He watched in frustration as she got out of the car, grimacing from the pain. He had learned from his experience with the lottery tickets that her gifts didn't work for personal gain, but it didn't seem right that she could heal others, but not herself.

"Oh, Wayne, it's beautiful!" she exclaimed. "I can see why you love to come here."

"This is where I always pitch my pup tent," he said, indicating a spot not far from a circle of stones around a bed of black cinders.

"It's so peaceful and quiet."

Indeed, the property had been Wayne's sanctuary for years, the perfect place for contemplation. He'd planned to build a cabin on it some day, but it had never seemed the right time to spoil the natural setting.

"Did I tell you about the time I saw the buck?" He described being awakened from a deep sleep at four in the morning by an awful sound. He'd peered through the mesh window of his tent and saw an enormous buck with six or seven does milling about. The sound he'd heard was the large stag's mating call.

"He was looking right at me from just over there," Wayne pointed toward the trees. "I could only hope that he wasn't confused!"

Anne laughed at his story as the two of them spread a blanket on the ground. She'd prepared a picnic lunch for the trip and set it out now at their feet.

"Are you hungry, Wayno?"

"Starving!" His appetite always seemed to increase in the fresh mountain air.

He helped Anne onto the blanket, then sat beside her.

"What is all this?" he asked as she took the lids off the plastic containers.

"I've made some wonderful vegetarian dishes that I know you'll love."

He blinked. "Vegetarian?"

"A nice healthy salad and some delicious barbecued tofu."

"Tofu."

"You've tried tofu, haven't you?"

"Does it come in a can?"

Anne laughed at his humor, but Wayne was only partly joking. He never had taken the time to improve his cooking skills. Canned food was still at the top of his grocery list. Since he'd met Anne, however, his diet had improved significantly. She was a wonderful, creative cook. Her meals were as much a feast for the eyes as they were for the taste buds. If she recommended barbecued tofu, then he was willing to try it.

He pierced a spongy square and popped it into his mouth.

Anne waited expectantly while Wayne chewed. Somewhere in the distance a twig fell through the branches. A squirrel skittered across the leaf-littered clearing. Wayne pushed the tofu around his mouth, not sure which was worse: the taste or the texture. He eyed the fire circle, wondering if he could spit the food out there, but Anne was watching him so hopefully he didn't dare. Finally, he forced it down and gave her a weak smile.

"Do you like it?" Anne asked.

"Let's put it this way," Wayne said as he reached for a drink. "I love you, and I'm thrilled to be here with you, but that was not a 'Wow' moment."

⊕⊕⊕

"Turn right, here." Anne pointed. "See? There's the gate." Her excitement grew as they approached the familiar entrance to Lily Dale. She'd been going there for decades, yet now she tried to view the Spiritualist camp through Wayne's eyes as he saw it for the first time.

"I hope you like it," she said. Her legs were bouncing again, if only slightly, and she had the distinct urge to giggle. If Rhonda were in the car, she would surely be rolling her eyes.

Just a few weeks earlier, Anne and Wayne had flown to Seattle, where Wayne had been asked to teach a class on writing to a group of federal employees. Anne had jumped at the chance to go with him. Rhonda was still at Fort Lewis with Chris, and they were expecting their first baby in just a few months.

Anne had been nervous, yet excited to introduce Wayne to Rhonda. They took Rhonda and Chris out to dinner their first night together. Anne thought things were going well until Rhonda pulled her aside when they got back home.

"Mom," she said, "what is *wrong* with you?"

Anne was taken aback. She had no idea what Rhonda was talking about.

"You're all giddy and giggly," her daughter continued. "I've never seen you like this."

Rhonda couldn't help but notice how her mother and Wayne kept looking at each other. Even though it had been years since her parents divorced, she still found it hard to see her mother enjoying the presence of another man. It was obvious that Anne and Wayne had a lot of fun together, but Rhonda also sensed a mutual respect that made it hard for her to dislike him. In spite of their apparent compatibility, there was one thing that Rhonda found hard to believe.

"I can't get over the fact that you're dating a priest," she admitted. "What the heck do you talk about?"

Anne did her best to explain that while they did have differences in their beliefs, their mutual love of God and the central role that faith played in their lives overcame all else. Anne knew that the tenets of Spiritualism crossed all religions. She hoped that with time, Wayne would see that he could maintain his core beliefs, yet expand them to include a greater reality.

Wayne's family found it equally hard to believe that he'd date any woman who wasn't Catholic. When he took Anne home for his family's annual Fourth of July reunion, his mother pulled Anne aside and sat her down for a serious talk. Even though she was now bent over from osteoporosis, Mother Knoll exuded a palpable inner strength.

"Now, Anne," she said gravely, "I can see that Wayne loves you, but you're not Catholic."

Anne returned the smaller woman's gaze. Mother Knoll knew that Anne was in her 60s and was the pastor of her own church. Unperturbed, Anne nodded her head and said, "Yes, Mother Knoll, but I promise to raise all of our children Catholic."

There was silence for a moment, then the older woman's head went back and she let out a belly laugh that was heard throughout the house.

Now, as they approached the entrance to Lily Dale, Anne pressed her hands on her thighs and forced herself to calm down. She waved at the guard as they passed through the gate.

"Turn right again and follow the road along the water."

Wayne slowed to avoid bouncing too hard through the ruts. "I can certainly see why you like it here," he said as they came to Cassadaga Lake.

"And there's my house," Anne said, pointing to the little white cottage with the pink trim.

"Oh, Anne," Wayne said as he got out of the car. "It's perfect for you!"

"It's kind of small."

"Don't be silly," he said, turning to face the peaceful lake. "With a view like this, you have all you need!"

They went in through the back door off the carport. Anne removed her shoes and asked Wayne to do the same, then they stepped into the cheery kitchen. Anne had upgraded all of the appliances, but the small room still had an old-fashioned feel. She led him on a tour through the first floor. The formal dining room had a large table with a lace cloth that matched the thick, white carpeting. The living room beyond was color coordinated with a lavender couch and armchairs that matched the floral wallpaper.

Wayne gazed around as if entranced. "I'm so impressed," he said. "You're a genius at décor."

She looked up at him through her eyelashes. "It's not very manly, I'm afraid."

"No, but it's so *you,* and that's what makes it perfect."

"This is where I give my readings," she said as she led him to a small parlor at the foot of a staircase just inside the front porch.

Two wooden armchairs with lavender cushions sat on a shiny floor of checkered tiles in pink and white. A large oil painting in an ornate gold frame hung on a pink wall across from the chairs.

"This is you!" Wayne said, taking in the portrait.

"Many years ago." The painting portrayed her in a white gown with gold-trimmed sleeves. Thick brown curls swirled around her face.

Portrait of Anne.

He gave her a kiss and said, "You're even more beautiful now."

Anne waved away his compliments and led him onto the enclosed porch. "This is my favorite place to sit."

"I can see why." An assortment of ferns framed a white wicker couch and chairs. The inviting pink cushions matched the pink floor and ceiling. Wayne plopped onto a chair and gazed through the wall of windows at the lake.

"I could sit here forever." he said, shaking his head. "It's simply magnificent."

"Yes, but it's also rather cold." Anne wrapped her arms across her chest and shivered. She didn't usually travel to Lily Dale in the fall, but she'd wanted to bring a carload of things to the house. The cool air reminded her why she spent only summers in western New York. "Come into the kitchen where it's warmer, and I'll fix us something to eat."

Wayne moved to a straight-backed chair at the wooden table along the kitchen wall. Anne poked about in the cabinets and set a few containers on the counter.

"I think I can make something from this," she said, "but first, if you'll excuse me, I have to use the bathroom."

She left Wayne sitting at the table and disappeared through a door next to the refrigerator. Seconds later the door opened and she stared pointedly at Wayne.

"I don't have many rules for my house," she said, "but one is: if somebody goes into the bathroom, whoever is in the kitchen has to either sing, whistle, or leave." With that, she smiled, went back in, and closed the door.

Wayne did a double take. He wasn't sure if Anne was serious or not until her voice rang out from behind the door.

"Sing, Wayne, sing!"

Unsure whether to laugh or drive back to Virginia, Wayne shook his head, then cleared his throat. He didn't know what he was supposed to sing, so he chose an old German love song. His father used to serenade his mother with the tune in his beautiful tenor voice, and it was one of Wayne's favorites.

"*Du, Du liegst mir im Herzen,*" he began. "*Du, Du liegst mir im Sinn . . .*"

The door to the bathroom swung open, and Anne stepped out, tears streaming down her face. She stared at Wayne, who looked back at her, puzzled.

"Did I do all right?" he asked.

"More than all right," she said, wiping away her tears. "You sounded exactly like my father when he used to sing that song to my mother."

Anne held on to the wall as she took one painful step after another toward the waiting room. Wayne jumped up to help her. The doctor she'd just seen was his primary-care physician. Wayne had prayed that he'd be the one to finally diagnose the cause of Anne's pain. From the look on her face, he knew they'd hit another dead end.

"Do you know what that man said to me?" Anne fumed as Wayne helped her into the car. "He said that since I've been to all these specialists and no one has been able to help me, he wants me to see a psychiatrist!"

"Oh, Anne." Wayne had never seen her so angry.

"I tore his referral sheet into pieces and threw it right back at him. I told him that if I were a man, he never would have suggested such a thing. He would find the cause!"

Anne was at her wit's end. She'd been suffering for seven years, but things had gone downhill frighteningly fast in the last 12 months. Wayne and Colleen were the only ones she allowed to know how much she was hurting. She still gave readings at her house, but she never let her clients see her walk or stand. She couldn't understand why her prayers were never answered, other than to make her more empathetic when dealing with others in a similar situation. She now understood firsthand the devastating effects of chronic pain. It had reached the point where Wayne had to push her around the grocery store in a wheelchair.

Wayne watched helplessly as Anne slipped into a deep depression. She'd shared with him the story of how she deliberately overdosed on pills as a teenager and had been drawn to the beautiful light. He was afraid that the woman he wanted to spend the rest of his life with would find that light irresistible now in the face of such physical agony.

"I just want to die," she told him one day, confirming his worst fears. "I don't want any more doctors, and no more diagnoses. I'm just going to sit here. If I get well, that's fine. If I die like this, that's fine, too. I'm ready."

"Please, Anne," Wayne begged. "Don't talk like that."

He came home from the university one day and told her about a chiropractor he'd heard of in Fairfax. Dr. Bill Erbe was supposed to be something special.

Anne was adamant. "No more doctors."

Wayne begged, sweet-talked, cajoled, and coerced until Anne finally relented.

On the day of her appointment with Dr. Erbe, Wayne carried her in his arms from the car to the exam room. The doctor greeted them with a firm handshake. His movie-star looks would make most women smile, but Anne was not in the mood.

Dr. Erbe got straight to business. He took a complete history of Anne's symptoms and what she'd been told by others to date. He had her go through a range of motions and moved his hands over her spine and joints. When he finished his exam, he simply said, "I want you to come back on Thursday and we'll discuss the next step."

Wayne carried Anne back to the car where she sat tight-lipped and somber. She believed in chiropractic and had been to several chiropractors, but all she could think was: *Here we go again.*

She didn't want to return on Thursday, but Wayne insisted. He carried her once more into the exam room. When Dr. Erbe entered, this time his smile was gone.

He put his arm around Anne's shoulder and said, "I really prayed about this, and I meditated."

What kind of doctor would admit that? Anne wondered. She shared a look with Wayne.

"I know what severe pain you have," Dr. Erbe continued. "I can see it, and I can feel it. Unfortunately, I can't help you."

Anne had started to feel hopeful, but the doctor's last words brought her hopes crashing down.

"Your problem is not within the scope of chiropractic. You need to go to a hip specialist."

"Hips?" Anne was confused. "My pain is in my legs and back."

The doctor nodded. "You have a congenital hip defect and a synovial cyst. You need a hip specialist."

"But how do you know that?" Wayne asked. "You didn't even take any x-rays."

Dr. Erbe shrugged. "The specialist will want to take his own x-rays. I don't want to waste your money by doing them twice."

What kind of doctor would think like that? Wayne wondered. He shared a look with Anne.

Dr. Erbe explained that he had used a simple process of elimination based on his experience and knowledge of applied kinesiology. When Anne asked if his prayers had helped with the diagnosis, the doctor was equally nonchalant.

"I pray about all of my patients. I pray for wisdom and for divine intervention to help them, and I always thank God for the tools he's given me."

Anne's intuition had failed her with all aspects of her painful problem until now. As Wayne carried her out of Dr. Erbe's office, for the first time she had a good feeling about the visit.

Wayne immediately made a call to the Georgetown University Medical Center and asked to be connected with their best hip specialist. The secretary for Dr. Bryan Evans came on the line, and Wayne explained the problem. He didn't know if his status on the faculty would help Anne be seen any sooner, but he was willing to do anything to get her help as quickly as possible. The secretary gave Anne the doctor's next available opening.

On the day of her appointment, Dr. Evans greeted Anne and Wayne in the waiting room. He asked Anne to walk along the wall and then to walk toward him. He studied her gait as she did so, then politely asked if she minded having some x-rays. Feeling optimistic for the first time in months, Anne readily agreed.

Wayne joined Anne in a treatment room as they waited for the results. Dr. Evans walked into the room and slid the x-rays onto the light box.

He turned to face them and said, "There's no diagnostic dilemma. Your problem is clear."

He pointed to the x-ray where a white bubble as large as an orange stood out like a wine stain on a white shirt.

"You have a synovial cyst as well as a congenital hip defect."

His diagnosis was identical to Dr. Erbe's.

"This is where your hip socket is supposed to be," he said, pointing at the photo, "only you have no socket; it's just bone on bone."

Anne and Wayne grimaced. It hurt just looking at the x-rays. The problem was so basic that any first-year medical student could have diagnosed it, yet because the pain was in her legs and back, none of the many doctors she visited had thought to x-ray her hips.

"So, I guess I don't need a psychiatrist after all," Anne said wryly.

"I don't know how you even walked in here," Dr. Evans said. "You need a hip replacement, and the sooner the better."

Wayne wanted Anne to schedule the operation immediately, but she refused. After seven years of misdiagnoses, she'd lost all trust in doctors. She insisted on seeing two more hip specialists. Only then, after the additional physicians confirmed Dr. Erbe's and Dr. Evans's findings, did she agree to have the surgery.

It was a warm morning in early September when Anne and Wayne sat at the sunny breakfast nook in her kitchen and discussed the next step. Wayne had always worried about finances, and now, with Anne facing a sophisticated and complicated operation, he expressed his concern.

"I fully respect your work," he said, "but I'm a college professor. Your source of income is 'full-time medium.'"

Anne crossed her arms. "I have perfectly good medical insurance."

"Yes, but mine is better. If we were married, you could have the benefit of my insurance and have your surgery at Georgetown."

After her painful divorce, Anne had pushed all thoughts of marriage out of her mind. With Wayne, she'd simply allowed herself to enjoy the fun, the friendship, and the wonderful romance. Now, she cocked her head. "Wayne, are you proposing to me?"

He threw out his hands. "I've known I was going to marry you since our second date. As far as I'm concerned, it's always been a done deal."

Anne rolled her eyes. "This is not very romantic, Wayno."

"Romance can wait," he said. "Your health can't."

Anne laughed. "I can tell you're a Virgo . . . very practical."

"We can have a fancy wedding later, but let's just go to the courthouse, then schedule your surgery right away."

Anne leaned back and inhaled. Her first husband had swept her off her feet and carried her to the courthouse. Now, because of her hips, Wayne might have to carry her as well. But this time, she'd have no doubts that she was doing the right thing.

"All right. Let's do it."

"You'll marry me?"

"Of course I will. I love you, Wayne."

"And I love you," he said as he helped her to her feet.

He wrapped her in his arms and held her there, savoring the feeling he'd longed for so many times during his lonely years as a priest and beyond. He could have stood there lost in the moment for an eternity, but he stepped back and said, "Let's call Dr. Evans."

The same single-minded focus that had made him a professor at Georgetown University was going to get his *wife* into Georgetown Medical Center.

Chapter 30

The newly married couple walked out of the courthouse into the bright September sunshine. Wayne hadn't stopped grinning since they walked in. *This is my wife,* he thought as he gazed at his beautiful bride, the answer to his prayers.

Neither he nor Anne had told anyone they were going to be married. They planned to have a church wedding presided over by both a Spiritualist and a Catholic priest after Anne recovered from her surgery. In the meantime, the short secular ceremony at the Fairfax County Courthouse united them legally, if not as romantically as Anne had hoped. They didn't know the witness who signed their license, but the justice of the peace was the same woman who had married Chris and Rhonda.

Anne slipped an arm around Wayne's waist as he helped her down the courthouse steps. Her smile faltered as a troublesome thought ran like a current of energy from her arm to her brain. She sensed that something wasn't right with Wayne's health . . . something under her hand, near his kidneys. She knew that Wayne had suffered from kidney stones over the years and wondered if what she was feeling was more of the same.

She pasted the smile back on her face and pushed her worries to the back of her mind. Nothing was going to put a damper on their wedding day.

Wayne lay his book on his stomach and looked at Anne resting beside him in the bed. He had so much to be grateful for. Her operation at Georgetown had been a complete success. Within three weeks of their wedding, Dr. Evans had removed the enormous cyst and replaced Anne's hip socket with a fully functional artificial joint. The postoperative pain was minor compared to the agony she'd suffered beforehand. Thanks to the surgery, Anne had gotten her life back overnight.

Wayne smiled at how peaceful she looked, until he noticed her arms and legs twitching. He thought she might be having a bad dream and wondered if he should wake her. Then, with her eyes still closed, Anne's lips parted and she spoke.

"Good evening, Wayne. We bring you greetings from Spirit."

We? He shook his head, startled. As feminine as Anne was, the voice he heard was higher in pitch than hers, almost girlish. The tempo was clipped—quite unlike Anne's normal cadence.

"We come to tell you that we are directing the instrument to do the work of Spirit on Earth—to bring humankind to spiritual awareness."

Wayne suddenly realized that he must be witnessing a visit by Anne's spirit guide, Sally. Anne had told him about the young woman who often spoke through her while in trance. The voice was exactly as Anne had described it, and Anne was most definitely in some kind of altered state.

"Are you Sally?" he asked tentatively.

"Our instrument often refers to us in this way."

It was the second time that Sally had used the word *instrument,* and Wayne realized she was referring to Anne. He'd had some unique experiences as a Jesuit, but this was quite a show. He didn't know how to react—what to say. Sally took the burden from him.

"Do you have any questions for us?" she asked.

Wayne had the fleeting image of a bottle lying on a sandy beach, and Sally was his genie. He sifted through his thoughts, realizing that he could ask anything he wanted. He thought about his finances—a perennial concern after so many years of giving all of his money to the Jesuits.

"Will we be able to pay our bills?" he asked, feeling somewhat foolish.

Sally gave a cheerful, high-pitched laugh and said, "Out of abundance."

Wayne listened, enthralled, as she went on to say a prayer not just for him and Anne, but for all creatures on Earth. He couldn't help but feel that Sally's reality was far greater than his own.

"We will take our leave now," she said. "Our instrument's energy is diminishing."

Wayne realized that in order to speak through Anne, Sally's spirit needed to tap into Anne's physical energy. Anne's strength ran down like a battery the longer Sally used her.

He waited, unsure who would speak next: Anne or Sally. The room remained quiet, then Anne's arms and legs began to twitch just as they had before Sally appeared. After about a minute, her limbs grew still; and she breathed in and out in the slow, steady rhythm of sleep.

Wayne set his book on the nightstand and turned out the light. Sleep didn't come as quickly for him as he stared into the darkness, reliving the unusual incident. He'd known when he married a medium that he would be exposed to new experiences, but he hadn't counted on Sally showing up uninvited. Wayne couldn't help but chuckle. He was just getting used to sharing his bedroom with Anne, only to find that his bed was more crowded than he'd expected.

Anne bustled about, moving almost effortlessly from the stove to the refrigerator to the table. During her recovery from the hip replacement, she'd slept in a hospital bed in the kitchen. The bed was gone now, and she gave thanks every day for her newfound mobility.

Her face lit up with pleasure at the sound of the front door opening and closing. Wayne was home from the university. "Home" these days was either his place or hers. They'd agreed to shuttle back and forth until they found a house to purchase together.

"Hello, Wayno."

He returned her kiss, but Anne instantly sensed his concern.

"We need to talk about something," he said as he took her hand and led her to a chair in the breakfast nook.

She lowered herself slowly onto the seat, bracing herself for the bad news his words portended.

"The results of my physical are back," he said. "The doctor did a sonogram of my left kidney and discovered a mass."

Anne flashed back to their wedding day when she'd put her arm around his waist and knew that something was wrong. She'd been preparing herself since that day for this moment.

Wayne cleared his throat. "He says it's almost certainly cancer."

Anne sat back hard, as if pushed against the chair. She was relieved that the tests had revealed what was wrong, but she'd never expected to hear the dreaded "C" word.

"What are they going to do about it?" she asked weakly.

"They're going to try to remove it surgically."

"And then?" She refused to allow herself to think about the treatments that often accompanied such a scary diagnosis.

"Then we'll see," Wayne said. He laid a hand atop Anne's. His fingers were cold, but Anne felt a comforting sense of reassurance that came not from Wayne, but from Spirit. As worried as she was, she had to trust that feeling, just as she'd done all her life.

The surgeon wanted to operate as soon as possible. Wayne delayed the surgery only a few weeks until the end of the fall semester. As soon as the last of his classes was finished, he entered the Georgetown hospital. A year earlier, it had been Anne in the bed with Wayne at her side. Now, their roles were reversed.

The wait during his surgery was torturous. Anne prayed continually, yet she couldn't help but wonder at how the world worked. She'd been an instrument of healing for countless others during her life, yet she'd been unable to heal either herself or her husband.

Finally, the doctor emerged from the operating room. He pulled the surgical mask from his face and revealed a tired smile. Anne's legs went weak with relief as he told her that they'd gotten all of the cancer and saved Wayne's kidney.

After a few days of recuperation in the hospital, Wayne was free to go home. There was no need for radiation or chemotherapy. The best remedy, according to the doctor, was to go someplace warm to heal.

Wayne envisioned Hawaii with its healing sun, sea, and sand. He had a student whose parents owned a restaurant there, and they'd issued him a standing invitation for dinner.

"We'll take them up on their offer," he said.

As soon as they got home from the hospital, he spread a map of the Hawaiian Islands on the table.

"I can't find the name of their town on my map," he said as his eyes scanned the tiny print.

Anne, who'd never been to Hawaii, stepped to the other side of the map and held her hand above it. She moved her arm in a clockwise circle several times, then plopped her index finger onto the paper.

"Is this it?"

Wayne looked where she was pointing and blinked up at her in surprise.

"That's it!"

She'd simply been showing off, hoping to impress him, and now she beamed. Still, the irony wasn't lost on her. She had succeeded with a simple trick, but had been unable to use her gifts when the stakes were far more critical.

The three weeks they spent on Maui proved to be the best possible prescription. For the first week, Wayne moved slowly and didn't have the strength to do much more than lie on the beach. The second week, he was well enough to enjoy dinner with his student's parents. They spent the third week snorkeling with the tropical fish in Hanauma Bay and touring the islands like a couple of honeymooners, thanks to a full dose of what Wayne called "Anne Sunshine."

⊕⊕⊕

Anne stood on the porch at Lily Dale and looked out over the lake. She'd just arrived from the airport in Buffalo. It felt strange to be at the little pink cottage alone, but Wayne had stayed back in Virginia. They'd been going back and forth all summer, but now the fall semester had started at the university. Wayne had no choice but to stay home to teach while Anne closed up the cottage for the season. The ringing phone startled her, and she hurried to pick it up before the answering machine kicked in.

"Anne, it's Wayne."

The tone of his voice put her on alert. She instantly thought of Rhonda, who had gotten out of the Army at the end of her obligated service and moved into a town house in northern Virginia. Chris was once again stationed overseas, and Rhonda was taking care of their young daughter alone. Anne had been thinking about Rhonda the day before with the simple worry that any mother has about her child. Now she feared that her concern might have occurred for a reason.

"Rhonda's in the hospital in Alexandria," Wayne said. "She's had some kind of stroke."

"A stroke?" Anne's mind raced. Rhonda was only 26.

Wayne explained that Rhonda had been Rollerblading in Washington with a girlfriend. They'd started home in the car when Rhonda began to babble about her father. Her arm shot out in front of her, then down to her side, then back out in front again. Finally, she'd slumped over in her seat with the right side of her face drooping. She was conscious now, but partially paralyzed.

Anne hung up the phone and paced. Wayne would take care of booking her a ticket on the next flight home, but it was already late. There wouldn't be anything until the morning. In the meantime, Anne did the only thing she could do: she prayed. In between her prayers, she picked up the phone and called everyone she knew who organized prayer ministries, followed by every group that engaged in prayer. She spoke to leaders of the Spiritualist Assembly, the Unity Church, the Science of Mind, and the Methodists. She didn't sleep at all that night and was ready at 5 A.M. when a neighbor two houses down drove her to the airport.

Wayne met her flight. He filled her in on Rhonda's condition during the short drive to the hospital. The doctors had done an MRI and had found several large masses in her brain. Anne wrung her hands in her lap. Rhonda had always been such a bright and happy child—the first to cheer up others when they were down. Now, Anne steeled herself to assume the same role.

They arrived outside Rhonda's room just before 9 A.M. With Wayne at her side, Anne took a tentative step forward. The sight made her heart sink.

That's my daughter, Anne thought, as she took in Rhonda's drooping face and right arm, which was drawn up against her side.

Rhonda opened her eyes. "Hi, Mom," she said groggily. "Hand me a pen. I can do a really good Bob Dole imitation."

The three of them laughed, but Anne quickly grew serious. Whether from the stroke or whatever drugs the doctors had prescribed, Rhonda was not completely aware of her surroundings and drifted in and out of sleep. Wayne took a seat in the corner, and Anne pulled a chair next to the bed. She sat at Rhonda's side and touched her daughter's forearm as she continued to pray. She slid her hand atop Rhonda's and slowly straightened each finger one by one. The fingers curled back into themselves when Anne released them to once again massage Rhonda's forearm. Suddenly, Anne experienced a surge of energy that propelled her to her feet. From his chair in the corner, Wayne watched as Rhonda's eyes opened wide.

No one said a word as Anne lowered herself back into her chair. Then, like an instant replay, the energy jolted Anne to her feet once again. She could see Rhonda's aura quite clearly, and it expanded as Anne held on to her arm.

Anne and Wayne glanced up as a nurse walked from the hallway toward the room. The woman stopped abruptly in the doorway and put her hands in front of her as if blocked by an invisible wall. Her face went from surprise to puzzlement, then she backed away and disappeared down the hall.

A third powerful surge passed from Anne to Rhonda. Anne saw a light in the corner of the room that was far more brilliant than the sunlight coming through the window. She stared, transfixed, as the light moved toward them, then swept across Rhonda.

As Anne and Wayne watched, Rhonda's fingers uncurled and her arm began to relax. Anne prayed ever more fervently, knowing that if a healing had taken place, it was a response to so many who had answered her calls for assistance.

By the next morning, the paralysis in Rhonda's face was gone, as was the weakness in her limbs. When the doctors performed a second MRI, they thought they'd mixed up the films. The first set of pictures showed ominous masses; the new set was perfectly clear. The doctors had no explanation. They sent Rhonda home from the hospital with a cane, but she never used it.

Chapter 31

Wayne checked his watch. The special session had been slated to last two hours, but they were well into their third hour and still going strong. The first time he'd invited Anne to Georgetown to talk to his students about Spiritualism and demonstrate her gifts, Wayne worried how she'd be received. The regular event quickly became one of the highlights of the semester for his students.

Anne stood at the front of the small auditorium and singled out the boyfriend of one of Wayne's brightest seniors. When she informed the young man that his grandfather's spirit was standing beside him, the boy looked skeptical.

Wayne couldn't blame him. He'd had the same doubts when first confronted with Anne's gifts. Since then, his experiences with his wife had stretched his understanding of reality far beyond what he'd been taught by the Jesuits. In spite of Wayne's advanced degrees and his long years of schooling, he was the first to admit that there was always more to learn. In a ceremony presided over by Anne at her Center for Spiritual Enlightenment, Wayne was inducted into the Spiritualist church. The former priest now called himself an *expanded Catholic*. The core of his beliefs would always be Catholic, but rather than contradicting his Catholicism, Spiritualism augmented his faith.

As usual, Anne was undeterred by the skeptics in the audience. "Your grandfather is most definitely here," she informed the young man, "and he's telling me that he's glad you liked the car he left you when he passed."

Wayne smiled at the boy's startled reaction and at his girl-friend's exclamations. It was obvious from their wide eyes that Anne's message had hit the mark.

The reason I left the priesthood is right there, Wayne thought as he watched his wife.

Anne caught his gaze and beamed back, making no effort to hide her affection in front of his students. She never failed to be amazed and thrilled by his total acceptance of who she was and what she did. The fact that he had the confidence to take her to a Jesuit university to demonstrate her mediumship showed a degree of support that went beyond anything she'd known was possible from a partner. She'd once endured a marriage where trust never entered the relationship. With Wayne, Anne had discovered trust and respect on every level: physical, emotional, and spiritual.

After three hours of lessons and demonstrations, Wayne called the evening to an end. His students were slow to leave, hanging around Anne as if she were a movie star. One young woman remarked that she saw a beautiful glow surrounding both Anne and Wayne when they stood together.

Wayne finally extracted his wife and drove her home. The large house they'd bought together in Springfield was close to the campus for Wayne and perfect for Anne to give readings in the cozy pink parlor. The large back deck overlooked their own private forest, a haven for the quiet reflection and contemplation that was so central to both of their lives.

They got home just as it was getting dark. They entered through the front door and crossed to the kitchen where the red light on the answering machine blinked a familiar greeting. Anne pushed the button as they took off their coats.

"Hi, Mom, it's me."

Rhonda's cheery voice filled the room. Anne and Wayne shared a knowing smile. Rhonda had suffered no lasting effects from her stroke. They were now the proud grandparents of four beautiful children.

"I was looking for Nana's old recipe book, and I can't find it," Rhonda said.

Margaret, Rhonda's grandmother, had died years earlier. The recipes in the book dated back several generations.

Wayne glanced around the kitchen, wondering if the book could be in the house, but Anne stared at the answering machine as Rhonda's recording continued.

"I need the recipes for the bread-and-butter pickles, the dill pickles, and the cinnamon rolls. Would you ask Sally if she can get them from Nana?"

Wayne's head whipped around and he let out a guffaw. Sally had visited him dozens of times since she first showed up in his bed. He never lost his sense of awe at being spoken to directly by a spirit, yet to Anne and Rhonda, asking Sally to contact a deceased family member about some lost recipes was no different from placing a long-distance phone call.

Seeing the look on his face, Anne giggled and held out her hand.

Wayne shook his head and echoed her laughter as he took her hand and led her toward the deck.

Feeling his fingers, a tingle ran up Anne's arm. It was the same pleasant jolt she felt each time he touched her. He did everything so lovingly, from helping her in or out of the car to moving the chair from the table so she could sit down.

"Look, a full moon!" he exclaimed as they stepped outside.

Anne squeezed his hand as they both gazed skyward. When she looked back at Wayne, Anne couldn't help but notice his aura. It radiated outward in beautiful purplish blue colors, blending perfectly with the shimmering moonbeams. She smiled. Wayne's spirituality was the first thing that had attracted her to him. There was nothing more spiritual than a purple or blue aura.

Wayne looked into Anne's eyes and felt their souls connect as he pulled her toward him. Wrapped in her arms, he recalled with painful clarity the insatiable longing that had led him to this very moment. He regretted not one day he'd spent with the Jesuits, but the vow of celibacy had nearly cost him the love of his life.

His need to leave the priesthood had always been more than physical. It was never for lack of faith. It was the need for this very thing . . . being able to throw his arms around his wife and show her that he loved her . . . feeling her arms around him and knowing that she loved him back.

His wife looked truly radiant in the glow of the moon. He nuzzled his nose in her hair and thought, *The reason I left is right here.*

Wayne and Anne today.

A Conversation
with Anne Gehman
and Wayne Knoll

From author Suzanne Giesemann:

The first round of interviews for this book took place at Anne and Wayne's cottage in Lily Dale, New York. They took me into their home and treated me like a member of the family. Never have I felt so blessed as when I sat between them at the start of each meal, my right hand in Wayne's and my left in Anne's, as one or the other gave the blessing. With a Catholic priest on one side and a Spiritualist minister on the other, I couldn't go wrong! I returned to my home suffused with love, and glowing for days from a weeklong dose of their wonderful energy.

What follows is a transcript of a uniquely insightful conversation that took place one evening between Anne and Wayne in response to my question about the similarities in their beliefs and how they deal with any differences. The deep love and respect they have for each other came through with every word and gesture. I share that evening with you now so that you may come to know this special couple and their philosophies even better. . . .

"I am a wealthy man!"

Wayne's voice booms from the doorway of the pink and white Victorian cottage, through a small park, and across the still waters of Cassadaga Lake. A passerby on the rutted gravel road glances left and right, then smiles warily at the white-haired gentleman with the sparkling eyes.

Arms spread wide, he repeats, "I am a wealthy man to be with my soul mate and enjoy a view like this!"

With a smile of satisfaction, he closes the French doors and crosses the porch to the white wicker love seat.

Anne has been waiting patiently, back straight, hands crossed demurely in her lap. When Wayne takes his place beside her, she reaches across and pats his leg, polished pink nails bright against his khaki shorts. The sleeve of her diaphanous pink poncho brushes his blue Hawaiian shirt.

Wayne turns to me and clears his throat. "In answer to your question, I felt from the start that while there were some aspects of Anne's spirituality with which I wasn't familiar, I wasn't uncomfortable with them. I was fascinated with them—specifically her mediumship and her psychic gifts. I was not brought up with those experiences at all."

He and Anne share a smile and he adds with conviction, "Anne's spirituality has made me a better person, spiritually."

She squeezes his leg and says, "And my relationship with Wayne has made me a better person as well."

Wayne squints, then shakes his head. "That's not the issue. We're talking about how your Spiritualism has changed me and how my Catholicism has changed you."

"Oh. Gosh." She shifts uneasily on the pink cushion.

The silence lengthens.

Her eyes shift upward, and she studies the pink paint on the ceiling.

He cocks his head and waits.

"Hmm . . ." she hums, still thinking.

"Wow," he says, as if they're alone. "You know what you're underscoring? I've been aware of this for some time."

She waits.

"Because of who you are—because you're a medium and a psychic par excellence, and because you are a pastor, I have essentially practiced your faith rather than mine."

"But we've been sharing our spiritual life from the time we met," she protests.

He hears her, but withdraws from the conversation, as if he needs time to digest his previous pronouncement.

She is insistent now. "And you'll remember that on our second date, I asked you to take me to a Mass in Maryland."

He leans back and crosses his arms. "But there is very little uniquely Catholic that I brought to you."

Her eyes go back to the ceiling, his to the floor.

It's he who speaks first.

"I've learned so much from Anne and from Spiritualism, but I frequently attend her church, not mine." His eyes grow moist. "And I miss mine."

"I'm conscious of that when we go to his reunions in Kansas, and the Church is so important to his family," Anne says.

"When I want to go to Mass, she never hinders me," he admits. "I go on special holidays, and if I wanted to go my separate way, I could. But for our mutuality, I decided to attend church with Anne."

He sweeps his hand toward the lake and says, "But the truth is, the two times when I truly experience God—not just pray to Him, but truly experience Him—are when I enjoy a view like this and when I attend Mass."

They drift off again, the initial question still hanging unanswered in the crisp evening air.

"I love Catholic churches," Anne says, trying again. "I love the architecture. I love the feel of them, the beauty." She pauses, then announces with certainty, "I'm sure I'm a better person because Wayne is Catholic."

He looks at her sideways.

She giggles.

He shakes his head and puts his hand on hers. The patient professor can wait no longer, and he answers my original question for her, "My influence on Anne—I hope—is to further confirm her in her faith."

She rears back and throws out her hands. "Exactly! Yes." She nods vigorously. "That's right!"

He beams.

She exhales.

They settle back on the love seat and rejoin hands. Their eyes drift downward to their laps. Both left ring fingers bear a matching gold band. He stares at his ring for a moment, then turns to me. His eyes are intense with the need to speak.

"I'm still a priest, you know."

The porch is still as his words hang in the air. It is Anne who finally breaks the silence.

"We should turn the lights on," she says.

Wayne gets up and crosses the porch.

"Lily Dale is known as the City of Light," Anne informs me as Wayne bends down and plugs a cord into a wall socket.

Strings of tiny white bulbs strung like icicles around the porch come to life, giving the room a magical feel. Wayne returns to the love seat. With his wife now satisfied, he resumes the conversation.

"When I talked before about my sense of God's closeness," he says, " I didn't mean I intellectually found God. I mean I experienced God. That's the only way I can explain it."

"Wayne," Anne shakes her head, "you talk about being in God's presence or feeling the presence of God, but I feel there's nowhere that God is not—that everything is an expression of God." She pauses, then holds her hands out and states emphatically, "God *is*."

"See," Wayne said, nodding. "That's where we differ."

"God *is*," she repeats.

"I agree with you," he says, "but I find God's presence particularly strong experientially in the presence of what we call the Blessed Sacrament in a Catholic church. This is where the host that has been transformed in Mass is maintained. It's my firm belief that when you receive a sacrament, it radically alters your identity. That's why I say that I'm still a priest: once ordained, you are always a priest."

He turns on the cushion to fully face her.

"When we visited the little churches in Kansas that were constructed by the German colonists, I could tell which churches were just preserved and which were still active places of worship. I could tell because I could experience the presence of the Blessed Sacrament or not."

"I didn't experience it as the Blessed Sacrament," Anne replies, "but I could just tell from the energy—the vibration—which ones were no longer active places of worship."

"I would actually test myself," Wayne says, "because a characteristic in a Catholic church when the Blessed Sacrament is present is a special lighted candle that's placed in a prominent position at the altar."

Anne tilts her head. "I didn't know that."

His excitement increases. "I remember telling you, 'The Blessed Sacrament is here—I know it.' Remember?"

"Yes." She nods.

"You were immersed in your own prayer," he reminds her, "so you may not remember."

"I do remember that, but I've always felt a certain need to feel that kind of connection with the outdoors. From the time I was a little girl with my father, and also with my spirit guides, I was always aware of God's expression through nature, and I didn't find any of those teachings with a church, through any dogma or creed."

"I also feel close to God as mirrored in the beauty of nature," Wayne agrees. "Do you remember how we found our home? We'd been looking for a year. One day after church you said you felt drawn to Springfield."

Anne nods at the memory.

"We found a wonderful tree-covered lot. We walked back among the trees and both felt God's presence so strongly there. We looked at each other and said, 'This is it.' We signed on the dotted line before we had any idea of a house structure to build among those trees."

"And we're blessed to this day," Anne says.

Wayne touches a finger to his lips and further considers his response. "Rather than rituals or dogma, do you know where we're most similar?"

"Where?" she asks.

"In our longing to be one with God."

He takes a breath, then adds, "It's one of the things I love most about you."

She lowers her eyes and flushes with pleasure.

"I don't denigrate ritual or dogma," he tells me. "I love the Catholic liturgy, the Mass, the sacraments."

He closes his eyes for a moment and smiles, as if savoring a private memory.

"This sort of thing—the sacraments—mean a great deal to me. I attend these sometimes at Georgetown or at a local church. And sometimes Anne goes with me."

She nods and Wayne continues.

"We've attended Mass, for example, at St. Peter's in Rome. They sang the same songs I used to sing in Latin, and it brought tears to my eyes, right?" He turns to Anne, who nods again.

"Some of the new songs in the Catholic Church strike me as silly, sung to the tune of 'Michael Row Your Boat.'" He shakes his head and frowns. "But the Gregorian chant and the Latin hymns . . . they're magnificent!"

"I love the Gregorian chant, too," Anne says. "In fact, before I knew Wayne, I listened to it a lot, and I still do, right, Wayne?"

He rolls his eyes. "She hasn't a clue what it means."

"No, I don't have the slightest clue." She grins.

"I know Latin," Wayne says, sitting taller. "I speak it."

"But I love the beautiful voices and the beautiful sound of the Gregorian chant," Anne says. "The vibration . . . the energy of it . . ."

Her voice drifts off, then she adds, "But when Wayne translated the words for me, I thought, *Oh my gosh! That doesn't mean anything!*"

Wayne's laughter fills the porch.

Anne crosses her arms. "So for me, it sort of lost its beauty, you know?"

Wayne collects himself and cocks his head. "Now, I find Spiritualism a bit lacking in ritual and symbolism."

Anne gives a slight shrug.

"I've said that before," Wayne prompts.

She raises an eyebrow. "Mm-hm."

"It makes me miss the experience. The Catholic Church has had centuries—two millennia, in fact—during which to fine-tune a resplendent, rich tradition of ritual and symbolism, music, architecture; and above all, an entire and magnificent library of theological, philosophical, and spiritual thought. Just look at the history of the Virgin Mary and the saints, for example."

"You grew up with that," she says. "It was deeply ingrained within you."

"Yes, but it's not just familiarity." He strokes his chin. "I think objectively there's a richness in the Catholic symbols and the ritualism. And I have to say that I love some of the hymns of Spiritualism, but some are so old fashioned . . . so outdated . . . so . . . fuddy-duddy."

Anne rears back, but Wayne continues: "And to me, that's a distraction from prayer."

"See," she says, looking offended. "I sort of feel that way about things you say and sing in the Catholic Church. There are a lot of words that are strung together that to me have absolutely no meaning whatsoever."

Wayne's shoulders shake in a silent chuckle.

"As a Spiritualist," Anne says, "for me, repeating prayers that you just learn—that have been handed down for centuries—has no meaning because it's not from the heart." She places a hand on her chest. "To me, prayer is spontaneous and from the heart—not something memorized—not something passed down through the centuries."

"See?" Wayne says to me, grinning.

"All that stuff that you repeat," she says to Wayne, indignant now. "I mean, that's nonsense!"

"See?" he repeats. "There are differences. I love and value the richness of Catholic traditions."

"You say the Spiritualist hymns are 'fuddy-duddy,'" Anne says, her dander still up.

"I said 'some of them,'" Wayne corrects her.

"Yes, well, as far as rituals, you know, in the beginning of modern Spiritualism there was an effort on the part of those in the spirit world to help humankind move away from ceremonies that were old and musty and didn't have meaning. But we do have a few things that are rituals."

"Oh, you do," he agrees. "What is most meaningful to me, which I've never experienced as a Catholic, is the ritualism of hands-on healing, which is a part of every Sunday service."

Anne nods.

"It's beautiful and meaningful," he affirms.

"Wonderful."

"Absolutely."

"So that, in a sense," she says, "may not necessarily be considered a ritual, but I do see it as service."

"The hands-on healing is fundamental to Spiritualism," Wayne tells me.

"And the reading of our Declaration of Principles is something else we do," Anne adds. "So those are two things that are sort of ritualistic."

He tilts his head. "Now, the reading of the Spiritualist principles . . . we were talking about dogma earlier . . . they actually are a creed, although you say otherwise. They're a manifestation of the identity of the Spiritualist faith."

"I guess you could call it that," Anne says. "But we don't use the term *faith*. We replace *faith* with *knowledge*. I hope that doesn't sound smug, but we think of it that way because we want to replace blind faith with knowledge."

Wayne pinches his lips together. He parts them only long enough to say, "That is a difference."

"Yeah," she insists.

He arches his eyebrows. "Yeah."

She holds her head high. "The knowledge comes from teachings directly from the spirit world."

"Wait a minute!" Wayne pulls in his chin. "I don't see that. It seems to me the only avenue in which Spiritualism replaces blind faith with knowledge is in evidential readings—when a medium passes along a message with specific details known only to the recipient. That's the only avenue."

"But the Declaration of Principles came directly to us from the spirit world."

Wayne shakes his head. "To an objective observer, that's an act of faith."

"You're saying that we accept all messages from the spirit world as an act of faith," Anne says, "and I don't think we do. We analyze what is said and—"

"No, you don't," he interrupts. "I would just like to complement what you're saying. May I?"

Anne doesn't realize he is trying to help her and says, "Supposing I gave you a message from the spirit world . . ."

"Which you have, occasionally. But Anne, where I see Spiritualism based on knowledge rather than blind faith, where I see that your assertion is absolutely right is in the evidential readings I just mentioned. That is the cornerstone of Spiritualism. You don't find that in any other religion. I've heard enough evidential messages so that I believe some of them—not all of them," he's quick to point out, "but some of them are coming from the spirit world. Absolutely."

Wayne turns to me now. "Do I believe that there are many mediums in Spiritualism who have the gift of serving as channels from the spirit world to denizens of this world? Absolutely. I don't believe that; I know it. The Spiritualist Principles are the Spiritualist equivalent of the Roman Catholic creed, I think. Now, most of them are based on . . . ," he pauses. "Boy, I'm on rocky ground here. I have to think this through further. . . ."

Anne waits patiently while he reflects. After a moment Wayne gives a definitive nod. "Most of the Spiritualist Principles are based on sound evidence. They are based on knowledge rather than blind faith. But some of them require faith as well as reasoning."

Anne's eyes shift upward, and her head bobs as she mentally ticks off the nine principles.

"In other words," Wayne says, "I do not believe that because the principles evolved from a medium that they are exclusively evidence to the mind and not dependent on faith. I don't see that. There's a lot of faith there."

Anne starts to protest. "I don't think—"

Wayne holds up a finger. "Excuse me." He turns back to me. "And also the very formulation and the number of principles have changed over the years."

"Yeah," Anne says, "because they've evolved."

Wayne again raises his eyebrows.

Anne's chin juts forward.

"What I'm saying is an oversimplistic generalization," Wayne says. "But I would say that the essence of what is unique to Spiritualism is based on knowledge rather than faith. I certainly believe that, but it also requires a good deal of faith."

"Well," Anne says, crossing her arms, "all of life does."

She sulks for a moment. Wayne remains pensive, then says, "Some people have the simplistic view that to be a Catholic, you have to believe everything."

Anne considers this for a moment, then says, "Your mother told your brother Devon that he'd be in purgatory if he married a woman who wasn't Catholic."

Wayne chuckles and shakes his head. "There is a great deal that is taught that does not require belief on the part of a good Catholic. For example, the dogma of purgatory, or the dogma of limbo, especially of unbaptized babies. One of my great Jesuit professors was asked several years ago about the dogma of limbo—that babies, totally innocent, because they were not baptized, have to exist in a limbo after they die and cannot enter paradise."

Anne listens with her head cocked to one side.

"And the man responded, 'That doctrine is currently in the shop for repairs.'" Wayne makes an exaggerated face and guffaws.

"I like that!" Anne exclaims. "That there's optional belief. I like that a lot!"

"Most Catholics don't even know that," he says, nodding.

Anne shakes her head. "Wow."

"For example, the dogma of limbo did not come to the Catholic Church from Scripture. It was reasoned to by theologians. Now we know," he pauses, "they were wrong!"

"Excuse me," Anne holds up a finger. "What about all of the things that were voted on by the Nicene Council in A.D. 325?"

Wayne takes a slow, deep breath and wrinkles his nose. "That's pretty close to fundamental."

Anne tilts her head. "I mean, in 325 they brought up this long list of things that they voted on as to whether or not they would be part of the Catholic Church or not, right?"

"Yeah, and then subsequently—"

Anne interrupts and starts ticking off the fingers of her left hand with her right. "Virgin birth . . ."

"Right, and—"

"Reincarnation . . ."

"Correct, then subsequently—"

She stops counting and gives him a challenging look. "Uh huh?"

"They were tested," he replies. "Not over a period of years, but centuries. They were tested by prayer, by theological discourse, and by subsequent councils and pronouncements."

Anne throws her hands out. "Now that's a major difference between Spiritualism and Catholicism then. Catholics would say, 'I believe because after all these centuries . . .' and Spiritualists would say, 'I *know*.'"

"Not quite true," Wayne says. "The passage of time does not determine an article of faith. Eventually, the Pope declares a principle an article of faith *ex cathedra*. When he does so, he speaks with infallibility, and Catholics then accept that pronouncement as an article of faith. However, such pronouncements are few and far between, and always as a fundamental principle."

"I *know*," Anne repeats.

"Honey, that's very accurate. That's very good. That's true. Another thing that's changed since I was growing up is that it used to be required to not eat meat on Friday. If you did, you committed a mortal sin. Now," he laughs, "you can go to a fish fry on Friday, but you can also have a steak, and there is no problem, officially."

"Because . . ." Anne prompts him with her hands.

"Because that was a man-made rule that came from the hierarchy. It did not come from Scripture, so the hierarchy can and did change the rules."

Anne crosses her arms and gives him a smug smile.

Wayne taps a finger in the air and turns to me. "You know, a couple of summers ago when we were in Rome, we visited the Coliseum. Of course it's all in ruins, but I obtained some literature that gave us re-creations of what it must have looked like. And Anne, with an intake of breath said, 'I've been there! I've seen this!'"

"A lot of people would interpret that as a past-life thing," she says. "I did not. I simply had experiences in my life where I was taken to various places by spirit guides and teachers. I would sit and listen to a dialogue in those places."

"You see," Wayne says, "this is what is so marvelous for me. There are views and experiences that are totally unique to Anne—that I was never exposed to and that are fascinating to me." He turns to face her. "For example, your being transposed to other lands and times—I've never had that. And when you are in communion in meditation with the spirit world, you are in communion with spirit *and* with spirit entities. That's new to me."

"You use the term *holy communion* to talk about a ritual . . . a sacrament," Anne says. "Holy communion to me is an experience of the holy communion with the Divine."

Wayne digests her words for a moment, then says, "You know, the root meaning of 'communion' is not 'mutual exchange of conversation'; it's 'being one with.'"

"'Being one with.'" Anne tests out the idea and nods. "My experience in holy communion, then, would be that meditative attunement process in a spiritual sense. I feel that every time I give a reading. I feel holy communion."

"That's wonderful," says Wayne.

"You know, there's so much talk these days about meditation, but when I first studied with Wilbur, we didn't use that term so much. That word came in vogue in the '70s when we began to see the blending of the East and West.

"When I meditate," Anne explains, "I try to clear my mind of all negativity and active thinking. If I'm at a retreat, I withdraw from the news. I enter into the silence and focus on some deep breathing. I spend some time outdoors, close to nature. All of your senses become very clear when you do this. You see and hear more acutely."

Wayne nods. "This is what we have in common. At Wernersville, in my early days as a Jesuit, when I'd sit outside on a bench looking at the sky, I was just overwhelmed with God's great beauty. There's no analytical thought." He throws his hands out and says, "It's just: 'Wow!'"

"I would seek greater attunement with the spirits around me," Anne continues. "And I would expect to project to other levels of consciousness—not necessarily out-of-body experiences, as people are always trying to do."

She cocks her head and asks, "Why would anyone want to do that? The body is so wonderful! But the whole reason for meditation is that it brings one into balance of body, mind, and spirit. It's an evolution of the soul. But it's not focused on self, because you come into a deeper realization that you are a part of the whole and a contributor to the whole. Right, Wayne?"

"Absolutely," he agrees with a vigorous nod. "These spiritual experiences are not intended to be forms of self-indulgence. We don't leave ourselves open to the touch of spirit simply to give us a pleasing experience. Spiritual experiences are for humankind. We're instruments."

"That's right," she says.

He repeats the phrase, enunciating each word: "We are instruments."

"Meditation and retreats are not for self-aggrandizement," she stresses. "They're for growth and greater awareness and deeper love."

"When we go on a retreat, we're not entering a spiritual spa," Wayne says, grinning.

"We may be," Anne counters, "but it goes beyond self."

"That's not the end in itself."

"The end," she says, "is to be a greater servant for Spirit—to use your spiritual gifts and awareness for the upliftment and benefit of humanity."

Wayne pats her leg. His face is etched with pride. "Everything that Anne has shown me as the Spiritualists' view regarding Christ has opened my eyes and made me so much more understanding of Jesus, and of so much that's in the four Gospels. There are so many wonderful instances there of Jesus as healer . . . healing the man born blind . . . and Jesus prophesying, and of transmission of energy. . . ."

"Such as when a woman touched Jesus's garments," Anne says, "and he felt the energy go out to her, and she was healed."

"That is one of so many wonderful instances," Wayne says. "And this is my point . . ." He pauses, clenches his fists, then raises his voice almost to a shout: "The Catholic Church doesn't seem to know what to do with these phenomena!"

"They don't have the slightest idea," Anne says softly.

"They don't emphasize them. I grew up thinking that things like healing and prophesying—that these are what happened back then; they don't happen any more. But Spiritualism knows what to make of them."

Anne nods.

"This is an avenue in which the Spiritualists can teach the Catholics," he says. "Yes. Yes! This is a fact!"

"We would say that Catholics see them all as historical events," Anne says.

"And not currently relevant," Wayne adds.

"But we Spiritualists see them as natural law."

"Yes," Wayne says with amazement in his voice.

"And natural law is unchangeable."

"Right!"

"It is always manifested the same way."

"It's universal and unchangeable," he adds.

Anne's enthusiasm grows. "So we know that the same experiences that Jesus had, according to natural law—"

"They continue right throughout history!" Wayne marvels.

"That's right!" she says. "And they continue for us, too, just as Jesus said, that 'greater things can ye do'!"

Wayne turns to face his wife and states with finality: "So the Spiritualists, with their experience and practice of gifts on the part of mediums and psychics, have a great deal to teach the Catholic Church, and the Catholic Church can enlighten Spiritualists in some respects."

Anne sings out, "Amen, Brother!" as the two high-five with their right hands.

Anne turns to me.

"Wayne was meant to be a teacher, you know."

"It's all I ever wanted to do," he says. "To teach."

"He got his Ph.D. from Harvard," she adds with obvious pride.

He flashes her a humble smile.

"He graduated *magna cum laude,*" she says, then rocks her shoulders and adds, "I graduated 'Lordy How Come.'"

The joke hangs in the air for a moment, then the two burst into laughter.

"Anne is a wonderful teacher in her own right," Wayne says.

She looks at him. "You said that Spiritualists have a lot to teach Catholics, but I think we have a lot to teach all of humanity. And one of the greatest things is the recognition that we are a spiritual being here and now. We don't wait until we leave the physical body. We are a spirit, temporarily within a physical form, and the time that we call death is simply a transition."

"As a Catholic," Wayne says, "I totally agree."

From somewhere down the lane, a dog barks. Anne peers outside into the darkness, then says, "You know, about ten years ago the Pope made the pronouncement that animals have souls."

"She's known that all along," Wayne says.

"As Spiritualists, we've always known that. Everything is soul force."

"Right."

She looks up and swirls her hands in the air. "Everything is spiritual energy, and the difference is simply the vibrational frequency."

"Absolutely," Wayne agrees. "You know, I have learned so much from Anne, but another area of difference is that Catholics believe that there are three persons—the Trinity—Father, Son, and Holy Spirit."

Anne raises her brows. "No daughters, you'll notice."

"That's right." He gives her a tolerant smile, then notes, "It's interesting that Spiritualism is overwhelmingly female, and the Catholic governing structure is overwhelmingly male."

"Getting back to your point," Anne says, "as a Spiritualist, I see the Trinity as body, mind, spirit. The body corresponds to the physical, material world; the mind corresponds to the collective consciousness; and the spirit to the Infinite."

Wayne points a finger. "That is *a* trinity, not *the* Trinity . . . the Divine Trinity."

Her face is set. "And I see body, mind, spirit also as divine, because everything is of God."

He shakes his head. "See, that has to be explained, because on the face of it you're describing pantheism."

"No, I'm saying what I said before: that God *is,* and everything is an expression of God."

"See, that's different."

Wayne crosses his hands in his lap. "She cannot refute me, nor can I refute her. So what's the attitude? I respect her views; she respects my views, fundamentally."

She reaches over and squeezes his hands. "I love you, Wayno."

He seems pleased, but slightly embarrassed. "I am a more spiritual person because of my exposure to Spiritualism. No question. But I'm going to make a statement."

She tilts her head.

"And this is hypothetical," he says, "to a degree."

"Okay." She cautiously drags out the word.

"If you were to go to God, I would go to Sunday Mass."

She blinks and keeps her lips knit together. "Mm-hm."

"And frequently attend Spiritualist church, also," he quickly adds, "but my principal Sunday religious participation would be Mass and communion. I would remain in my spiritual roots."

"But you don't want me to die yet, do you?" she jokes, but her brows are pinched.

He gives a small chuckle. "No, that's why I said it hypothetically. Certainly, I don't want you to die."

"All right," she pouts, "but don't leave me for very long. . . . Gosh, let's not talk about that."

He takes her hand and laughs. "How can I leave you? You're a medium!"

Anne holds up a finger. "I want to get back to what you were saying—that you would remain in your Catholic roots if I were to die."

Wayne grimaces as if he's sorry he raised the subject.

"But you'd still be a Spiritualist, too, wouldn't you?"

He nods. "I'm comfortable as a Spiritualist *and* as a Catholic. The one irreconcilable difference we have is our different views on the nature of Jesus Christ. That's irreconcilable."

At this, Anne throws back a shoulder and says, "Well, Jesus told *me*. . . ."

Wayne blinks in shock, then seeing her comical expression, he chuckles.

She joins him in his laughter.

"She's pulling my leg," he says, as if to make sure I know that.

He squints as he tries to remember what he was saying, then gives up and laughs some more. He looks at Anne sideways and says, "What did Jesus tell you?"

Anne grows serious. "Well, see, we see Jesus as the great medium, the great healer, the great psychologist, the great philosopher, and teacher. We take very seriously what he said, that 'those things which I do, ye can do also . . . even greater things can ye do.' He was referring to the spiritual gifts, and those spiritual gifts are very beautifully written in Paul's letters to the Corinthians, okay?"

"Okay."

"When Jesus said, 'The Father and I are one,' he was referring to the oneness of each individual with God, with the Infinite. We believe in salvation from spiritual ignorance as we follow his pathway. Then, indeed, there is enlightenment. We would think of the blood of Jesus as being the work of Jesus."

Wayne pulls his chin into his neck and gives her a startled look.

"In other words—his ministry, his work," Anne explains.

"'Blood' is 'the work of'—that's the direct translation from the Aramaic."

Wayne frowns. "Okay. That's your view. You've got a right to your view . . . even though it's wrong." He waits half a second, then lets loose a burst of laughter.

"Well, I think it's right," she says, raising her chin. "And if it's not right, what difference does it make in the overall pattern of things? The fact is, we're all spiritual beings. We all have our individual pathway. We all have personal responsibility toward our unfoldment; and our growth spiritually, psychologically, and intellectually."

Wayne turns to me and says, "This is why I married her. She's a strong lady." He pauses. "And opinionated."

Their laughter fills the porch.

"So yes, we have irreconcilable differences," he confirms, "but they're irreconcilable intellectually. We reconcile them by mutual admiration and respect."

"Exactly!" she says. "We simply recognize that we think differently about some things."

He clasps his hands. "And I respect her for it, and she respects me for it."

"That's right," she says. "It's sort of like sound or color. We don't know when we hear a particular sound if we hear it the way the other does, or when we look at a particular color if we're seeing it the same."

"Her pink is not my pink," Wayne says, raising his eyes from the pink floor to the pink ceiling.

She pats his leg. "It's really blue, Wayne. It's really your favorite blue."

The sound of the phone brings the conversation to a halt. Neither Anne nor Wayne moves to answer it. After four rings Anne's recorded voice fills the air, followed by a live female voice.

"Mom? It's me. Are you there?"

Anne's face lights up. She excuses herself and hurries to the small desk in the corner of the porch. Wayne watches her as she picks up the phone and covers the mouthpiece with her hand.

He turns to me. "That's Rhonda."

He listens for a moment, then determines that Anne might be a while.

"May I take this time to talk about marriage and the priesthood? It's a subject about which I feel very strongly . . . for obvious reasons."

He coughs into his hand, then begins.

"I'm absolutely not against celibacy in the priesthood. It's a beautiful life. At its best, it means a total commitment of self to God and the people of God." He glances at Anne, who has turned her back.

"But celibacy is difficult and takes special grace and a special personality. Not many men can do it. That's why, in my view, the Church would be so much richer with a celibate clergy, able to imitate Christ in all respects, plus a married clergy like St. Peter. In the early Church, there was no rule of celibacy. That didn't occur until the 12th century."

Anne returns from her phone call. "Everything's fine," she tells Wayne under her breath. She settles onto the couch and places her hands in her lap. Her mind seems elsewhere as Wayne resumes the conversation.

"There are hundreds, probably thousands, of churches in the United States that have had to close due to the drastic shortage of priests. I look at that statistic and the closing of parishes as more than a statistic—it's very saddening. I realize that if the Pope and the Church hierarchy allowed married priests, there would be such a run that they wouldn't be able to handle them all. Isn't that right, Anne?"

"I'm sorry. What are we talking about?"

"We're talking about how many more priests there would be if it weren't for the issue of celibacy."

"Oh, yes." She's back now and nods her head vigorously. "Like your students."

"That's right. So many of my students at Georgetown have told me they would love to be priests and would sign up immediately. The only impediment preventing them from signing up is the rule of celibacy. And you must realize that celibacy is an institutional rule; it's not a divine mandate."

"And your female students . . ." she nudges him with her elbow.

"That's right. Students I've had for 36 years who are so intelligent and spiritual . . . they would love to be priests and function in the church."

"It's only a matter of time," Anne says.

Wayne agrees. "I see a number of serious obstacles for women becoming priests, but women being ordained is a historical inevitability. It may not happen in my lifetime, but it will eventually happen."

Anne pats his knee. "You're wonderful."

He shrugs. "I am convinced that the church would be infinitely more rich, responsible, and effective with a married clergy and female priests—along with the traditional celibate priests and nuns—in the pulpit, as experienced guidance counselors, in the confessional, in private sessions, and in public retreats or workshops."

"The best of both worlds," Anne says.

"Absolutely. From my perspective now as a married man, I honestly believe I am in a much better position to offer more enlightened counseling and much more enlightened sermons or homilies from the pulpit. There's no question. And I think that being married, the advice I would offer would be more credible with the people of God—especially with married couples."

Anne's smile turns wistful.

Wayne toys with the ring on her finger. "Anne is right. She is absolutely right. The best of both worlds would have been to be married to Anne and to be a priest."

He takes a sip of water. "Do you remember awhile back when the Pope said that other churches are defective as churches? That's the Catholic view."

Anne frowns and nods. "I remember that."

"That does not mean that other churches don't have validity," he says. "That does not mean that there aren't tremendous modes of cooperation, mutual respect, and mutual love."

"In other words," she says, "whatever a person believes is right, if they believe it strongly . . ."

"He didn't say they were defective," Wayne explains. "He said they were defective as churches."

"Wow." She shakes her head. "I can't agree with that at all. I don't think there's any one church that is not defective, because they're all made up of human beings."

"Sweetheart, I totally agree. But the nature of defining a church is an intellectual proposition, okay? If you take *defective* in its broadest sense, everybody's defective."

"Yeah," she sniffs.

"The question is, how do we, in modern society, escape tribalism? That's the hard thing, isn't it?"

"Mm-hm."

"I said this before: the issue of Jesus represents an irreconcilable difference between the two of us on an intellectual plane, but reconcilable on the basis of mutual respect. I really believe this. If we cannot—not just Anne and me, but humankind—if we cannot maintain mutual respect when there are intellectual differences, then all civilization is tribal."

Anne nods.

"It's tribal!" he says again. "Then the only people that matter are those in our tribe. And this is why we have such problems in the world today. We don't all have to be Spiritualists or Catholics, but we do need mutual respect, while maintaining the integrity of one's personal identity."

They join hands and look at each other for a moment. Finally, Wayne turns to me. "We may have our differences of belief, but where Anne and I are still very much together, as I said when we first started this discussion, is the emphasis—not on ritual, not even specifically on dogma—but on our love affair with God."

Anne's fingers whiten as she squeezes his hand. "Yes. All right."

"It's what we have in common," Wayne says, "and it is an adventure that only continues and evolves through time and eternity."

Spiritualism's Declaration of Principles[1]

Originally adopted by the
National Spiritualist Association

We believe in Infinite Intelligence.

We believe that the phenomena of Nature, both physical and spiritual, are the expression of Infinite Intelligence.

We affirm that a correct understanding of such expression and living in accordance therewith, constitute true religion.

We affirm that the existence and personal identity of the individual continue after the change called death.

We affirm that communication with the so-called dead is a fact, scientifically proven by the phenomena of Spiritualism.

We believe that the highest morality is contained in the Golden Rule: "Do unto others as you would have them do unto you."

We affirm the moral responsibility of individuals, and that we make our own happiness or unhappiness as we obey or disobey Nature's physical and spiritual laws.

We affirm that the doorway to reformation is never closed against any soul here or hereafter.

We affirm that the precepts of Prophecy and Healing are Divine attributes proven through Mediumship.

Discussion Questions for Reading Groups

1. In the Preface, Anne recalls when Wilbur taught her that a *prediction* could be changed and a psychic could intercede, whereas *prophecy* is that which is already set and can't be changed. What do you think of these concepts? If you agree with them, what types of things would be unchangeable? Why do you think some things can be changed and others can't?

2. As a young child, Anne is introduced to the faith of the Chippewa Indians and that of the Pentecostals. Both worship quite differently from the Mennonites Anne had grown up with. Anne comes to realize that all three groups worship the same God. Do all religions worship the same God?

3. Is it possible to distinguish between a subjective perception of God and the objective reality of God? For example, what are the differences between the names of God, Spirit, Supreme Being, Yahweh, Allah, and so forth? What is the objective reality of God? The Jewish faith describes God as "He Who Is," that is, the Un-nameable. Is God male, female, both, or neither?

4. Thirteen-year-old Anne watches her tears blend with rainwater and realizes that in essence, "all is one." What is meant by the spiritual concept of *oneness?* How can we apply this in our daily lives?

5. At age 14, Wayne reads the work of Thomas Merton and decides to become a Trappist monk. Why does a life of seclusion, prayer, and contemplation hold such appeal for some men and women, and what purpose does monastic life serve?

6. While first living alone, Anne attempts to take her own life and has a near-death experience. The NDE is as beautiful for Anne as for those who nearly die from other causes, and she feels compelled to return to her body and share the experience with others. From a spiritual perspective, why is suicide not the answer to depression and other problems?

7. Anne reunites a brother and sister with help from their deceased mother in the spirit world. What is the possibility that many seeming coincidences and random thoughts that we have are the result of effort and intervention on the part of spirit guides? How would things change for you if you accepted this concept as fact?

8. While a student at Harvard University, Wayne's friend sends out more than 200 letters of application for teaching positions. Wayne sends only one, to Georgetown University. His acceptance is the fulfillment of his life's vision. What is the value of having a personal vision? Have you identified your own?

9. Anne spends a year investigating the subject of reincarnation. She decides that she can't put faith in the theory as it is often presented. She ultimately comes to believe in the re-embodiment of soul force which carries fragments of memory. What are your thoughts on reincarnation?

10. Much of what the Spiritualists believe comes from spirit messages. Is this a valid source of information? Can it be trusted?

11. Wayne's tenant Elisa tells both Anne and Wayne that the two are soul mates. What is meant by this concept? Do soul mates actually exist?

12. Anne's daughter Rhonda is healed from a stroke after Anne lays her hands on Rhonda's arm. Anne claims that she is only an instrument for healing energy. Do healers actually heal the sick? If so, how do they do it?

13. Rhonda asks her mother to have Anne's spirit guide Sally contact her deceased grandmother to find some lost recipes. If you were able to contact the spirit of someone on the Other Side, who would you contact and what would you ask?

14. Wayne considers himself an *expanded Catholic*. He feels that being exposed to Spiritualism has further strengthened his faith. Do you think it's possible to incorporate the beliefs of Spiritualism with your religion? With any religion?

15. Wayne feels that the Catholic Church would be more responsible and effective with a married clergy and with female priests. Do you agree? Why or why not?

16. A recurring theme throughout the book is that there is no death. How would things change for the world if more people understood and accepted this belief?

17. Anne and Wayne admit that there are irreconcilable differences in their spiritual beliefs, yet they have a healthy, loving relationship. What can we learn from them about acceptance and tolerance on a larger scale?

Acknowledgments

I am deeply humbled and eternally grateful to God and the spirits that guided me in writing this book. I know in my heart that I was directed from the moment of its inception until I typed the final words. I was also helped along the way by many souls still with me here in person. I would especially like to thank:

My husband and soul mate, Ty, for your never-ending love and support. You are my greatest treasure.

My sister and best girlfriend, Janice Clay, for your chapter-by-chapter reviews and endless encouragement.

My agents, Bill Hammond and Bill Dorn. Thank you, thank you for keeping the faith.

To the family, friends, and acquaintances of Anne Gehman and Wayne Knoll for your wonderful memories and for telling your stories so honestly.

And, of course, my thanks to Anne and Wayne for your friendship, your love, and your openness in sharing your lives and life lessons with me and the readers of this book.

Endnotes

Chapter 5

[1] Thomas Merton, *The Seven Storey Mountain* (New York: Harcourt Brace and Company, 1948), 242.

[2] Merton, 227.

[3] Merton, 242.

[4] Merton, 281.

[5] Merton, 352.

Chapter 8

[1] Arthur Findlay, *The Rock of Truth* (London: Psychic Press, 1933), 139.

[2] Findlay, 143.

Chapter 11

[1] http://www.jesuits.ca/Join_us/vow_day.php

[2] Ibid.

Chapter 17

[1] http://www.bluesforpeace.com/martin-luther-king.htm

[2] http://www.fallrivervocations.org/ministries/ordination_rite.htm

[3] Ibid.

Chapter 22

[1] http://www.nps.gov/eise/historyculture/eisenhower-at-gettysburg.htm

Chapter 28

[1] http://fatherjoe.wordpress.com/stories/something-strange-in-the-house/

Addendum

[1] *Spiritualist Manual,* National Spiritualist Association of Churches, (Revision of August, 2002), 32.

About the Author

Suzanne Giesemann is a writer and motivational speaker focusing on personal excellence and spirituality. She is a former Navy Commander who served as a Commanding Officer and aide to the Chairman of the Joint Chiefs of Staff on 9/11. An avid sailor and U.S. Coast Guard licensed captain, she and her husband, Ty, have sailed their 46-foot sloop *Liberty* across the Atlantic Ocean and throughout the Mediterranean. Her other books include *Conquer Your Cravings; It's Your Boat Too: A Woman's Guide to Greater Enjoyment on the Water;* and the memoir *Living a Dream.*

Website: **www.SuzanneGiesemann.com**

We hope you enjoyed this Hay House book. If you'd like
to receive our online catalog featuring additional information
on Hay House books and products, or if you'd like to find
out more about the Hay Foundation, please contact:

Hay House, Inc.
P.O. Box 5100
Carlsbad, CA 92018-5100

(760) 431-7695 or **(800) 654-5126**
(760) 431-6948 (fax) or **(800) 650-5115 (fax)**
www.hayhouse.com® • **www.hayfoundation.org**

Published and distributed in Australia by: Hay House Australia Pty. Ltd.,
18/36 Ralph St., Alexandria NSW 2015 • *Phone:* 612-9669-4299
Fax: 612-9669-4144 • www.hayhouse.com.au

Published and distributed in the United Kingdom by: Hay House UK, Ltd.,
292B Kensal Rd., London W10 5BE • *Phone:* 44-20-8962-1230
Fax: 44-20-8962-1239 • www.hayhouse.co.uk

Published and distributed in the Republic of South Africa by:
Hay House SA (Pty), Ltd., P.O. Box 990, Witkoppen 2068 *Phone/Fax:*
27-11-467-8904 info@hayhouse.co.za • www.hayhouse.co.za

Published in India by: Hay House Publishers India, Muskaan Complex,
Plot No. 3, B-2, Vasant Kunj, New Delhi 110 070 • *Phone:* 91-11-4176-1620
Fax: 91-11-4176-1630 • www.hayhouse.co.in

Distributed in Canada by: Raincoast, 9050 Shaughnessy St., Vancouver, B.C.
V6P 6E5 • *Phone:* (604) 323-7100 • *Fax:* (604) 323-2600 • www.raincoast.com

<u>**Take Your Soul on a Vacation**</u>

Visit **www.HealYourLife.com®** to regroup, recharge, and reconnect with
your own magnificence.Featuring blogs, mind-body-spirit news, and
life-changing wisdom from Louise Hay and friends.

Visit **www.HealYourLife.com** today!

Mind Your Body,
Mend Your Spirit

Hay House is the ultimate resource for inspirational and health-conscious books, audio programs, movies, events, e-newsletters, member communities, and much more.

Visit **www.hayhouse.com®** today and nourish your soul.

UPLIFTING EVENTS

Join your favorite authors at live events in a city near you or log on to **www.hayhouse.com** to visit with Hay House authors online during live, interactive Web events.

INSPIRATIONAL RADIO

Daily inspiration while you're at work or at home. Enjoy radio programs featuring your favorite authors, streaming live on the Internet 24/7 at **HayHouseRadio.com®**. Tune in and tune up your spirit!

VIP STATUS

Join the Hay House VIP membership program today and enjoy exclusive discounts on books, CDs, calendars, card decks, and more. You'll also receive 10% off all event reservations (excluding cruises). Visit **www.hayhouse.com/wisdom** to join the Hay House Wisdom Community™.

Visit **www.hayhouse.com** and enter priority code 2723
during checkout for special savings!
(One coupon per customer.)

HAY
HOUSE

HAYHOUSE
RADIO))
radio for your soul™

HAY HOUSE
Wisdom